Linux in Small Business: A Practical Users' Guide

JOHN P. LATHROP

Apress™

Linux in Small Business: A Practical Users' Guide

ISBN (pbk): 1-893115-46-1

Printed and bound in the United States of America 12345678910

Editorial Directors: Dan Appleman, Peter Blackburn, Gary Cornell, Jason Gilmore, Karen Watterson

Technical Reviewer: Kurt Wall

Managing Editor: Grace Wong

Project Manager and Production Editor: Kari Brooks

Copy Editor: Nicole LeClerc

Compositor: Diana Van Winkle, Van Winkle Design Group

Artist: Kurt Krames

Indexer: Carol Burbo

Cover Designer: Tom Debolski

Marketing Manager: Stephanie Rodriguez

Distributed to the book trade in the United States by Springer-Verlag New York, Inc., 175 Fifth Avenue, New York, NY, 10010 and outside the United States by Springer-Verlag GmbH & Co. KG, Tiergartenstr. 17, 69112 Heidelberg, Germany.

In the United States, phone 1-800-SPRINGER, email orders@springer-ny.com, or visit http://www.springer-ny.com. Outside the United States, fax +49 6221 345229, email orders@springer.de, or visit http://www.springer.de.

For information on translations, please contact Apress directly at 901 Grayson Street, Suite 204, Berkeley, CA 94710.

Phone 510-549-5930, fax: 510-549-5939, email info@apress.com, or visit http://www.apress.com.

The source code for this book is available to readers at http://www.apress.com in the Downloads section.

For my wife, Mariann

In gratitude for her endless patience while I Linuxed.

Contents at a Glance

Contents

About the Author

expatriate *adj, n, v* **1 :** living abroad, esp. for a long period

John Lathrop's first computer experience was in 1969, writing Fortran for a PDP 8 that used paper tape to store and transfer data. (You can see one of these machines, on loan from a museum, actually plugged in and running in the 2001 Australian film *The Dish*.) He has been involved with PCs since buying an IBM PS/2 Model 25 in the 1980s.

Mr. Lathrop is a confirmed expatriate. Serving in the southern Philippines (in microlending) for the U.S. Peace Corps led him subsequently to a long career in the Middle East, developing computer training programs for the military and for private businesses. He became interested in Linux early on, and even abroad he was an early Linux adopter, using the new OS in 1996 to manage a UNIX Web server in Pittsburgh, Pennsylvania, from the Persian Gulf. Since returning to the United States in 1998, he has written two Linux books and consulted for several Linux companies in America. His consultancy, Linux Leap, provides business assessments, solutions for Linux integration, and computer training.

Mr. Lathrop currently divides his time between Calgary and California. He remains interested in overseas markets.

About the
Technical Reviewer

Kurt Wall first touched a computer in 1980 when he learned Fortran on an IBM mainframe of forgotten vintage; things have only gotten better since then. These days, Kurt is a full-time Linux and UNIX author, editor, consultant, and programmer. He has written five books about Linux and UNIX programming and system administration, he's working on his sixth, and he's the technical editor for over a dozen other Linux- and UNIX-related titles.

When he isn't working on a writing project, Kurt enjoys cooking, gourmet coffee, music, racquetball, science fiction, current affairs, staying up late, and sleeping even later, the latter of which makes a day job quite a challenge.

Currently, Kurt lives and works from his home in Indianapolis, Indiana. He can be reached via e-mail at kwall@kurtwerks.com.

Acknowledgments

I would like to thank the following people for their help with this book. First, my brother, Thomas Patrick Lathrop, Internet and network coordinator, Division of Information Technology, San Francisco State University. Linux is a child of UNIX, and Linux enthusiasts, administrators, and writers, particularly those from a DOS or Windows background, keep returning to UNIX (somewhat unwillingly), rather like grown children returning to the family home. Thomas Patrick has been a UNIX administrator since the earliest days that UNIX was seen as enterprise-capable, and he eased my frequent returns to the fold.

At Apress, Publisher Gary Cornell commissioned this book, and Editorial Director Karen Watterson made many helpful contributions, not the least of which (especially prized by an author) were her enthusiasm and encouragement.

This, my second Linux book, would not have seen the light of day without the efforts of Apress' editorial and production staff, including Jason Gilmore, the open source editor, and especially Kari Brooks, the indefatigable project manager and production editor. I wish I had a dime for every vial of midnight oil she's burned.

My technical editor, Kurt Wall, Linux consultant, writer, and editor, brought an attention to detail to the manuscript that one normally associates with hardened proofreaders. Any errors that remain are definitely mine.

Red Hat, Inc., has produced, under the leadership of Edward C. Bailey, some of the best documentation in the business. Despite his workload at Red Hat, Ed was as ready to give assistance with this book as he was with the first. The current Red Hat Linux product documentation manager, Sandra (Sam) A. Moore, helped me greatly in sharing her personal—and very clear and detailed—notes on NFS installations.

Also at Red Hat I want to thank Mike Evans, VP of business development. He is one of those managers who finds time in a busy schedule to respond promptly to queries, find answers, and distribute product to authors.

Finally, I want to thank Noelle Higgins, *née* Cullen, of Sliabh Glass, Kilmore, near Limerick, Ireland, who many years ago on the southern shore of the Persian Gulf suggested that I write a *non-fiction* book.

Preface

My first PC was an IBM PS2. It was built like a Sherman tank. The prospect of learning how to use this heavy and very advanced piece of machinery was daunting. Fortunately, it came complete with documentation almost as bulky as the computer itself. The docs were bound in thick, paperboard ring binders reminiscent of mainframe manuals, and their mass and solidity held promise: I felt certain that here lay the secrets of this computer.

But I could hardly understand a single sentence. The documentation might as well have been Greek. It had been written by IBM engineers, for other IBM engineers. The result for the novice was impenetrability.

Many beginning Linux books today take it for granted that the reader is, at the very least, familiar with UNIX conventions. As a result, these books are just as impenetrable for the Linux novice as that IBM documentation of many years ago was for me—and today's Linux novice may well be a Windows system administrator. I have therefore tried to write a *Windows-friendly* Linux book that will be an easy and practical introduction to the Linux operating system. My target audience is the professional Windows user, the Linux student, and the Windows sysadmin who is interested in learning the newer operating system. For the Windows user trying out a Linux desktop, this will be the only book on the subject needed. For students and sysadmins, this book will be a useful introduction to many facets of Linux, especially those that come under the heading of networking. Later, network and system administrators may want to pick up one of the specialist volumes on DHCP, Samba, Apache, Sendmail, and so on.

According to IDC, a market research firm, small businesses already represent 48 percent of all Linux server installations, and Linux penetration into the small- and medium-sized business market is expected to grow. Small business is a primary market for this book, and I've drawn the scenarios used in this book from the small business environment. However, individual workgroups in a large firm can be very similar to a small business, and the workgroup is often one of the first places a system administrator will experiment with Linux. So I hope this book will find its way into larger companies as well.

One of the reasons I wrote this book was the number of young Microsoft sysadmins I've met over the past few years who tried to become acquainted with Linux, and who ended their initial experiments in frustration at installation problems, poor hardware support, and so on. These "teething problems" have been largely overcome with the latest Linux releases. When it comes to hardware compatibility, Linux may now be considered a more mature platform than Windows XP.

However, there's no doubt that a computer operating system designed to emulate UNIX brings both advantages and disadvantages to the more recent generation of PC users and administrators. One of these disadvantages is UNIX's traditional reliance on command-line administration. It's now many years since most computer users were weaned from dependence on the command line, and the veterans' boast that Linux will still run a DOS version of Lotus 1-2-3 from the 1980s, which didn't even support a mouse, is irrelevant (and eccentric) to today's GUI-centric computer audience.

I've tried to address this issue by showing that many common administrative tasks in Linux can now be performed in a familiar Windows-style environment. Many readers will be surprised to discover that in Linux today, point-and-click tools for basic administration exist not only for a Web server, such as Apache, but even for BIND, the domain name system (DNS) server. The mouse, if not yet taking over, is at least rearing its head and beginning to roar.

This is even truer in the realm of desktop productivity applications. "Linux on the desktop" has, during the past 2 years, gone on a roller-coaster ride in the press, in venture capital boardrooms, and among developers. It has gone from being hyped, not once but several times, in the sage pages of *The Economist*, to being scornfully dismissed by some angry (and suddenly out of work) programmers. But through both the ups and the downs, developers at Red Hat, Ximian, OpenOffice.org, Sun Microsystems, and many individual development groups have kept on working, until now Linux actually is a capable desktop productivity platform.

Like most Linux users, I'm convinced that the OS is here to stay, both as a server and as a desktop solution, in the enterprise and in small- and medium-sized businesses. I don't think that is a pipedream. No less a company than IBM is putting serious resources into promoting Linux in all three corporate environments. I hope that this book, by providing an easy and practical introduction to Linux, will further its adoption by the market—and help ensure your success in implementing it.

CHAPTER ONE

Introduction

This is a results-oriented book. Its goal is to show small businesses, corporate workgroups, and in fact any small- to medium-sized organizations how they can, today, adopt Linux both as a server solution and as a workstation solution. There are three good reasons for doing this:

- To save money

- To achieve a higher degree of stability and simplicity

- To take advantage of certain definite benefits of "open source" software

The advantages of the Linux operating system have for years proven conclusive for the IT departments of major corporations, for ISPs, for e-commerce companies, and for retail chains with hundreds of point-of-sale terminals. And Linux has been administered by the highly trained staffs of these companies and organizations.

This book is written around the assertion that Linux is now user-friendly enough for the new Windows system administrator, and even the ambitious "designated computer person" in a small office or workgroup, to introduce it into their organizations. In short, Linux has matured to the point where its benefits are available to the average office—for the potential of thousands of dollars in yearly savings and far fewer support and upgrade headaches.

Who Should Read This Book

This book is written for several audiences:

- The MS Windows system administrator who wants a quick, results-oriented introduction to Linux and how to deploy it in a mixed Windows/Linux LAN environment

- The small business owner interested in upgrading and expanding his or her IT systems and saving money at the same time

- The manager or IT decision maker in a host of organizations that can benefit from Linux adoption, from schools to government offices to NGOs

- The computer student

Linux in Small Business: A Practical Users' Guide is meant to be an easy-to-use guide and resource. Although written primarily for use as a stand-alone text, it can easily be used in conjunction with a Linux class or seminar. It does not attempt to replace the many highly technical books already on the market devoted to covering in-depth subjects such as Internet security and e-commerce. Rather, it is a practical introduction to Linux in business today.

This book is not written for system administrators with UNIX or Linux experience. They will want a more technical volume.

Navigating This Book

Linux in Small Business: A Practical Users' Guide is organized into parts and lessons.

Chapter One is this introduction.

Chapter Two is devoted to Linux installation.

Chapter Three is an introduction to the Linux desktop, particularly GNOME.

Chapter Four shows how to connect to the Internet, through DSL or dial-up access.

Chapter Five, a very long part with many lessons, shows how to use Linux as a LAN and intranet server in a small business or workgroup, especially in a mixed Linux/Windows environment.

Chapter Six introduces some issues—both business and technical—to consider when evaluating whether or not to use Linux to self-host a Web site or corporate e-mail.

Chapter Seven shows how Linux is being used, and how it can be used, as a legitimate workstation solution for small businesses, organizations, or the corporate workgroup.

Chapter Eight is an introduction to Linux system management.

Chapter Nine is an introduction to that old bugbear: the Linux command line.

All lessons are presented in a step-by-step procedure, with screen shots selected to illustrate the instructions. There are three appendixes, the second of which provides a useful table of every configuration file mentioned in the book: where it is mentioned, what it does, and which program is used to configure it.

Presentation Plan

This book uses Red Hat Linux version 7.2. Red Hat is the market leader, and 7.2 is their latest offering as of late 2001.

I start from the premise that the professional Windows user knows little or nothing about Linux, other than it could be a way to increase productivity and lower computing costs in his or her firm—both accurate assumptions. And, since the Windows user is unlikely to be adept at command-line operations, I concentrate the presentation on ways to manipulate the system via the desktop, in a graphical, point-and-click manner that is most familiar to the reader.

This means that configuration-file editing and command-line operations in general only come up when absolutely needed. For reference, an entire chapter on command-line operations is included at the end of the book.

In order to make configuration, particularly LAN configuration, easier, I have written a number of configuration files, which are available for download from my consultancy's Web site, `http://www.linuxleap.org`.

The book and the lessons in it are designed to be friendly, unintimidating, easy to read, and quick to learn. Material is presented in easily digestible chunks. The presentation is oriented toward the subject matter: In lessons where exercises would be useful, exercises are given, and in lessons that would benefit from a scenario, a scenario is presented. Nearly all of Chapter Five, for instance, is presented in an extended scenario.

Finally, the book is peppered with real-life examples of how Linux is being adopted today.

Linux Benefits

The benefits of using Linux in a small firm or workgroup are exactly the same as using it in an enterprise. It all comes down to cost. The cost of traditional computing starts at purchasing hardware and continues through software purchase, licensing fees, hardware and software upgrades, support, training, and finally disposal. Of all these, licensing fees, upgrades, and support are the most notorious. Fees increase as the company grows and, although an expensive irritant, are at least foreseeable. Software upgrades come more frequently than they should, are often incompatible with previous versions, and too often require expensive hardware upgrades. Support has been cited as the worst cost of all, for it is least manageable: upgrades are likely to require more time—and more downtime—than planned, and breakdowns due to viruses and general instability cost time and money.

With Linux, these costs either do not occur at all or are greatly reduced. Most of the software is free—or, for convenience, it can be purchased once and then loaded onto as many computers as desired. With few exceptions, there are no licensing fees. Software upgrades can be downloaded for free over the Internet and seldom require hardware upgrades. Support is likely to be less expensive also, because less is needed for the following reasons:

- *Immunity to Windows viruses.* Ninety-nine percent of computer viruses are written for the Windows operating system. One of the main reasons behind this concentration is that Windows is far easier to write viruses for. Linux, out of the box, has security features that defeat most common viruses.

- *Stability.* Although the latest versions of Windows are more stable than previous versions, a badly written application—or even a badly written device driver—can still destabilize the entire operating system. This is far less likely to happen on the Linux platform, due in part to its more advanced memory management. If an application does crash in Linux, the chance of it bringing down the entire system is remote.

- *Security.* Although security is unlikely to be as much of a concern in a small office as it is in a major enterprise, it is still a concern, particularly if the business is thinking of implementing its own external Web site or e-commerce site. Here again, Linux scores.

- *Modest hardware requirements.* An older machine, such as a Pentium 133 (and even older machines), that would have an almost impossible time with a recent version of Windows can run Linux very successfully as an Internet server for dozens of workstations.

Table 1-1 gives an easy-to-read cost comparison of Linux and Microsoft.

Table 1-1. Cost Comparison for Linux versus Microsoft

COSTS	LINUX	MICROSOFT
Initial Costs		
Hardware purchase	Yes	Yes
Operating system purchase	Optional	Part of hardware purchase price
Applications purchase	Optional (no cost for free software)	Yes
Recurring Costs		
Licensing fees	No	Yes
Hardware upgrades	Seldom	Regularly
Operating system upgrades	Optional	Yes
Applications upgrades	Optional (no cost for free software)	Yes

Cost comparisons of Linux versus Microsoft are always so overwhelmingly favorable to Linux that they lead to the following questions: What is open source, or "free," software? How is it produced and supported? What makes it better than traditional proprietary software?

Open Source Software

The common perception of software developers, particularly open source software developers, is not that different from the perception of hackers in general: primarily young men with astonishingly low muscle tone, poorly developed social skills, narrowly focused interests, low self-esteem masquerading as arrogance, and a disdain for business. Anyone who has worked in Silicon Valley will recognize that stereotype.

However, the programmers leading the open source effort are in fact professionals—developers, consultants, academics, and company officers—many of them now entering middle age. They are people working in Linux primarily for the love of it, who are motivated by the desire to be team contributors and produce the best work they can to refine the best computer operating system in the world.

Red Hat (http://www.redhat.com) is a publicly traded company, showing an operating profit, busy consolidating its market share, and inserting its tentacles into every nook and cranny of the Linux OS, database, consulting, and software training business it can find. Like every business, it's in business to make money. And it makes a significant amount of its income by selling open source software.

The term *open source* refers to software that is distributed with its source code under a license that allows that code to be modified by the user. Generally, such software is copyrighted under the GNU General Public License (GPL). That does not mean that all software copyrighted under the GPL is free of charge. It means

- The program must be distributed with its *source code,* the computer code that enables a programmer to see exactly how it works, and to modify it.

- The program can legally be examined and modified by anyone.

- The program, either original or modified, can be redistributed, for a charge or for free, but must be redistributed under the same license.

The boxed Linux distribution you may have bought retail, at a computer store or bookstore, is an example of open source software. You paid for it, and you received the added value of documentation, an easy-to-install CD, and possibly a period of free support. You can now load that copy of Linux onto as many machines as you want. You can give it away. If you want, you can modify it and sell the modified version. The only things that are absolutely necessary under the GPL are that you include the source code of your modifications and either sell or give it away under the same license.

You may be wondering, How does good software get produced under such a license? Books have been written on this subject.

The majority of open source software is written by programmers who are interested in writing it because it is useful, because it is a challenge, because it is a creative act that brings its own rewards, and because it enhances their standing in their professional community. Some open source software is written as a business proposition, because the company involved hopes to make money by selling value-added products or services. Often in these cases, the corporation acts as a "maintainer," with a core of programmers that work with a highly distributed (i.e., worldwide) group of volunteers contributing to the same project.

It is easy to see that the quality of open source software benefits from the fact that its developers are writing it because they want to. Often the work is voluntary toil, undertaken and performed with pleasure, with the goal of observing the completed product with pride.

Open source software thus brings three advantages to the market:

- It is likely to have fewer bugs. In general, the code will be better written than that found in proprietary software.

- It is likely to be released as a production version only when it is ready.

- Fixes will be added to the latest release as soon as they are made, which will typically be as soon as they are discovered to be needed. This is in contrast to proprietary software, where a nonlethal problem is likely to be fixed according to a marketing and product release schedule.

Open source software, however, because of its strong engineering focus and the distributed nature of its producers, also brings two disadvantages:

- It tends to be more oriented toward the UNIX engineer and programmer than the average computer user.

- It is almost impossible for a commercial firm like Red Hat to release a new Linux version, according to a normal marketing and product release schedule, with every program guaranteed to be bug-free. This is because very few Linux developers work strictly to Red Hat's (or any company's) product release schedule.

The first of these disadvantages has begun to change. Developers are, more and more, taking pride in creating user-friendly programs. GNOME is an example of this trend. The second disadvantage, however, is less likely to change, and will continue to bedevil commercial release plans.

The Greening of Linux

Linux's reputation—which was well deserved during its first few years—as a command-line operating system, a type of system most computer users migrated away from in the early '90s, kept it from a wider market. That reputation kept it not only from the consumer market, but also from the younger end of the system administration market—a market largely shielded from the command line.

All that is now changing. Linux is now just as easy to install as Windows and often faster. Every Linux distribution is coming out with new GUI tools for system administration. The two major Linux desktops, GNOME and KDE, are both approaching the ease of use and finish of Microsoft Windows. And the development of office applications has reached a point where many standard office functions can be done perfectly well in Linux.

In GNOME, just as in other desktops, the user points and clicks a mouse to open a menu, start an application, or use a utility. As with other desktops, GNOME can access and manipulate files anywhere on the network through file managers. And, as with other desktops, Linux/GNOME has a full suite of office applications to choose from. Table 1-2 presents some of the applications this book covers and their Windows counterparts.

Table 1-2. Application Comparison for Linux and Microsoft

LINUX	MICROSOFT	FUNCTION
Office Applications		
StarOffice Writer	Word	Word processing
StarOffice Calc	Excel	Spreadsheet
StarOffice Impress	PowerPoint	Presentation
Evolution (in development)	Outlook	Calendaring/scheduling/e-mail
Internet Applications		
Netscape Navigator	Internet Explorer	Web browser
Netscape Messenger	Outlook	E-mail
Utilities		
Nautilus or GMC	Windows Explorer	File manager
Internet Configuration Wizard	Network and Dial-up Connections	Dial-up Internet connector
Network Configuration	Internet Connection Wizard	Network configuration utility
Graphics		
The Gimp	N/A. Adobe Photoshop is the Windows alternative	Drawing and graphics manipulation program
Multimedia		
XplayCd	Media Player	Music CD player
RealPlayer	Windows Media	Streaming video and audio player

It should be noted that, just as the entries under Microsoft applications are far from inclusive, there are many more applications available in Linux/GNOME than appear in Table 1-2.

The State of Linux Today (and Tomorrow)

This book is being published during a period of recession in the IT industry. Linux has not been immune to this general downturn. However, as the industry consolidates, the major players gain strength and market share. And new software start-ups still appear.

A peculiar strength of Linux, and of the open source software world in general, is that improvement and innovation are not always tied to market conditions. The Linux kernel—the central part of the operating system—continues to improve, literally weekly, and the latest versions are available for free download all over the Web. Major networking and application programs that ensure Linux's usefulness in a mixed Linux/Windows network environment and that define its use as an office workstation continue to be developed by open source programmers committed to their projects.

Linux already has a significant share of the ISP and e-commerce server market, and a reduction of that share is unlikely. Linux's share of the government, school, and small- and medium-sized business server market continues to increase, and it is finally penetrating the workstation market as well. It is gaining strength internationally, particularly in developing countries, such as China, that are not yet wedded to other operating systems.

Linux is, in fact, unusually well suited to weather an economic downturn, and even to prosper during it, due to its cost advantages, which rise as the size of the enterprise adopting it increases.

In short, Linux is here to stay.

CHAPTER TWO
Installation

This chapter of the book concentrates on obtaining and installing Linux, but it first starts with some background on different versions of Linux and of Linux desktops. Chapter Two consists of three lessons:

- Lesson 2-1. The Different Flavors of Linux and the Linux Desktop

- Lesson 2-2. Obtaining Linux Preinstalled

- Lesson 2-3. Installing Linux Yourself

Those who simply want to quickly install Linux—Red Hat 7.2 is the version covered by this book—should turn to Lesson 2-3, and then go back and read Lesson 2-1 at their leisure. There is a combined lesson review after Lesson 2-1 and Lesson 2-2, and a review after Lesson 2-3.

LESSON 2-1.
THE DIFFERENT FLAVORS OF LINUX AND THE LINUX DESKTOP

Isn't Linux a single operating system (OS)? If so, why are there so many "distributions" (and what exactly is a "distribution")? Is one distribution better than another? Which is the best desktop to use?

Linux Distributions

Since Linux is an open source operating system—in effect, free—it can be distributed by anyone, by any Linux company, and by any publisher. Selling Linux CDs in a computer store or a bookstore is the so-called retail distribution channel, and it is the most cost-effective way to make money with Linux.

For this reason, a number of Linux companies have sprung up (and just as they continue to spring up, others fade away) to sell their own versions of the operating system. These different versions of Linux are the so-called distributions. A Linux distribution sold retail will include the operating system and perhaps some applications on CDs, along with printed documentation and a period of free telephone or Web-based support. The boxed sets of these companies all look different, but all have certain basic things in common. Their similarities and differences are summarized in Table 2-1.

Table 2-1. Similarities and Differences in Linux Distributions

SIMILARITIES	DIFFERENCES
The Linux Operating System (OS)	Kernel version
	Installation routine
	OS configuration
	Post-installation configuration tools
X Window System	Desktop (either GNOME or KDE)
	Applications

Fundamentally, all Linux distributions are the same in that they use the same operating system. And, if two different distributions are using the same X Window desktop, they will look much the same as well. However, it is common for different distributions to try to customize their versions of Linux for specific market segments, such as server clusters for ISPs, file and print servers, and developer and office application workstations.

Although new small distributors are constantly entering the market, they generally do not succeed in grabbing market share from the established firms. They come and they go. And, since this is a period of market consolidation (late 2001), even some of the larger and more established distributions have either recently failed or are on the verge of failing. In such a market, however, the strong are in a better position to survive. Of the following four distributors, Red Hat is now profitable and Mandrake has successfully completed another round of funding.

The major distributors in America and Europe (as of late 2001) are as follows:

- *Red Hat Linux.* Very well financed and businesslike, Red Hat is quickly becoming the standard distribution. They have a large share of the retail and the corporate markets. They are the slickest and most corporate-looking of the distributions, and they are building a revenue-generating training program. In addition, their online update service (covered in Chapter Nine of this book) promises to become a major factor in attracting both corporate and home users to the fold. Their default desktop is GNOME.

- *Caldera.* The potential surprise story of distributors, Caldera is very well established and has a strong distribution oriented toward the ISP and enterprise-level markets. They also have strong support among resellers and consultants. Their one problem has always been the retail channel—

the physical isolation of Utah (where they are based) does not encourage a global, or even national, perspective of product marketing. However, a recent merger and commercial additions to their enterprise product line are strengthening Caldera's position. Their default desktop is KDE.

- *Mandrake.* As the major French distribution, Mandrake has the majority of the French market. They started as a knockoff of Red Hat, but they have since gone their own way. They have some good ideas regarding ease-of-use enhancements, but their distribution still suffers from rough edges. A recent management shake-up may lead to a more focused strategy. Their great strength is their retail distribution arm. Their default desktop is KDE.

- *SuSE.* As the major German distribution, SuSE has a large share of the German market.

A volunteer-driven distribution called Debian has many adherents, but little retail market share. Of the two companies that chose a year ago to base their commercial distributions on Debian, Storm Linux and Corel, one has folded and the other has sold its Linux business.

Red Hat was chosen as the basis for this book for several reasons. It is a distribution oriented toward business, rather than the casual user or computer hacker. The installation routine is arguably the industry's best, with few quirks and few obstacles for the Windows user. (In fact, many Windows users may find Red Hat Linux easier to install than Windows!) Many of the most important server programs, such as Sendmail, Samba, and Apache, are configured to start up with either only slight adjustments or right out of the box. In addition, Red Hat's network management program ensures easy upgrade and maintenance. Finally, it is important for commercial users to buy products from a company that is likely to last. Red Hat is very well capitalized, has an increasing share of the market and, unlike so many open source firms, is profitable. It is likely to be around for the foreseeable future.

Red Hat and Journaling Filesystems

The latest Red Hat distribution (7.2, covered by this book) uses a journaling filesystem, a feature that up to now was limited to high-end UNIX systems.

Why is this important?

In the unfortunate case of an unplanned system shutdown (a system crash), a journaling filesystem will usually result in greater data integrity and a much faster reboot. The journal keeps track of changes as they are made, greatly lessening the chances of data loss. And because e2fsck, the Linux version of

Microsoft's ScanDisk, does not have to be run when the system comes back up, the reboot will be much faster than usual.

From the server point of view, the inclusion of a journaling filesystem not only positions Linux as an even more viable solution for the enterprise-level market, it also brings enterprise-level quality to small- and medium-sized business, at a fraction of the cost of a UNIX system. For workstations, it brings an unmatched level of data integrity.

Linux Desktops

Whereas Windows users are locked into Microsoft's proprietary desktop (the set of icons, menus, and so on that the screen displays), Linux users have a choice between two. The two competing desktops for the Linux operating system are GNOME and KDE. How can a single operating system have two different desktops?

Linux originally functioned solely as a command-line OS, and many Linux servers are still set up that way. In Linux, the OS itself is separate from the software that runs the desktop—which is just one thing that makes it very hard for an application crash, for instance, to crash the operating system. However, few people today—even few system administrators—are happy to be faced with only a command-line interface, and early on various desktop solutions were developed. There were several on the market just a few years ago. Now the field has narrowed to just two. GNOME and KDE do exactly the same thing, and they even look quite similar. Both are open source, and both are being continually improved by the voluntary teams dedicated to them. Certain applications run better in KDE than in GNOME, and certain applications run better in GNOME than in KDE. All such applications are of secondary importance: The most important applications run well in both. GNOME probably takes the palm in user configurability. Which desktop you want to use is a matter of personal choice, for although the major distributions have different default desktops, they also all let the user choose which one he or she wants to use at start-up.

This book uses the GNOME desktop, because it is Red Hat's default, it is very configurable, and it also has somewhat more industry support among large companies that are beginning to deploy and support Linux.

GNOME itself comes in several different flavors. The differences among them are not very significant—they mostly boil down to variations in appearance and some minor functionality. A company called Ximian, founded by GNOME's original developers, makes available their version, which is highly customized and full-featured, with a number of add-on programs. It can be either downloaded (they have an excellent online installation routine) or ordered on CD. Red Hat has its own version, which, although vanilla in taste, has virtues similar to the distribution it runs on: It is businesslike and reliable.

LESSON 2-2.

OBTAINING LINUX PREINSTALLED

Obtaining Linux preinstalled is the easiest way to get started with Linux servers and workstations. The benefits are considerable.

- It saves time.

- You know that all your hardware (including video cards and modems) is Linux compatible and that there will be no surprises.

- There is frequently a warranty and/or service offering.

There are many companies to choose from. They range in size from the Linux-aware, privately owned local computer store (a disappearing species for years) to Dell, IBM, and Compaq, the biggest PC retailers in the world. In addition, you may choose between Linux specialists (i.e., companies that sell only Linux and Linux products) and larger companies whose Linux offerings consist of only one small line.

It is axiomatic that a large company can usually undercut a smaller firm in the same line of business. This is due to the economies of scale. This axiom does not hold true if the smaller company is willing to take a serious loss in order to build market share, or if the larger firm is confident enough of its position—probably a semimonopoly position—to unjustifiably raise it prices. But it does hold true most of the time, and investigation will reveal that larger firms selling preloaded Linux systems generally offer better prices than smaller firms.

There are more issues to consider, however, than just price. A dedicated Linux company may offer better support than a firm selling primarily Microsoft products. The cost and quality of support is a complex variable in the cost equation, and the corporate purchaser needs to consider it seriously.

Of the system examples that follow, two are from major retailers and the last is from a dedicated Linux independent.

Dell

Dell is, as of late 2001, the largest PC retailer in the world. It offers a full line of Linux servers from its excellent Web site, many of which can be ordered preloaded with Red Hat Linux. An entry-level small business server, with an 850MHz Intel Pentium III processor and 256MB of memory, a 20GB hard drive, two network interface cards, and Red Hat Linux preinstalled was recently quoted at $959. This is a very good value, and Dell also offers service and support.

Compaq

Compaq also offers a range of Linux servers. Their Web site has an interesting feature that enables users to do a price comparison of the same system hardware preloaded with a Microsoft solution or with a Linux solution. A recent quote for a server with similar specifications as the Dell server (see previous section), with Microsoft's Small Business Server 2000 and five client access licenses (CALs), was $1,299 more than the identical system with Red Hat Linux preinstalled—and no client licenses ever required.

QLI Tech Linux Computers

This independent Linux specialist offers a full range of servers, desktops, workstations, and laptops, all specially designed for and preloaded with Linux. Notebooks, complete with internal network cards and 192MB of RAM, start at $1,731.

Lesson Review

The preceding lessons were an overview of information necessary for the Linux specialist to know and interesting for the casual user. You learned

- What a Linux distribution is and the basic similarities and differences common among them all

- The major commercial distributions as of late 2001

- Why Red Hat was chosen for this book

- There are two different desktops, GNOME and KDE, and why this book is written around GNOME

- Like Linux itself, GNOME comes in several different versions

- Why and how to buy preinstalled Linux systems

LESSON 2-3.

INSTALLING LINUX YOURSELF

Installing Linux has never been easier. Problematic as recently as two years ago, it is now pain-free. Even installing Linux in a dual-boot, Linux/Windows configuration is easy provided enough free disk space is available (see the Note later in this section).

Not only has the software gotten better, but the documentation, too, is much improved over just two years ago. (That is to say, the documentation sold with the retail product. Free, open source documentation is still very uneven.) In fact, the various installation guides and getting started guides now sold with the major distributions are often as good as Microsoft's efforts in this field.

However, it is easy to get bogged down in the details, especially for the novice, and the subject of installing Linux onto a Windows computer is still poorly covered. Therefore, this lesson is in three sections, each one addressing a different reader or a different situation.

Which Section to Read First

There are three sections to the installation instructions:

1. Quick Install Guide

2. Installing Red Hat 7.2 in Detail

3. Disk Partitioning Guide

Table 2-2 shows which section or sections each user should read.

Table 2-2. A Guide to the Installation Instructions

USER	SECTION(S)
Experienced Linux user	Quick Install Guide
New user	Installing Red Hat 7.2 in Detail
Installing Linux on a PC with Windows, with free disk space (see Note)	Installing Red Hat 7.2 in Detail
Installing Linux on a PC with Windows, without free disk space (see Note)	First, Disk Partitioning Guide, then Installing Red Hat 7.2 in Detail

NOTE *When you install Red Hat Linux on a Windows machine, the installation routine will give you a choice: either remove Microsoft Windows or keep it, and set up the computer to dual-boot Linux or Windows. That is, when you start the computer, you will be prompted to choose which OS you want to run. This way, you can switch between one operating system and the other simply by rebooting the computer.*

However, to keep your current OS and install Linux on the same hard disk, you must first have enough free space on your hard disk—free space on which to install the new operating system.

Free space has to be understood clearly.

*The Windows OS occupies a space on the hard drive that has been specially formatted for it called a **partition**. Normally, this partition occupies the entire hard disk.*

*To install Linux, it is not enough to have free space on the Windows partition. You must have free disk space **outside** of the Windows partition. (The only way of getting around this is not suitable for a production system.)*

This means that, if you want to install Linux on a Windows machine, you must first either remove the Windows OS or reduce the size of its partition.

If you have doubts about this, please go first to the "Disk Partitioning Guide" section at the end of this lesson.

Quick Install Guide

The following steps are quick instructions for installing Red Hat Linux 7.2. A complete installation, which this book recommends, requires almost 2GB of disk space free. You will want more space for additional application programs. If you are installing on a machine running Windows and you want to keep the Windows operating system, the free space must be outside the Windows partition.

1. Reboot with CD number 1 in the machine.

2. The initial screens are self-explanatory. At the Install Options screen (see Figure 2-1), choose Custom, unless you are doing an upgrade from a previous installation or you are a qualified system administrator installing a pure server.

3. On the next screen, titled Choosing Your Partitioning Strategy, choose the option "Have the installer automatically partition for you."

4. The next screen, Automatic Partitioning, is the most important. If you are installing Linux as the sole operating system, choose "Remove all partitions on this system" (see Figure 2-2). If you are installing on a Windows machine, and you intend to keep that OS, choose "Keep all partitions and use existing disk space" (see Figure 2-3). Checking the Review box allows you to see a graphical representation of your partitions on the next screen.

5. Click the Next button to move on to the Boot Loader Installation screen (see Figure 2-6). Select the "Use GRUB as the boot loader" option. In addition, click the option to install the Boot Loader record on the MBR (unless you are dual-booting a Windows NT system or already have a separate multi-OS boot program, in which case choose the second option: /dev/hda1). Finally, check which OS you want to boot automatically.

6. The next screen, GRUB Password, allows you to add extra password security. You will already need to remember one to enter your system; if you want to remember two, add that here.

7. On the Network Configuration screen, enable DHCP if your computer uses it. If your computer will have a static IP address, type that in as well as the hostname. The netmask, network, and broadcast addresses will be configured automatically upon entering an IP address. The gateway and DNS addresses can be added if desired (see Figure 2-8). Note that all of this can configured and reconfigured quite easily after installation.

8. On the firewall screen, choose "No firewall." For the reason behind this, see the "Installing Red Hat 7.2 in Detail" section.

9. Install the language support you desire and set the correct time. Enter your root password and add users if desired (see Figure 2-9).

10. Accept the Authentication Configuration screen as is.

11. Choose all packages by selecting Everything at the bottom of the screen (see Figure 2-10).

12. Check the automatically probed settings for your video card, and change them if necessary.

13. Insert the second Linux installation CD when prompted.

Installing Red Hat 7.2 in Detail

These instructions are somewhat more detailed than the instructions in the "Quick Install Guide."

1. First, make sure that you have enough free disk space. This book suggests installing everything, which takes almost 2GB of hard disk space. Applications such as StarOffice will take more, so it is a good idea to have 3GB free. (This seemed like so much once, but who would hesitate now?)

2. It is not necessary to install Linux on a "virgin" PC. You can easily install it onto a Windows machine, either by automatically deleting the Windows OS and replacing it with Linux or, as long as there is enough free disk

space available outside of the Windows partition, by installing Linux alongside Windows, creating a dual-boot computer. If you choose the second option, you may have to "shrink" the Windows partition. For instructions on using third-party programs to repartition your hard disk, see the "Disk Partitioning Guide" section at the end of this lesson.

3. Insert the first Linux CD into the computer and reboot.

NOTE *If your computer won't boot from a CD.*

Nearly all modern computers will boot from CD—if yours does not, it is either because the computer's setup routine needs to be changed or simply because it is an older machine and incapable of booting in this fashion. If that is the case, then there are several alternatives, the simplest and most direct being to boot from a Linux boot disk. This disk can be made quite easily—look at Appendix A, and then return here.

Following the initial welcome screen, the installation program will provide you with language selection, keyboard, and mouse screens. They are all self-explanatory.

4. The Install Options screen (Figure 2-1) is the first requiring user input. There are five different types of installation to choose from:

    • Workstation

    • Server

    • Laptop

    • Custom

    • Upgrade Existing System

    The Workstation, Server, and Laptop installation routines all have built-in limitations: The Workstation and Laptop installations automatically disable certain useful networking capabilities, and the Server installation does not install a number of useful applications—it is purely a command-line interface solution. For these reasons, I suggest that most users install everything. That means choosing the Custom installation option. Table 2-3 clarifies this recommendation.

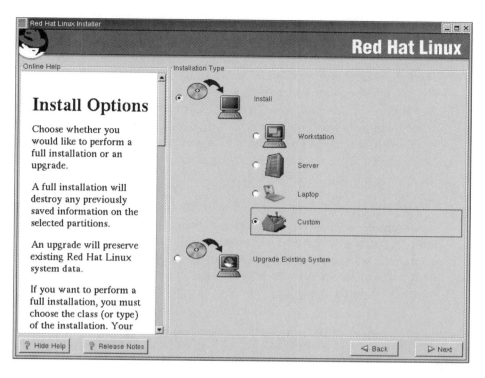

Figure 2-1. The Install Options screen, with Custom selected. This is the correct option for most users.

Table 2-3. Installation Option Guide

TYPE OF USER	DESIRED OUTCOME	SUGGESTED INSTALLATION OPTION
All	Desktop workstation	Custom
All	Laptop workstation	Custom
All	Dual-boot Windows/Linux	Custom
All	SOHO or business server	Custom
All	An upgrade	Upgrade
Professional UNIX/ Linux sysadmin	Command-line server	Server

Choose Custom and click the Next button.

5. On the next screen, titled Choosing Your Partitioning Strategy, most users should choose the option "Have the installer automatically partition for you." Choosing to manually partition with disk druid allows the user to manually configure RAID devices and the size, number, and location of partitions—the UNIX sysadmin will feel right at home. For everyone else,

the automatic procedure will work fine, creating and sizing partitions according to your disk size and amount of RAM.

6. The following screen, Automatic Partitioning, is the most important. If you are installing Linux as the sole operating system, choose "Remove all partitions on this system" (see Figure 2-2). This option will completely erase a Windows partition before creating new Linux partitions. If you are installing on a Windows machine, and you intend to keep that OS, choose "Keep all partitions and use existing disk space" (see Figure 2-3). Check the Review box to see a graphical representation of your partitions on the next screen.

   Two examples of that screen are given. Figure 2-4 shows a partition setup after choosing to remove all previous partitions. This is a single OS, Linux-only solution. Windows has been deleted. Figure 2-5 shows a dual-boot partition setup, with the Windows partition retained and new Linux partitions created alongside.

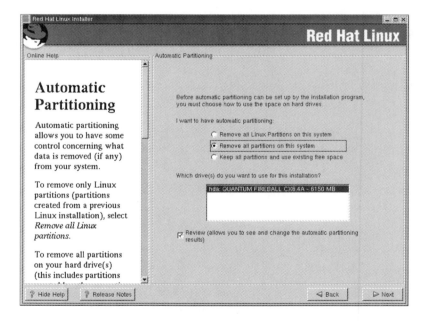

Figure 2-2. Installing Linux as the sole operating system with the "Remove all partitions on this system" option

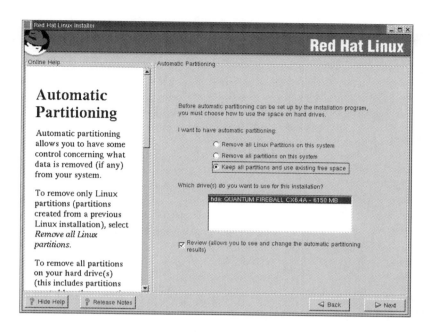

Figure 2-3. Installing Linux without destroying the Windows OS

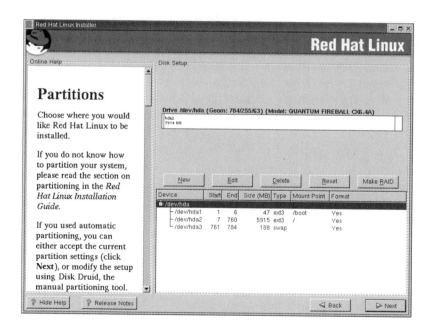

Figure 2-4. The Windows partition removed, for a Linux-only computer

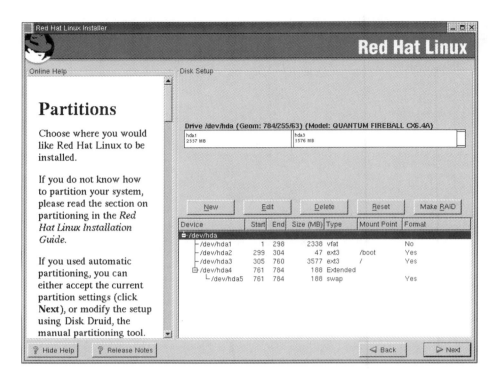

Figure 2-5. Both Windows and Linux on the same computer

7. Click the "Next " button to move on to the Boot Loader Installation screen (see Figure 2-6). Up until the latest Red Hat version, LILO was the boot loader—the program that lets the user choose which OS to start. GRUB is its replacement. Click the radio button next to the "Use GRUB as the boot loader" option. In addition, unless you are dual-booting a Windows NT system or already have a separate multi-OS boot program you want to keep (such as Boot Magic), select the option to install the Boot Loader record on the MBR. Finally, check which OS you want to boot automatically.

8. The next screen, GRUB Password, allows you to add extra password security. This is a good idea in a highly secure environment, but since a password is already necessary to log onto Linux, it will be overkill for many users.

9. The Network Configuration screen that follows gives you the opportunity to configure your computer's networking information during installation (it is not necessary to do it now—it can always be done later or changed). If your computer is not on a network, you can skip this screen entirely.

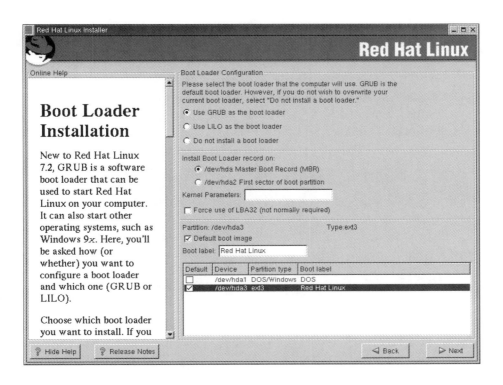

Figure 2-6. Installing GRUB on the MBR and Linux as the default OS on a dual-boot machine

NOTE *The Network Configuration screen is for configuring Ethernet networking and has little to do with configuring an Internet connection. Configuring stand-alone Internet connections is covered in Chapter Four; configuring Internet connections across a LAN is covered in Chapter Six.*

Most of the work of configuring a workstation connected to a LAN is done for you. If your network uses a DHCP server, check the "Configure using DHCP" box, check the "Activate on boot" box, and fill in your computer's hostname in the corresponding blank. (You may have to uncheck the DHCP box before you are able to enter the hostname. If that is the case, check the box again after entering the hostname.) If your computer has a static address, check the "Activate on boot" box and fill in your computer's IP address and hostname. Network, netmask, and broadcast addresses will be filled in automatically for you as you tab down. Gateway and DNS addresses can be added if you want or configured later, after the installation.

Figure 2-7 shows a computer attached to a DHCP server on a local LAN, with the hostname, gateway, and primary DNS information filled in. Figure 2-8 shows a computer configured with a static network address, 192.168.0.4, and the hostname of dell.hanifa.net. The network will be activated on booting. All the other numbers shown in Figure 2-8, except for the gateway and DNS, were automatically filled in by the installation routine.

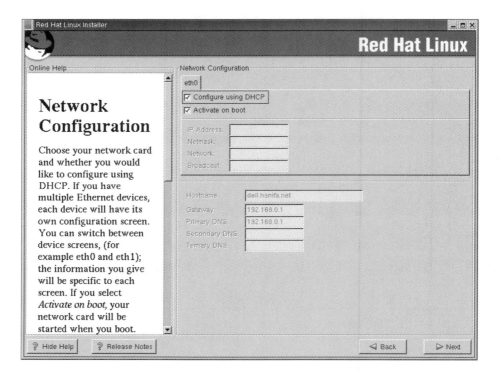

Figure 2-7. Computer configured to get its IP address from a DHCP server

10. The next screen, Firewall Configuration, offers to set up security between you and the outside world on the Internet. However, the program that this tool configures (ipchains), is not compatible with the more recent iptables program that this book suggests for the server—it is always best to use the most recent security software. Therefore, you should select "No firewall." Server setup is covered in Chapter Five, and security issues are covered in Chapter Seven.

11. The next two screens are largely self-explanatory. Linux supports many different languages, and you may load as many as you want and choose

your preferred default if it is different from the installation language. It is important to set your computer's time to your correct location, and you can do this either by using the map(s) provided (clicking the arrows next to "view" presents several maps to choose from) or by clicking the UTC Offset tab and choosing your time zone according to its difference from Greenwich Mean Time (now called Coordinated Universal Time, or UTC).

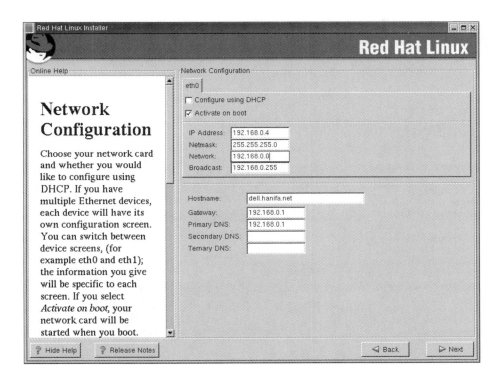

Figure 2-8. Computer configured for a static IP address

12. The Account Configuration screen is where you set up the root user's (the administrator's) password, and it is also where you can add other accounts with their own passwords.

    Linux is by nature a multiuser system, and in Linux all users have passwords—that is a fundamental rule. Another fundamental rule is that not all users are alike: A typical user cannot easily change system settings or even gain access to certain directories—a built-in security feature. The one user who has total access and can change or configure everything is called the *root user:* the system administrator.

Every Linux system starts with this root user, and he or she needs a password. You can add other users as you see fit, first during installation and later once the system is up and running.

In Figure 2-9, the root user has entered his/her password and also included account names and passwords for two other users

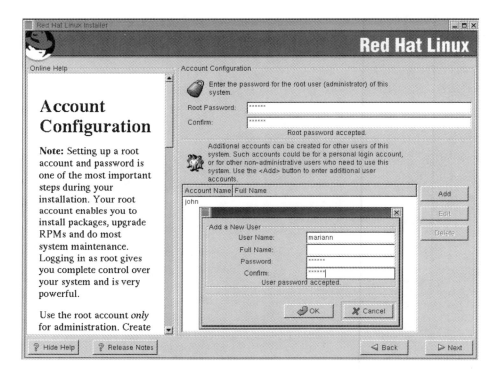

Figure 2-9. Adding account names and passwords

13. The next screen, Authentication Configuration, can be accepted as is.

14. The Selecting Package Groups screen is critical—it is why you use a custom installation instead of a preconfigured workstation or server installation. By far the simplest thing to do, to ensure functionality, is to install everything. Unneeded services and programs can always be turned off later, after installation.

    To install everything, simply pull the vertical scroll bar to the bottom of the screen and select Everything. This is shown in Figure 2-10.

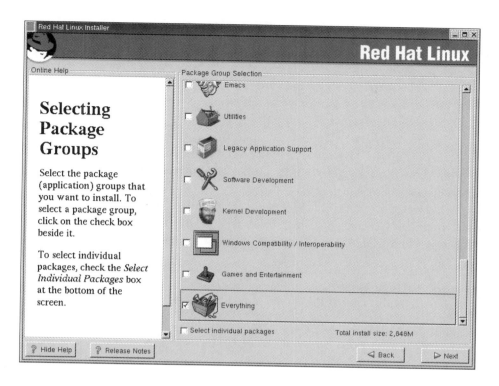

Figure 2-10. Installing all software packages—the safe way to go

15. At this point the semiautomatic routine starts to configure the X Window System—the system that runs GNOME. If it does not automatically select your correct video card, the correct amount of video card RAM, and your monitor, you can select them yourself (if your exact video card or monitor is not listed, choose either a similar one from the same manufacturer or one of the generic models). You can also choose whether to start Linux at the command line or graphically. I strongly suggest the command line.

16. And now, after you click the Next button a couple more times, sit back and wait. The actual installation will take a few minutes. You will be prompted to insert the second CD when necessary, and when finished, you will be prompted again to insert a blank floppy for a boot disk, which is handy to have if for some reason the system becomes corrupted.

    When finished, the CD will automatically eject, and your computer will reboot. If you decided to keep a prior Windows installation, you will be prompted to choose which operating system to boot.

Disk Partitioning Guide

To install Linux on a computer with another operating system already installed, you need to create free space on the hard disk. This can be done either by eliminating the partition holding the current operating system or by reducing the size of the partition and installing Linux in the space freed.

In the first case, deleting the current partition, the current OS and all data is irrevocably destroyed. This is the simplest solution, but also the most destructive. However, if you don't need the old OS on that computer and you have all the data backed up elsewhere, it is the best solution.

In the second case, the old OS remains on the drive. Although Linux and Windows cannot normally be run at the same time, the user may boot the OS he or she wants to run each time the computer starts.

NOTE *For the first-time Linux user experimenting with the OS, the scenario labeled "The Second Case" may be the best to follow for a first installation. Although somewhat more costly—a third-party program such as PowerQuest's PartitionMagic has to be purchased—it has the advantage of being nondestructive, which can be useful early on in an assessment procedure.*

The First Case: Deleting the Current Partition

Prior to Red Hat version 7.2, this method needed a command-line operation. It no longer does. The latest Red Hat Linux distribution enables the user to delete the Window partition during the installation process.

Follow the installation procedure outlined in the "Installing Red Hat 7.2 in Detail" section. In step 6 of that section, choose the "Remove all partitions on this system" option. This will delete the Windows partition, thus freeing up the entire disk for the Linux installation. A graphic representation of the new partition setup is shown in Figure 2-4.

CAUTION *If you choose the "Remove all partitions on this system" option and go forward with the installation, there's no way of going back and retrieving your Windows installation or data—short of heroic efforts well beyond the scope of this book.*

The Second Case: Reducing the Size of the Partition

This second scenario does not destroy the current Windows installation, but only reduces it, thus creating room for the Linux installation.

Various distributions approach this problem in different ways. Mandrake ships with its own graphical repartitioning tool as part of its installation routine. It works, but it is so confusingly presented that many newcomers to Linux and to partitioning in general will find in it little benefit. Caldera's eDesktop product used to ship with a stripped down version of PartitionMagic. Red Hat ships with FIPS, a command-line repartitioning program with many limitations. This is not the solution.

The solution is a third-party program such as PartitionMagic. It is not expensive, its design is intuitive, it loads into Windows, and if you don't want to run it manually, a wizard is available to create free space for you.

This is the solution I suggest to everyone who needs it, regardless of experience level. The procedure is as follows:

1. Obtain PartitionMagic and load it into Windows.

2. Reduce the size of the Windows partition.

3. Install Linux.

The Linux installation program will automatically create its own partitions from the free space available.

There is one special point to remember: If you decide to use PowerQuest's own boot manager (called BootMagic), when you load Linux, at the Boot Loader Installation screen (see Figure 2-6), choose to install GRUB (Linux's own boot manager) to the Linux boot partition, not to the MBR.

Figure 2-11 shows PartitionMagic displaying a single hard disk with a single large partition, and a Windows installation. This is a typical workstation scenario. Figure 2-12 shows the same system after reducing an almost 10GB Windows partition to 4.5GB and freeing up space for a Linux installation. Figure 2-13 shows the same system after a successful installation.

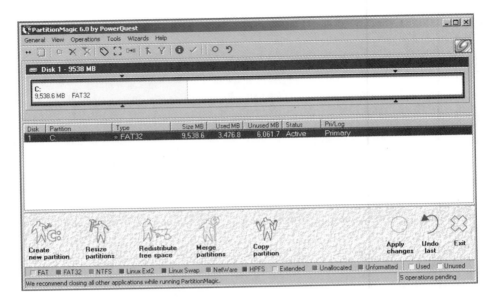

Figure 2-11. PartitionMagic displaying the typical pre-Linux setup: one big Windows partition

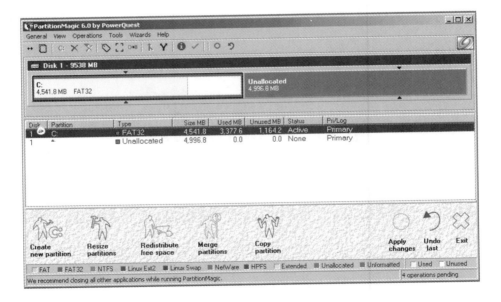

Figure 2-12. Reduced by half, with free disk space created

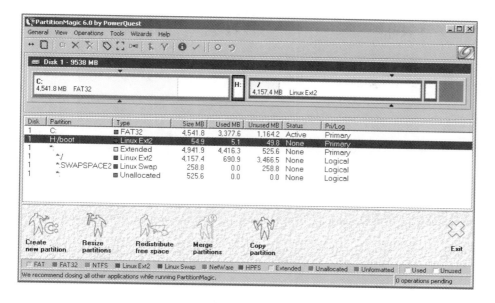

Figure 2-13. Two operating systems on the same machine

Lesson Review

The last two lessons were devoted to obtaining and installing Linux. You learned

- Some of the advantages of obtaining a computer preinstalled with Linux and some of the issues involved in choosing which firm to use

- About three companies, one a pure Linux shop, the others huge online retailers, that offer preinstalled Linux systems

- Some considerations to keep in mind when installing Linux on a Windows machine

- How to quickly install Red Hat 7.2

- The details of installation, including network and package selection

- The details of disk partitioning: what it is, when you need to do it, and how to do it best

What's to Come

To come is an introduction to Linux and the desktop and an initial exploration of the OS you just installed. The next section includes the following:

- How to log in, start the desktop, and log out

- A brief tutorial on accessing CDs from the command line

- An introduction to the Linux desktop environment, including the menu structure and window controls; the Linux desktop paradigm; and file and disk management

CHAPTER THREE

An Introduction to Linux and the Desktop

Many Windows users, and even many Windows system administrators, are intimidated when first faced with the bleak and baffling Linux command line. But there is little reason for the average user, and only somewhat more reason for the sysadmin, to spend much time there. Nearly all common operations in Linux can be performed in the comfort of a familiar Windows environment.

Chapter Three consists of four lessons, with a review at the end of Lesson 3-4:

- Lesson 3-1. Logging In, Starting the Desktop, and Shutting Down

- Lesson 3-2. Initial Configuration with Setup at the Command Line

- Lesson 3-3. Accessing CDs and Floppies from the Desktop and from the Terminal

- Lesson 3-4. An Introduction to the Linux Desktop

The procedure in Lesson 3-2 need only be performed once, and Lesson 3-3 is included so that users have some understanding of what goes on behind the scenes when they point and click at the CD and floppy icons on their desktop.

Reality Byte:

SECRETARIES USE LINUX, TAXPAYERS SAVE MILLIONS

Walk into the Largo, Florida, city hall and look at the two computer screens behind the reception desk. Receptionists, administrative assistants, and division fire chiefs here all use Linux instead of Windows, and most of them don't really notice one way or the other. But the elected officials who are responsible for Largo's IT budget certainly know about and notice Linux, because using Linux instead of Windows is saving the city a lot of money.

"The secretaries will never be able to figure it out." If that is so, then Largo employee Judy must be one of the world's smartest office workers. She is sitting at her desk, happily accessing an online city directory that lists all employees, vendors, and other important contacts.

Sysadmin Dave Richards points out that Judy does not technically have a computer of her own. She is using an NCD thin client that accesses a hefty server running Red Hat 7.1. Judy can move to any other desk, use her logon name and password on that desk's terminal, and voila! That desktop suddenly becomes "her computer."

But to Judy, what happens behind the screen doesn't matter. All she knows is that she clicks a program open and uses it for her work, keeping dozens of programs open at a time. She uses Windows at home but says, "I spend more time on the computer at work than at home, so I guess I'm really more comfortable with this system than with Windows now."

Dave and fellow sysadmin Mike Pearlman are even bigger fans of Largo's thin client system than Judy. Their 10-person IT staff supports 800 users running 400 devices (as Dave calls the thin clients). There is no way they could adequately support that many users and devices with such a small staff if they ran Windows on individual desktops. Dave says that if they had gone that route, "We'd be doing nothing but running around fixing PCs all day."

If Largo ran Windows 2000 as a server operating system, Dave says they'd have to run "a substantial server cluster" instead of a single machine, because "NT [or 2000] gets flaky when you run more than 40 clients, while Linux can handle hundreds." Dave has no exact figure for the cost of an adequate Windows server array for Largo's civic needs; it was obviously so much more expensive than the Linux alternative that it was never seriously considered.

On the client side, Dave estimates the current system, compared to Windows desktops, gives Largo direct hardware savings of about $300,000 per year, figuring that they'd have to swap out one-third of the city's desktops every year "just to stay current, not to increase productivity" if they ran Windows, a proposition Dave doesn't think would make the city's elected officials—to whom he reports—dance with joy.

Largo's computer-using workers are not, by and large, geeks. They are accountants, purchasing agents, and bookkeepers. They are rescue workers and police and fire personnel, managers and clerks, and so on. They are chosen for their skills in those areas, not for their ability to map out large-scale thin client networks or keep up with the latest Red Hat security patches. The point is, 800 Largo city employees, who are probably no more adept with computers than their counterparts elsewhere, use Linux all day, every day, without thinking about its significance.

by Robin Miller

LESSON 3-1.

LOGGING IN, STARTING THE DESKTOP, AND SHUTTING DOWN

IN BRIEF

1. Log in with your user name, or as root, and your password.

2. Start the X Window System with the startx command.

3. Shut down or reboot the computer with the poweroff or reboot command.

EXPLAINED

The first step is to log in.

The login procedure is identical whether you chose to start up Linux at the command line or graphically. The user is prompted, when Linux starts, to enter a login name and password. At this point it might be a good idea to consider the advantages and disadvantages of logging in normally as the root user (the system administrator).

....

Root versus Normal Users

Traditionally in the UNIX world, a world inhabited largely by network administrators, only the administrator had permission to log in as root. There was a very good reason for this.

The root user can utterly destroy a UNIX or Linux setup just by entering a few keystrokes and pressing the Enter key. (Note: From the command line and the root directory, the command is rm -f -r *. There is no recovery.)

An administrator responsible for maintaining a network of many users was therefore wise to restrict the root login to him- or herself. And even the administrator seldom logged in as root unless it was necessary. The downside was too great. Many UNIX administrators, early in their careers and in moments of fatigue, accidentally entered the command that would destroy their entire installation and would lead to even more fatigue-filled hours building it all up again.

So still today with Linux, if you are the one responsible for maintaining a LAN, either at home or in the office, you should log in as root only when necessary. And of course you should restrict the root user password—and the administrative tasks necessary for the root user—to yourself.

....

For this initial login, start the system as the administrator. Type in **root** as your login name, press the Enter key, and then enter your password. Pressing the Enter key once again starts Linux at the command line.

There is not a great deal to see. A few stark white letters and symbols against a black, unilluminated background. It is the experienced system administrator's darling, but it is empty and forbidding to most other computer users.

Fortunately, the user need not linger. Start the desktop by typing **startx** and pressing the Enter key. The terminal vanishes and the GNOME desktop appears (see Figure 3-1).

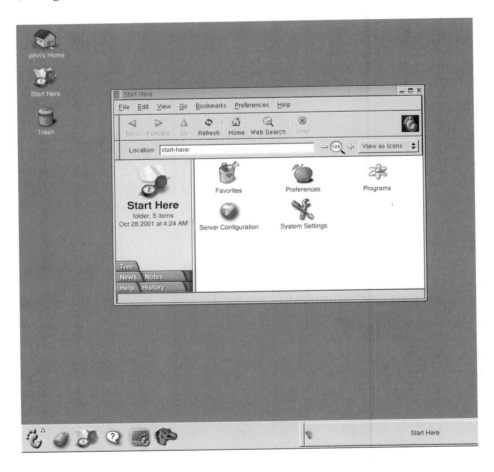

Figure 3-1. Starting GNOME for the first time

TIP *When you type commands at the command line, even simple ones such as startx, it is imperative that case be observed: A capital letter is very different from a lowercase letter in Linux. To start the X Window System, you must type **startx**—all lowercase. A single capital letter will cause the command to fail.*

The Desktop, GNOME, or the X Window System?

The first of these terms is both generic, meaning the Windows- or Mac-style screen that almost all users expect to see when they start up their computer, and specific, when it refers to the specific desktop program running (GNOME is one example, and KDE is another).

The desktop in Linux is composed of two major programs, one running on top of the other. The first is the X Window System. This provides the desktop's foundation. To the average user the X Window System is an invisible underpinning—you need only get involved with it if its configuration file needs tweaking. The second is the desktop program itself, which includes icons, menus, and desktop configuration programs. Red Hat's default, and the desktop used in this book, is GNOME.

The Start Here window in the middle of the screen opens automatically the first time that GNOME is started. Its System Settings and Server Configuration icons provide an entry to Internet and LAN setup, and much more. They are covered fully in Chapters Four through Seven.

You log out of the desktop in much the same way you log out of Microsoft Windows: First close any open programs, and then click the Start button at the lower left-hand side of the screen (the footprint icon), choose "Log out" from the bottom of the pop-up menu, and click Yes when prompted.

The average user is given two commands to shut the computer down: poweroff and reboot. (The system administrator has a third: the shutdown command, which is capable of many customizations.) Rebooting is likely to be used primarily by the administrator—Linux does not need the frequent reboots that Windows systems often require. The average user is more likely to use poweroff.

In both cases, the word is the command. To reboot the computer, type **reboot** and press the Enter key. To power off the computer, type **poweroff** and press the Enter key.

Linux is a very stable operating system—it's not unusual for servers to keep going for months. Even reconfiguration seldom requires a reboot. Most shutdowns will be to save electricity.

LESSON 3-2.

INITIAL CONFIGURATION WITH SETUP AT THE COMMAND LINE

Although most system configuration can be done within GNOME, in a Windows environment, soundcards and the X Window System (the latter only if reconfiguration is necessary) must be configured using Setup, a command-line utility program. Setup is an older program, and most users will prefer using the GUI configuration tools available within GNOME. However, since it is necessary to use this program for initial configuration, it may as well also be used for checking system services.

"System services" refers to programs that are set to automatically start when the computer boots up. The default settings are very seldom optimal for either a server or a workstation. Generally, some services that are unneeded are set to run, while others that are needed are not turned on. Naturally, every service that is necessary should be started automatically. However, starting a service at boot-up that you are unlikely to require (for instance, starting the Apache Web server in a firm that has no plans to self-host its own Web site) will use up a certain amount of RAM that otherwise would be free. (Starting unneeded services can also be a security risk: see Chapter Seven.) Of course, different users and administrators in different situations will have different requirements. Each administrator will have to make his or her own decisions about which programs he or she wants started at system boot-up, on the server, and on the Linux workstations.

Checking system services with Setup need only be done once. To start it, just enter **setup** at the command line and press the Enter key. Use the down arrow key to scroll down the list to "System services," tab to the Run Tool button, and press Enter again.

Check a service by pressing the spacebar to configure it to start at system boot. Table 3-1 gives suggestions for services to check for a server and for a workstation.

Table 3-1. Suggested Services to Start at Boot

SERVICE	SERVER	WORKSTATION
anacron	X	X
apmd	X	X
atd	X	X
autofs	X	X
crond	X	X
dhcp	X	

Table 3-1. Suggested Services to Start at Boot (continued)

SERVICE	SERVER	WORKSTATION
gpm	X	X
httpd	X	
identd	X	X
ipop3	X	
iptables	X	
keytable	X	X
kudzu	X	X
lpd	X	X
named	X	
netfs	X	X
network	X	X
nfs	X	X
nfslock	X	X
pcmcia		X (necessary for laptops)
pop3s	X	
portmap	X	X
postgresql	X	X
random	X	X
sendmail	X	
smb	X	X
syslog	X	X
telnet	X	X
webmin	X	
wu-ftpd	X	X
xfs	X	X
xinetd	X	X

After system services are properly configured, Setup can be used to configure the computer's soundcard. And, if there has been a problem with the X Window System, that can also be reconfigured with Setup. Most other system configuration parameters are more easily done with the range of GUI tools available.

After you set system services, it is a good idea to reboot.

LESSON 3-3.

ACCESSING CDS AND FLOPPIES FROM THE DESKTOP AND FROM THE TERMINAL

Command-line operations are covered in detail in Chapter Ten. This lesson covers how to access CDs from both the desktop and the terminal—the latter being a good thing for everyone to learn, since it makes operations at the desktop with CDs that much clearer.

IN BRIEF

1. CDs and floppies need to be mounted after insertion and unmounted before ejection.

2. In GNOME, accessing CDs and floppies is purely point and click.

3. Mount and unmount CDs either from the terminal or from GNOME—not both.

Mounting and Unmounting CDs and Floppies

In the traditional UNIX/Linux system, CDs, like all removable media, are mounted and unmounted from the command line. *Mounting* simply means being able to read to and write from removable media: a CD or a floppy disk. In the past, reading a CD, for instance, was a two-step procedure: First, the CD was inserted, and then it was mounted.

In the modern Linux desktop environment, things have changed. GNOME effectively takes over what used to be a manual operation, and it makes the mounting (at least of CDs) completely automatic. A CD is mounted and ready to read as soon as it is inserted. GNOME mounts the CD itself and, depending on the kind of data on the CD, a file manager (for text and data) or an audio player is automatically started—the CD is automatically both mounted and read.

However, this automatic mounting overrides the command line. It is possible, and in fact often desirable, to run command-line programs at the same time as

GNOME, either by opening a terminal window within the desktop (rather like opening an MS-DOS window within Windows 2000), or by switching to a full-screen terminal. You can switch to a full-screen terminal from within GNOME by depressing the Ctrl and Alt keys together, and at the same time pressing one of the function keys from F2 to F6. In this way, it is possible to keep up to five terminals open at once, while running the desktop on F7. Switch back to the desktop by pressing Ctrl+Alt+F7. It is not desirable, however, to attempt to mount or unmount a CD at the command line while GNOME is running. Such an attempt will generally fail, and it may leave the desktop in a confused condition: Is the CD being accessed or not? In the worst scenario, the CD may stubbornly refuse to be unmounted.

For this reason, try to access your CDs either from GNOME or from the command line, but not from both at the same time.

Mounting and Unmounting CDs and Floppies from a Terminal

To understand more fully how GNOME treats removable media, it's a good idea to know what's going on the background. The best way to understand this is to know how to manually mount and unmount a CD or floppy disk.

At the terminal, there is a four-step procedure to follow:

1. Insert the CD or floppy disk.

2. Mount the CD or floppy disk with the mount command.

3. When you've finished, unmount the CD with the umount command.

4. Eject the CD.

Here is a typical command line example:

```
mount /mnt/cdrom
```

This mounts the CD from the terminal. It can now be accessed via /mnt/cdrom. For a floppy:

```
mount /mnt/floppy
```

The floppy can now be accessed via /mnt/floppy.

Unmounting at the command line is very similar. To unmount a CD, for instance, before ejecting it, type the following:

```
unmount /mnt/cdrom
```

The CD is now ready to be ejected.

Mounting and Unmounting CDs and Floppies from GNOME

Mounting and unmounting from GNOME is much easier. CDs are mounted automatically as soon as they are inserted. However, they must still be unmounted correctly, even within GNOME. The procedure is to right-click the CD icon, and then choose the menu item at the very bottom of the pop-up menu: Unmount Volume. The CD is then automatically ejected.

A floppy is slightly different. After insertion, click the floppy icon on the panel. This automatically mounts the floppy disk, and a floppy icon appears on the desktop. Right-clicking the icon brings up another pop-up menu, from which you can open the floppy in the Nautilus file manager or in some other program. In order to unmount the floppy, just click the panel icon again.

Instructions and illustrations on how to insert a floppy icon on the panel and on using CDs and floppies within GNOME are given later in this chapter.

LESSON 3-4.

AN INTRODUCTION TO THE LINUX DESKTOP

Although there are a few differences, the Linux desktop—in this case, GNOME—will be comfortably familiar to Windows users. Things work much the same. And the Linux paradigm of multiple desktops makes multitasking more transparent and easier than ever before.

This lesson contains a brief introduction to desktop features. Details on using Linux as a workstation solution are covered in Chapter Eight.

The Main Menu Structure and Window Controls

Access the main menu by clicking the main menu button (the footprint at the bottom left-hand corner of the screen) once. The various submenus open up as the mouse pointer hovers over them. In Figure 3-2, the pointer is hovering over Programs, opening up that submenu.

The main menu has three command icons: Run, Lock Screen, and Log Out. The first opens a small dialog box, where you can either choose the program you want to run from a list or enter its name. The second brings up the screen saver, hiding the desktop. Only when the current user's password is entered will the desktop reappear. The Log Out command closes GNOME and returns you to the original login screen.

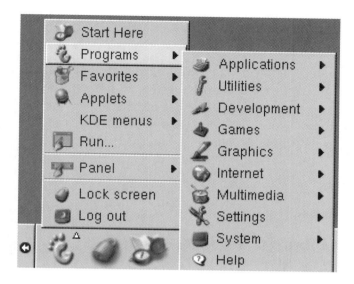

Figure 3-2. The main menu and the Programs submenu

There are four submenus within the main menu (five, with the addition of the KDE menus, if you have chosen to install everything). Programs is the first submenu, and it organizes the dozens of programs that come with every Linux distribution into several categories. (GNOME is a highly organized desktop. Dividing programs into separate categories makes them easier to find in the menu structure and avoids the "ticker tape" appearance of an endless submenu.) Figure 3-2 shows these categories, from Applications at the top to System at the bottom. Most are self-explanatory, such as Applications (meaning office and productivity applications), Games, Internet, and Multimedia. However, three categories, all dealing with configuration, need some explanation.

- *System.* These are the configuration tools for Linux and GNOME. Here you'll find tools to set up Internet access, the LAN, printing, and many other aspects of the system. This is the most important of the three configuration submenus.

- *Settings.* These are the configuration tools controlling the actual look and feel of the desktop, as well as the default appearance and behavior of applications.

- *Utilities.* This is something of a grab bag of relatively minor configuration tools. Many can be found duplicated elsewhere.

The main menu's other three submenus are Favorites, Applets, and Panel. Favorites is a folder for programs you use often—although many users will prefer to place those programs on the desktop as application launchers. Applets is a category of small programs—most of them utility programs—that can be added to the *panel,* which is the horizontal bar at the bottom of the screen. The Panel submenu presents several programs for panel configuration.

Hands On:

LAUNCHING A PROGRAM WITH THE MAIN MENU'S RUN COMMAND

To run a program using the main menu's Run command, follow these steps:

1. Click the main menu's Run icon.

2. With your mouse, drag the slider down to, and highlight, the Calendar program in the Available Programs box.

3. Click the Run button.

The Gnome Calendar program appears, as shown in Figure 3-3. This is an easy-to-use calendar and appointment program with a variety of views (day, week, month, or year) that can remind you of your appointments with a visual alarm, an audio alarm, by opening up a program, or by sending you (or someone else) an e-mail. Like all programs in GNOME, it can be started with the Run command, or you can start it from a menu by navigating from the main menu to Programs ➤ Applications ➤ Calendar.

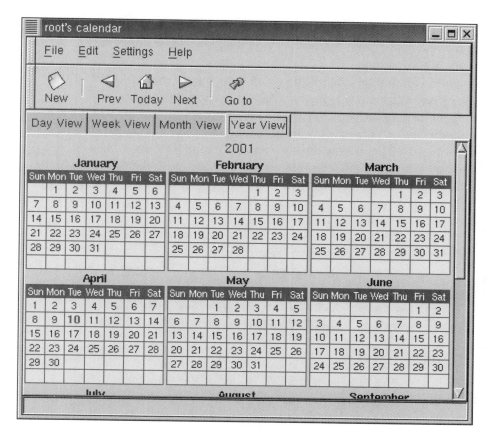

Figure 3-3. The GNOME Calendar program

Using Window Controls to Resize and Close Programs

Each application window in GNOME has three buttons in the upper right-hand corner: a Minimize button, a Resize button, and a Close button.

The Minimize button (the button with the single line) reduces the window to an icon on the tasklist. The Resize button (the one in the middle) maximizes the application window when it is first clicked and reduces the window to its original size when clicked again. The Close button (the button with the X) closes the program.

A window control menu opens when the user clicks once on the application window's upper left-hand corner. Some of the menu items simply reproduce the actions of the Minimize, Resize, and Close buttons, but others provide additional functions. For instance, the History menu item remembers, for future GNOME sessions, the exact desktop placement of the application.

Right-clicking an application's entry on the tasklist on the panel brings up a window with the "Kill app" command. This is useful when an application, for one reason or another, refuses to die—an example of application misbehavior that occurs seldom in GNOME, but that you want to be prepared for. Such an application is likely to exhibit other, even more antisocial traits, such as hogging the computer's processor. In this case the Kill app command comes in handy, closing down even the most stubborn and unruly program.

Hands On:

RESIZING, CLOSING, AND DESTROYING A PROGRAM

Practice resizing, closing, and destroying programs using the application window buttons and menus.

1. Click the Calendar program's Minimize button and restore it by clicking once on the tasklist's Calendar button at the bottom of the screen.

2. Practice resizing the program using the Resize button.

3. Close the program with the Close button, and then reopen it using the menu (Start ➤ Programs ➤ Applications ➤ Calendar).

4. Kill the program by right-clicking the tasklist at the bottom of the screen and choosing Kill app.

The Panel, the Pager, and the Linux Desktop Paradigm

The panel is the horizontal bar stretching across the bottom of the screen that holds a variety of program launchers and applets. The most important applet is the Pager, which is used to switch desktops—a new paradigm for the newcomer to Linux.

Linux lets you work as if your computer screen was actually just one of several computer desktops—as if your screen represented one of four connected terminals (the default number is four, but it can be higher). Using the Pager, you switch from one desktop to another. This is an excellent way to organize your work when multitasking. It is similar to having a desk large enough to organize your different tasks in different areas, all within easy reach. You can devote each desktop to a specific task and the application program or programs needed for that task.

Figure 3-4 shows an example of how this works. It appears at first that only one program is running, a graphics manipulation program called The Gimp (similar to Photoshop). However, the panel at the bottom of the screen shows a seven-button tasklist, which indicates several more programs running. At the bottom right is the four-window Pager (a similar tasklist and Pager are shown in greater detail in Figure 3-5).

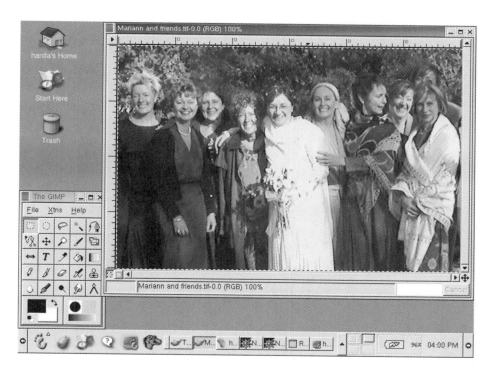

Figure 3-4. The Gimp running in one desktop, with the tasklist showing other running programs

Figure 3-5. Closeup of the Tasklist and Panel

In fact, the screen in Figure 3-4 shows only one of four running desktops. Each of the other three desktops has one program running. If you could see all four desktops indicated by the Pager in Figure 3-4 and Figure 3-5 simultaneously, it would look like Figure 3-6. If you look at the desktops starting with the one in the upper-right corner and moving clockwise, their programs are as follows:

- The Gimp (control panel and image)

- The Nautilus File Manager

- RealPlayer 8, showing the launch of the Mars Odyssey spacecraft

- Netscape Navigator, showing a photograph from The Guardian

You can switch to the desktop and the program of your choice either by clicking the appropriate Pager window or by clicking the program button on the tasklist. It is important to remember that although only one desktop is being displayed at a time, the programs in all four desktops are open and running in the background.

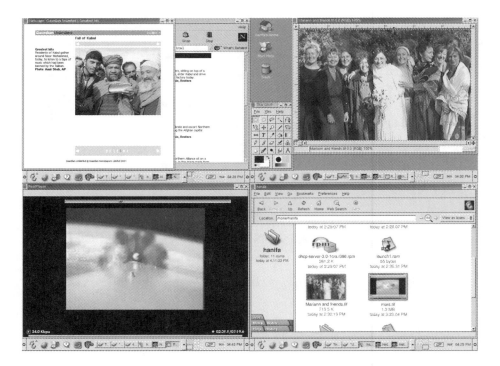

Figure 3-6. Four desktops running at once

Hands On:

OPENING PROGRAMS IN DIFFERENT DESKTOPS USING THE PAGER

Open three different programs, one per desktop, and cycle from one to the other using the Pager.

1. Click the main menu button and navigate to Programs ➤ Applications. Click Calendar.

2. Move the mouse pointer to the Pager's upper right-hand window, and click once. The Calendar program will disappear because you are now at a different desktop.

3. Open the terminal emulation program by clicking the Terminal icon on the panel.

4. Go back to the Pager and click the window directly beneath it.

5. Click the main menu button again and navigate to Programs ➤ Multimedia. Click XPlayCD. This is one of two music CD players that come with GNOME.

Cycle from one desktop to another using the Pager.

Reality Byte

An accountant has to regularly import spreadsheets from StarCalc into documents produced in StarWriter. She finds it convenient to keep both programs open in one desktop.

To avoid clutter and to separate tasks, she runs her calendar in another desktop. Finally, she likes to keep abreast of the news—particularly the financial news—and runs Netscape Communicator in its own desktop, usually tuned to CNNfn.

Customizing the Panel and Its Applets

You can easily customize the panel to make it easier to use, and you can add a number of "applets" to make it more useful.

Hiding the Panel and Changing Its Position and Size

The panel can be hidden automatically—that is, whenever the mouse pointer is not right above it, or explicitly, when you click either end. You can choose the behavior you want by clicking the Start button and navigating to Panel ➤ Properties ➤ Hiding Policy. It is a good idea at this time to click Hide Buttons and choose "With pixmap arrow."

Using the same menu, the user may choose between seven different panel sizes. In addition, if a "Floating panel" is chosen as the type, you may choose to have the panel positioned vertically along the side of the screen, rather than horizontally. If, during your experiments, you seem to have got it stuck along the top of the screen, don't worry: You can drag it back down with the mouse.

Adding Virtual Terminals

The Pager can be configured for more than just four separate desktops. Depending on the amount of RAM your system has, you may want six or more. In order to "add" desktops to the Pager, follow these steps:

1. Click the Start button and navigate to Programs ➤ Settings ➤ Sawfish Window Manager ➤ Workspaces.

2. To add two virtual desktops to the Pager, for a total of six, configure Workspaces as shown in Figure 3-7.

3. To enable *edge flipping*—that is, to switch to an adjoining desktop simply by moving toward it with the mouse—click the Edge Flipping tab and check the box next to "Select the next desktop when the pointer hits the screen edge."

 NOTE *You may have to restart GNOME for changes to take effect.*

In addition, you can add a tasklist arrow to the page by right-clicking the Pager and selecting that feature from the pop-up window.

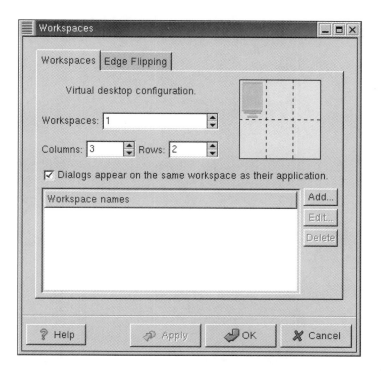

Figure 3-7. Adding virtual desktops to the Pager

Adding Floppy Disk and CD-ROM Icons

A panel icon for the floppy disk greatly simplifies mounting, accessing, and unmounting floppy disks. To add this "applet," follow these steps:

1. Click the Start button and navigate to Panel ➤ Add to Panel ➤ Applet ➤ Utility ➤ Drive Mount.

2. To change the icon's orientation, right-click the icon, choose Properties, and check the box next to "Scale size to panel."

You can also add panel icons in the same way for CDs and even disk partitions. Figure 3-8 shows the Drive Mount Applet property window for a CD-ROM applet.

The panel can be customized almost without limit. You can add application icons and the date and time, and several utility applets are available, including a humble date and time clock.

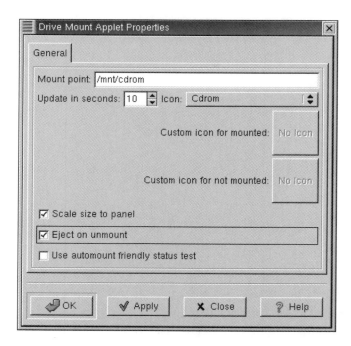

Figure 3-8. Adding a CD-ROM applet to the panel

Desktop and Panel Icons and Applications

Several of the most important applications have icons on the desktop or the panel. These include the Nautilus file manager and Mozilla, the default Web browser.

The Nautilus File Manager

Double-clicking the Home icon in the upper left-hand corner of the screen opens the Nautilus file manager. This program provides a point-and-click method of browsing the file system—both local and network—and of copying, moving, opening, renaming, and deleting files. File manipulation is performed as follows:

- *Moving files.* Select the file in the right window and, holding down the right mouse button, drag it to the destination directory. From the pop-up menu, choose Move.

- *Copying files.* Follow the same steps for moving a file, but hold down the left mouse button instead.

- *Selecting more than one file.* Use the mouse and the Shift key.

- *Opening, renaming, and deleting files.* Right-click the file and choose the action desired from the pop-up menu.

The Nautilus file manager will browse and copy files to and from any NFS share or Windows mount point that it has permissions for, thus providing easy access to the network. You can customize it in many ways: You can resize the panes, select a variety of different view types, and so on. In addition, Nautilus will automatically show thumbprints of many graphics file types, as well as fragments of text from text files, and identify other types of files with specific icons. An example of this is shown in Figure 3-9.

Nautilus does, however, have one severe drawback—most severe for users with older hardware. Nautilus is slow. In a Microsoft environment, Nautilus would be considered "bloatware." It is still under development, and we can hope for better in the future. In the meantime, there is an alternative for those who seldom use graphic file managers and value speed. It is the GNU Midnight Commander file manager, or GMC for short.

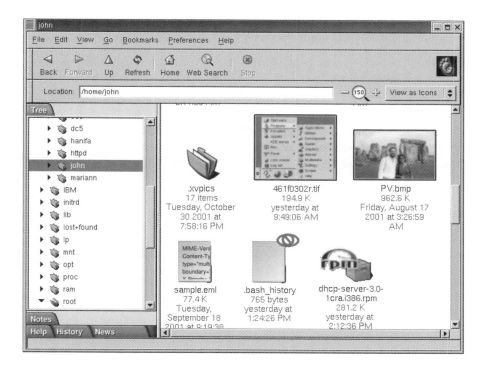

Figure 3-9. Nautilus displaying directories in tree view in the left pane and files in icon view in the right, thumbnailing a bitmap and TIF graphic, and identifying hidden and RPM files.

The GMC File Manager

GMC was Nautilus' predecessor; Nautilus was built from GMC's foundations. By modern standards it is a somewhat stripped-down GUI, but what it loses in graphics features, it makes up for in speed and stability. Certainly, if your main use for a drag-and-drop file manager is to move and copy files, you might be better off with GMC.

To open GMC, click the Start button and select Run. Type in **GMC** and click the Run button. You will notice immediately how much faster this older but still useful file manager is. Some of its operations, however, are slightly different.

File manipulation is performed as follows:

- *Moving files.* Select the file in the right window and, holding down the left mouse button, drag it to the destination directory.

- *Copying files.* Follow the same steps for moving a file, but hold down the Ctrl key instead.

- *Selecting more than one file.* Use the mouse and the Shift key.

You can also open files within GMC by clicking them with the right mouse button, selecting Open With, and then choosing the desired application.

Mozilla and Terminal Emulation

The panel holds several icons, the two most important of which are probably the icons for Mozilla and for terminal emulation.

Mozilla is the new suggested default Web browser for GNOME, although in fact it doesn't have to be your default. You can choose from two installed browsers, and download a third, all descendants of Netscape: Netscape version 4.78, Mozilla, or Netscape 6.2. Chapters Six and Eight cover using these different browsers as e-mail clients and their individual strengths and weaknesses. In brief, consider the following three things when choosing amongst them:

- Netscape version 4.8 is definitely the most stable and the fastest choice, but it supports only one POP e-mail address.

- Mozilla is the open source version of Netscape 6.2—there is little practical difference between the two.

- Although Mozilla will automatically "migrate" e-mail settings from Netscape 4.8, automatic migration does not work in reverse. So if you think you may want to use both, or experiment, it's best to start with 4.8.

Generally, all these programs perform well as Web browsers, although Netscape version 4.8 is much faster and somewhat more stable. If you need a multiple-POP server e-mail client, go with one of the later versions. To open Netscape, click Start and navigate to Programs ➤ Internet ➤ Netscape.

Terminal emulation means opening up a command-line terminal from within GNOME. This is different from opening one of the full-screen terminals by pressing Ctrl+Alt at the same time as one of the function keys from F2 to F6. (Remember to return to the desktop via the F7 key.) The function key method opens an actual terminal; the icon on the panel opens a virtual terminal. In practice, however, they are very similar, and a terminal emulation window can be very handy for all kinds of system administration purposes.

For a short tutorial on command-line operations, see Chapter Ten.

Floppy Disks and CDs: A Simple Scenario

Adding floppy disk and CD icons to the panel was covered earlier. I strongly suggest that all users add the floppy icon at least—it greatly simplifies dealing with floppy disks. There follows a simple scenario showing how CDs and floppies can be accessed in GNOME.

Say a user wants to play a music CD at the same time he inspects the contents of a floppy disk. He first inserts the CD. Since he is running GNOME, the CD is automatically mounted, and the GNOME CD Player automatically starts. If the CD had contained data or text or other nonmusic files, Nautilus would have opened instead.

While the music is being played, the user decides to look at the floppy. He inserts it, and then he clicks the floppy icon on the panel once. That mounts the floppy (part of the icon changes color to reflect its mounted status). A floppy icon also appears on the screen. He right-clicks the screen icon and chooses Open from the pop-up menu. The Nautilus file manager starts up, displaying the contents of the floppy disk.

This user is curious enough about the command line to want to experiment. He decides to view the contents of the floppy from both Nautilus and a virtual terminal. He clicks the virtual terminal icon on the panel and navigates to the /mnt/floppy directory, using the change directory command presented in Chapter Ten.

Figure 3-10 shows all of this going on at once. In the upper left, the CD player is playing the mounted CD. Below it, the Nautilus file manager is displaying the contents of the floppy disk. To the upper right, a virtual terminal is open, displaying the floppy's contents at the command line. The panel's floppy icon, used to mount and unmount floppy disks, can be seen next to the Start button.

It is important to remember that in GNOME mounting and unmounting of CDs is automatic, but mounting and unmounting of floppies is not. In this scenario, when the user wants to stop the music, he will stop and close the CD player and that will automatically unmount the CD. It can then be ejected in the normal way, by pressing the Eject button.

However, before ejecting the floppy disk, the user should first close both the virtual terminal and the file manager. Only after he is sure the floppy is not being accessed should he unmount it by clicking once on the panel's floppy icon and then ejecting it.

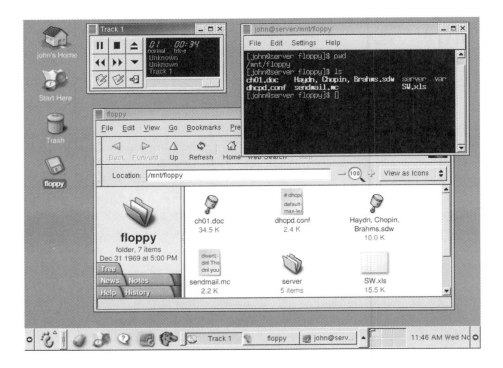

Figure 3-10. Playing music CDs and examining floppies in both Nautilus and in a virtual terminal

Lesson Review

These lessons were devoted to an initial exploration of Linux and the Linux desktop. You learned

- How to log into Linux and some of the issues to consider in deciding whether to log in as the root user (the system administrator) or as a normal user (using your personal user name)

- How to start up the desktop (GNOME) and exit both it and Linux

- The importance of case and of spacing at the command line

- How to check and configure the services you want to start when you boot the computer

- How to mount and unmount CDs at the command line and from within GNOME

- How the desktop's main menu is organized, and how to use the Run command in the main menu to start applications

- The theory behind multiple desktops and how to use the Pager to multitask with several applications running in different desktops: the new desktop paradigm

- How to launch important applications directly from the panel and the desktop

What's to Come

In the next chapter, you learn how to configure your Internet connections, whether you're an individual user or you're setting up a LAN Internet server. The next chapter includes the following:

- Configuring Ethernet cards and making sure that your modem will work in Linux

- Configuring a variety of dial-up and DSL connections

Connecting
to the Internet

The first thing that most users will want to set up in Linux is their Internet connection. This lesson covers setting up dial-up and DSL modem connections. Configuring Internet LAN connections, including setting up an Internet server so that several computers can use one connection, is covered in Chapter Five.

This chapter consists of three lessons, with a review at the end of Lesson 4-3:

- Lesson 4-1. Configuring New Networking Hardware

- Lesson 4-2. Configuring Dial-up Internet Access

- Lesson 4-3. Configuring DSL and Cable Internet Access

LESSON 4-1.

CONFIGURING NEW NETWORKING HARDWARE

To access the Internet you will need either a regular modem for a dial-up connection or an Ethernet card connected to a DSL modem or cable modem for a DSL or cable connection. If you are installing either a modem or an Ethernet card *after* installing Linux, you should run Kudzu, the hardware detection and configuration tool.

Kudzu should have been automatically configured to run upon system start-up or configured by the user to run at start-up (see Chapter Three, Lesson 3-2). However, it can easily be run manually within GNOME. Log in as the root user and start GNOME by typing **startx**. Open a virtual terminal by clicking the Panel icon and typing **kudzu**. Kudzu will start, and if new hardware needs to be configured, it will prompt the user. If the hardware is already recognized by the system, the program will automatically exit.

To make sure your Ethernet adapter is being recognized, type **ifconfig** in the same terminal and press Enter. There should be two paragraphs of information, one labeled "lo" (on the left) and the other "eth0." (If you are installing on a server with two Ethernet cards, there should be a third paragraph of information labeled "eth1.") If the "ethX" lines show up, Linux is recognizing your Ethernet cards.

Occasionally, however, usually on older systems, a card will not be recognized—even the automatic detection program will fail. If this should happen, your first resource should be the Linux Hardware Database, a link for which can be found at Linux Leap's Web site (`http://www.linuxleap.org`). This site has up-to-date information on hundreds of Ethernet cards, modems, and every other kind of computer hardware, and their compatibility—or lack of compatibility—with Linux. It also has many software drivers, with instructions on how to configure them for specific cards.

Older machines will sometimes already have the correct driver for their card on the system, but the driver will not be loaded at start-up. This can be solved simply by adding a line to the /etc/modules.conf file. In the following example, the card being used is one of the many generic Ethernet cards that uses the "tulip" driver to be correctly recognized and configured by the operating system. To force the system to use this driver, the sysadmin could use the gedit program (click Start and navigate to Programs ➤ Applications ➤ Gedit) to add the following line to the /etc/modules.conf file:

```
alias eth0 tulip
```

Rebooting the system would then result in automatic recognition.

However, the vast majority of mainline PC Ethernet cards are now automatically recognized at start-up. Most users will have no trouble, either with PCI Ethernet cards or with PCMCIA Ethernet cards. Modems, however, are another story. (See the "Linux and the Trouble with Modems" sidebar for more information.)

....

Linux and the Trouble with Modems

Linux supports nearly all "traditional" modems, but it has trouble with so-called *Winmodems*—newer, inexpensive modems that are always internal and rely on the Windows operating system to work. This means, oddly enough, that the older your PC and its built-in modem, the more likely it is to work in Linux.

How can you make sure a new computer's modem will work with Linux, and what should you do if you discover that your old computer's modem does not?

First, remember that almost any external modem will work just fine. They can still be easily found, although there aren't as many available as there used to be. Most new PCs are now sold with an internal modem.

If you want to buy a new computer with an internal modem, first make sure that the modem is compatible with Linux, as follows:

- Buy your computer from a Linux hardware vendor, such as Dell or IBM, or one of the smaller Linux vendors. This is the easiest and most trouble-free method.

- If you decide not to buy from a Linux hardware vendor, check the compatibility of your proposed new system's internal modem by calling up the distributor and asking for technical support. Plan on a lengthy wait.

- If your distributor cannot help you, turn to the "Winmodems are not modems" Web site (http://www.idir.net/~gromitkc/winmodem.html). This site gives a very long and detailed list of modems that will definitely work in Linux, those that may, and those that will not.

If you are stuck with a computer with a Winmodem that doesn't seem to work in Linux, don't despair. The Linmodems.org site (http://www.linmodems.org) carries information on software drivers available, both from modem vendors and from the open source community, to make some Winmodems work. And you can always buy an external modem and plug it into your computer's serial port. They are still available, are not expensive, and will probably prove to take less processing time away from your computer than the internal modem and be more stable.

LESSON 4-2.

CONFIGURING DIAL-UP INTERNET ACCESS

Dial-up access, which means accessing the Internet through a normal modem and telephone line, is fast being phased out in small businesses in favor of 24-hour, high-speed connections. Even in the small office/home office (SOHO), dial-up access is being supplanted by the faster DSL. However, dial-up access is still common and will probably remain so for years to come.

Until recently, configuring dial-up Internet access was a task involving the manual editing of a number of configuration files. For most users, that is no longer the case. Red Hat Linux 7.2 has two Internet configuration wizards that go a long way toward automating the configuration process. The newest one, however, is geared toward the German market and has a few problems with the PPP Dialer, another, very convenient program to use, so this book advises the use of the older program, the Dialup Configuration tool. This tool is not found on the desktop, or even in the menu, in 7.2. You must start it with the Run command.

Click Start and then Run. In the Run Program window, click the Advanced button and type **rp3-config** in the box. Click the Run button. The first screen to appear is shown in Figure 4-1.

Clicking the Next button brings up the Select Modem screen if the operating system has not yet identified and configured your system's modem. Click the Next button again and the program scans every port on your computer for a modem. When the program finds and identifies your computer's modem, it displays a Modem Found screen. From here you can accept the device or ask the program to look for another. If desired, you can modify the modem information, but that shouldn't be necessary. Click the Next button once again.

Figure 4-1. The opening screen of the Dialup Configuration tool

The following screen (see Figure 4-2) prompts you to type in your ISP's telephone number and account name. The account name can be anything you like. It should serve as an easy identifier if you have more than one dial-up Internet account. The telephone number is the number your modem should dial to connect with your ISP.

After another click of the Next button, the program prompts you to enter the user name and password for the account. Your ISP provides this information—they may call your user name your "login name." (Note: Your account password is different from your e-mail password. Check out your ISP's information.) The next screen is called Other Options. The AT&T Global Network is one of the largest ISPs, with connections, as its name implies, all over the world. Choose that if it is your ISP; otherwise, choose Normal ISP.

The final screen actually creates the account. Check the information, and if it's correct, click the Finish button.

Now check if the program has correctly configured your modem and your ISP account. In the Internet Connections screen, click the Debug button. This actually has your modem dial your ISP (you will, of course, need to have your telephone line connected to your modem) and brings up another screen titled "Trying to connect." If everything works (as it should), you will see a list of messages scroll down the screen, ending in "Starting pppd. . .". Both screens are shown in Figure 4-3.

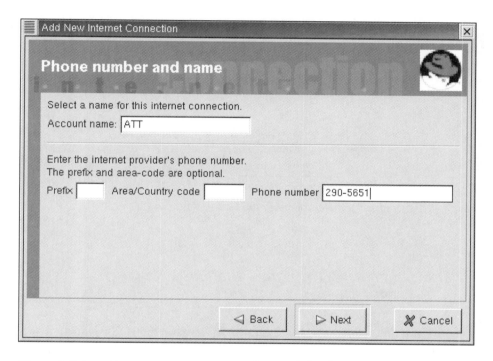

Figure 4-2. Inserting an account name and your ISP's telephone number

To close both screens, click the Cancel and Close buttons.

The previous procedure sets up a dial-up Internet connection for the first time. For everyday use, there's a much easier way to initiate the connection.

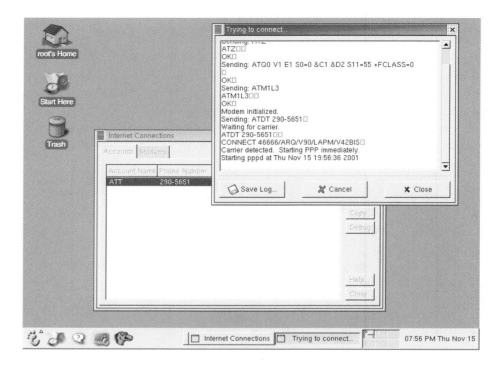

Figure 4-3. A successful test—connecting via a modem to an ISP

Connecting to the Internet the Easy Way: Using the PPP Dialer

Open the main menu and navigate to Applets ➤ Network ➤ RH PPP Dialer. Click the Dialer.

A pop-up window will appear that prompts you to choose an interface; there may be several to choose from. Pick the one you just configured—it will be the account name you entered previously. Click the OK button, and when prompted to start, choose Yes.

The PPP Dialer tool, an applet, will appear on the panel. The green light indicates that your connection is active. Managing your connections with this tool is simplicity itself:

- To connect, click the unlit light once.

- To disconnect, click the lit green light once.

Figure 4-4 shows the PPP Dialer during an active connection. The green light is on, as is the time counter, and the red and green moving graphs indicate that the computer is both receiving and transmitting data. This applet is very versatile and can be easily configured to show either the time connected or the cost, either per connection or accrued. To configure this, or any panel applet, click it once with the right mouse button and then click Properties with the left button.

Figure 4-4. The PPP Dialer during an active connection

LESSON 4-3.

CONFIGURING DSL AND CABLE INTERNET ACCESS

DSL and cable Internet connections are increasingly popular in SOHOs and small businesses, since they are both inexpensive and fast. The advantages and disadvantages of DSL vs. cable are somewhat difficult to pin down. Theoretically, cable should provide higher speed, while DSL should provide more stable speed and service. In reality, however, both speed and reliability will depend on the individual service provider.

DSL and cable connections require DSL or cable modems (different animals from traditional dial-up modems) and an Ethernet card. The Internet service provider should provide the modem (although some give discounts if the customer provides their own), but the customer will often be expected to provide their own Ethernet card.

Until recently, DSL and cable connections, like all Internet connections, were configured at the command line by manually editing a number of configuration files. Although in the odd case tweaking may be necessary, most of the time Internet configuration can be done via GUI tools in GNOME or KDE.

Cable Setup

Cable modem setup, in general, is the same as DSL bridged setup, which is described in the following section. Cable users should read the DSL introductory section and then the "Setting Up DSL: Bridged, Dynamic IP" and "Setting Up DSL: Bridged, Static IP" sections. However, there are many local peculiarities, depending on the provider. For this reason, cable users may also want to refer to the

Cable Modem Providers HOWTO, which you can find on Red Hat Europe's Web site (`http://www.europe.redhat.com/documentation/HOWTO/Cable-Modem`). (For some reason, a great deal of useful documentation is on the company's European, rather than their American, Web site.)

DSL Setup: An Introduction

How you configure your DSL setup in GNOME depends on what kind of DSL service you have. The two most common types of service today are Bridged and PPPoE. The major difference, from the user's point of view, between Bridged and PPPoE (point-to-point protocol over Ethernet) is that the latter requires authentication via a user ID—a login name—and password. Both types can be subdivided into static or dynamic IP connections.

NOTE *Static and dynamic DSL connections refer to **IP addresses** (a set of numbers which form your Internet address), which either don't change (static) or may change (dynamic). In each case, your DSL provider provides them. Most individuals and SOHOs have a dynamic address. It is inexpensive and provides reliable access. It is also easier to set up, since your server (the computer at your provider's office through which you connect to the Internet) automatically provides your computer with the address it needs. A static address is preferable if you are going to run a public Web server or you want to run your own Internet e-mail server.*

If you don't know which kind of address you have, it is almost certainly dynamic—static addresses are more expensive.

Although you will probably know, or be told, whether you are getting a static or a dynamic IP address, you will probably not be told what kind (Bridged or PPPoE) of DSL service is being provided. Or at least the information will probably not be volunteered. You will have to ask. It is necessary to know which type of service you have been offered, since different services need different setup tools. Table 4-1 shows which program you should use for which service.

Table 4-1. DSL and GNOME

DSL SERVICE	GNOME SETUP TOOL
Bridged—static or dynamic IP	Network Configurator
PPPoE—static or dynamic IP	Internet Configuration Wizard, then Network Configurator

To make matters slightly more complicated, if you ask your DSL service provider if they support Linux, they may well answer "No!" This doesn't mean that their service will not work with Linux. If it works with Windows, it will work with Linux. It means that their technicians don't know how to set up their DSL service with a Linux computer.

However, all the technician has to do is set up the wiring from the wall to the DSL modem and from the modem to your computer. You can do the rest.

Setting Up DSL: Bridged, Dynamic IP

First, a dynamic IP setup. Open the main menu and navigate to Programs ➤ System ➤ Network Configuration. Click the Network Configuration menu item. The Configurator program has four tabs along the top, Hardware, Devices, Hosts, and DNS, which open up their own windows. You need only look at DNS and Devices.

Click DNS. For a dynamic address DSL connection, just make sure that the computer's hostname and domain are entered in the correct boxes, but that all other boxes are empty (see Figure 4-5). The missing information, which goes into the /etc/resolv.conf file, will be provided by the server upon connection.

Next, click Devices. In the example shown in Figure 4-6, which is typical of a LAN Internet server, there are two Ethernet cards: eth0 and eth1. The first is the LAN Ethernet card (it has its own IP address), and the second is the DSL Ethernet card (you will have only one card—the card for DSL Ethernet—if your computer is not part of an internal network). Click your DSL Ethernet card to select it, and then click the Edit button. A smaller window opens, labeled Ethernet Device, which has three tabs: General, Protocols, and Hardware Device.

Under the General tab, check the box for "Activate device when computer starts." Then click the Protocols tab and the Edit button. In the TCP/IP Settings window, check the box for "Automatically obtain IP address settings with" and choose "dhcp." Part of the multiwindow process is shown in Figure 4-6.

Click the OK buttons to exit the various windows, and then the Close button. When you're prompted to save changes, choose Yes.

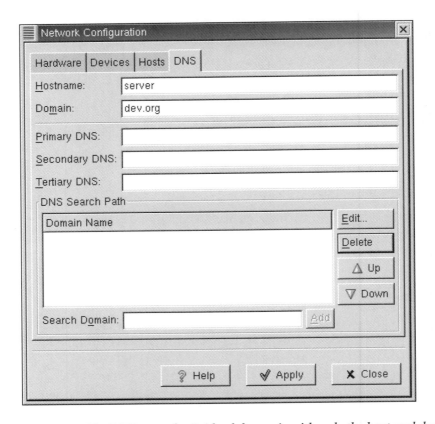

Figure 4-5. The DNS setup for Bridged dynamic with only the host and domain names entered

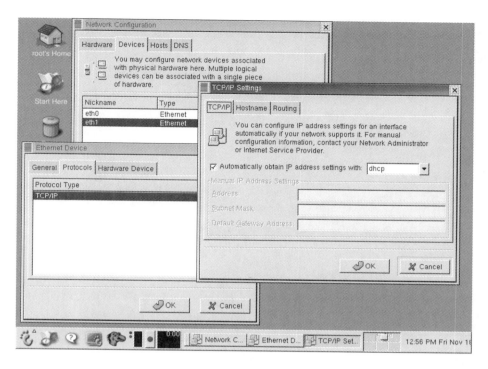

Figure 4-6. Setting a dynamic DSL connection to start at boot via DHCP

Setting Up DSL: Bridged, Static IP

A small business setting up a DSL static IP connection is probably doing so in the context of setting up both an Internet server for the LAN and either a self-hosted Web presence or an Internet e-mail server. In such a scenario, the firm will have its own domain and its own nameservers (it may provide one nameserver itself). The configuration procedure is similar to a dynamic IP DSL connection—there is just more information to enter. In the Network Configurator's DNS window, you will have to enter the addresses of the firm's nameservers and your domain name under the DNS Search Path, as shown in Figure 4-7. The domain will be an actual name, while the nameservers will be two sets of four numbers, with each number separated by a period.

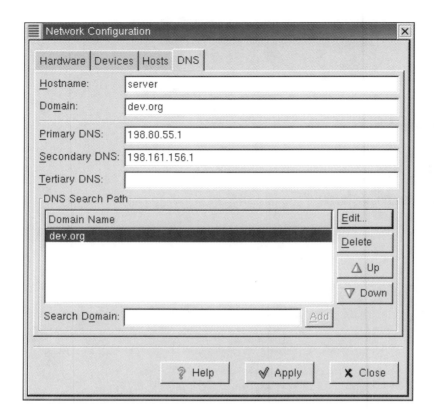

Figure 4-7. Setting up DNS for a Bridged static DSL service

Next, click Interfaces. If this machine is a LAN Internet server, there will be two interfaces: eth0 and eth1. One will carry the IP address for the local network, and the other will be for the incoming static IP DSL line. The DSL line can be configured exactly as in Figure 4-6. The protocol is still DHCP—it is just a static instead of a dynamic address.

When you've finished, save your changes.

TIP *A common problem with static IPs is that, upon connecting, the client's domain name and nameserver entries (yours) get overwritten to reflect the domain name and nameservers of the ISP. This happens during the boot phase and is a fait accompli by the time you log in.*

*What is happening is this: Your ISP is overwriting the contents of the /etc/resolv.conf file. Red Hat's default is to accept this behavior. However, this can be changed simply by downloading from the Linux Leap Web site (*http://www.linuxleap.org*) and copying to your machine a slightly customized version of the file that brings up the network at system boot:* **/sbin/ifup**. *Or, you may use gedit or some other text file editor to edit the file yourself. Change the following:*

```
if [  -n "${DYNCONFIG}"  ];  then
  PUMPARGS=$PUMPARGS
  DHCPCDARGS="$DHCPCDARGS  -n"
```

to

```
if [  -n "${DYNCONFIG}"  ];  then
  PUMPARGS= "-d"
  DHCPCDARGS= "-R"
```

Setting Up DSL: PPPoE Dynamic IP

As noted above, the main difference from the user's point of view between Bridged and PPPoE DSL connections is that the latter type requires a login name and password.

Open the main menu and navigate to Programs ➤ System ➤ Internet Configuration Wizard. At the first screen, select xDSL Connection and press Next. If the program cannot find an Ethernet card (either because it hasn't yet been configured, or perhaps because you are using a laptop with a PCMCIA Ethernet card), you will be presented with the Select Ethernet Adapter screen. Otherwise, you will go directly to the Configure DSL Configuration screen, where you will enter your ISP's name, and your login name and password. Click Finish to set up the account. The screen will look something like the one shown in Figure 4-8.

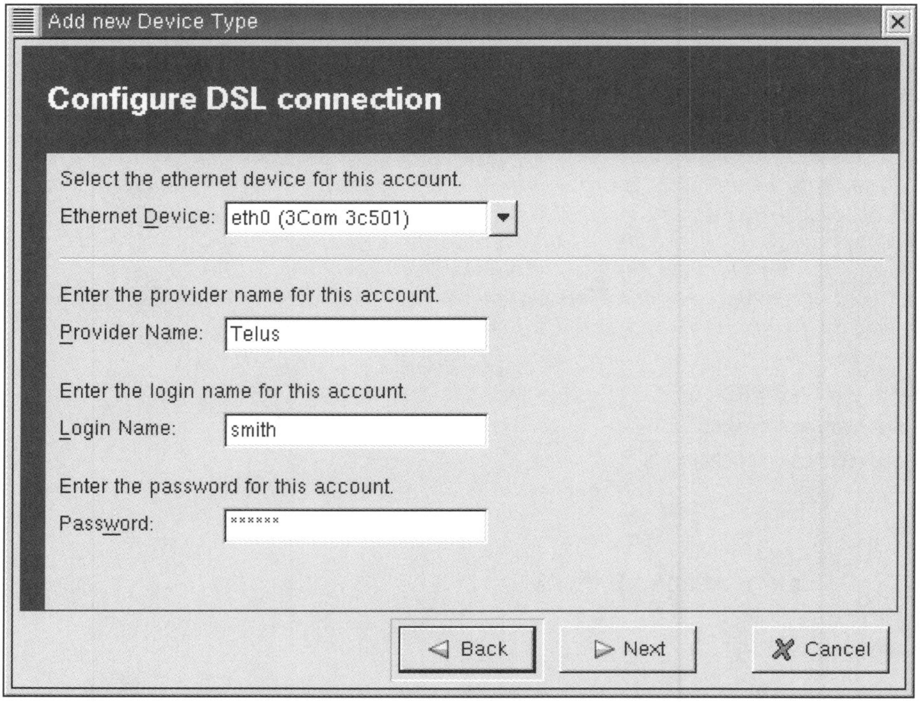

Figure 4-8. The Internet Configuration Wizard's setup for PPPoE dynamic DSL

Now open up the Network Configurator, click the Devices tab, and select the nickname (which will be on the same line as "xDSL" under Type) of your provider. Click the Protocols tab and the Edit button. Check the box for "Automatically obtain IP address settings with dialup." Several of these windows are shown in Figure 4-9. When you've finished, click the OK button and save the configuration.

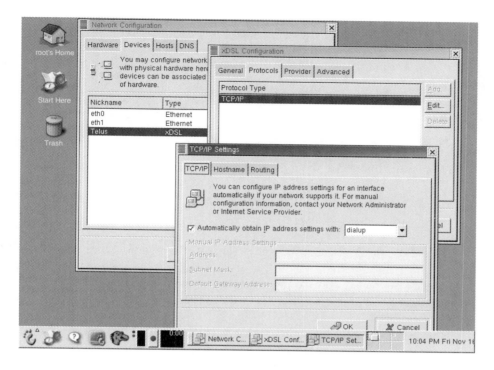

Figure 4-9. Setting up PPPoE dynamic DSL in the Internet Configuration Wizard

Setting Up DSL: PPPoE Static IP

This procedure is exactly the same as for dynamic service, except that you have to enter the DNS server addresses your ISP supplied. These addresses will be two sets of numbers, each set consisting of four numbers separated by periods, asd shown in Figure 4-7.

There is no need to use a program such as the PPP Dialer to connect via DSL. Your computer connects automatically every time it starts, and the Internet connection stays on as long as the computer stays on.

Lesson Review

The three lessons in this chapter were devoted to configuring Internet access. You learned

- How to configure new networking hardware if everything works right the first time—and if it doesn't

- How to make sure that the modem you want to buy will work with Linux

- How to use the Dialup Configuration program to configure your computer for dial-up Internet access

- How to use the PPP Dialer program to log on and log off the Internet

- How to use the Network Configuration program to configure the most common types of DSL service: Bridged dynamic and static

- How to use the Internet Configuration and Network Configuration programs to configure both dynamic and static PPPoE DSL service

What's to Come

Linux is still used primarily as a server, and the next chapter shows you how to set up a Linux LAN server. It covers the following:

- Setting up hardware and determining a workable scheme for LAN IP addresses

- Setting up a DHCP server for the network

- Setting up a domain name server

Laying the Foundations: Linux As a LAN Server

Linux shines as a server. As a LAN server, you'll most likely use Linux for the following:

- Accessing the Internet across the LAN

- Sharing files

- Sharing printers

- Sending and receiving local e-mail

As a small business intranet server, you can effectively use Linux for the following:

- Hosting a company Web site

- Sharing data from a server-based database

Setting up these applications is covered in the next chapter. First, the foundations must be laid. You should start by *designing* the LAN, taking into account how, and why, it will be used. Next, you need to connect computers physically, and you have to install and configure software, both on the server and on the client machines.

This chapter covers the basics: hardware setup, determining IP addresses, and setting up DHCP and DNS. (If you need an explanation of these terms, read on—they're described in the sections that follow.)

Traditionally, setting up a server, especially a Linux/UNIX server, has been considered the role of a highly trained system administrator. This book takes the view that any reasonably computer-literate employee can set up such a server and can maintain a mixed Linux/Windows LAN for a small firm or workgroup.

Server setup has been made easier by recent improvements in mouse-driven LAN configuration tools, which now extend even to domain name servers. Some configuration, however, still does entail editing certain text files. But text file editing is no more difficult than word processing, and to make the process easier, you can download many configuration files from the Linux Leap Web site (http://www.linuxleap.org).

The system administrator is not left out of the equation. This book presents enough detail to be useful as a primer for the administrator new to Linux who desires to understand how it all works, and who may want or need to customize and enlarge his or her LAN for a growing organization.

 NOTE *This chapter is mostly concerned with configuration issues, and so, where it is not explicitly stated, it is assumed that the user is logged in as the root user (the system administrator).*

Presentation

Examples aid the learning process by offering practical illustrations to the text. This and following chapters use both a fictional scenario (inspired by a real company in Calgary, Alberta, Canada) and real examples from around the world.

Chapter Five is organized into the following lessons:

- Lesson 5-1. Hardware and Addresses

- Lesson 5-2. Setting Up a Dynamic Server and Clients

- Lesson 5-3. Setting Up a Domain Name Server for the LAN

The Scenario

Development, Ltd., is a small company specializing in project management for domestic (Canadian) health projects, and Canadian and U.S. funded developing world health projects. It does not engage in long-term contracts; rather, it concentrates on producing project viability studies and management reviews. In short, it's a highly specialized firm in a narrow niche market.

Several years of quiet success have brought Development, Ltd., name recognition, and it suddenly finds itself with much more business than it can handle. The owner and CEO has long made do with one part-time and seven full-time employees; she is now faced with adding six new full-time employees and six new computers.

Currently, she has an elderly NT server functioning as a file server and workstation, and several older client machines that she upgraded a year ago to Windows and Office 2000. They are slow, but stable. Her ISP provides her with an ADSL line, five company mailboxes, and hosting for the company's Web site.

Windows XP worries her: She foresees expensive hardware upgrades, and she has a feeling that she's going to be paying for features her employees neither want nor need. She understands that if she upgrades her desktops she should probably upgrade her server, and since she wants to institute an intranet, she's considering BackOffice 2000. However, the license is going to cost almost US$4,000 for five clients and another US$200 for each additional client. She may well need new hardware on top of that. Finally, she wants local e-mail for all employees, but she's run out of the free mailboxes supplied by her ISP.

In short, she has a suspicion that she's locked into a software and hardware model of rigid and regular upgrades, and solutions that, for a small firm like hers, are expensive.

Her new office manager (who is keen to make her mark and has recently read this book) convinces the CEO to try a different approach. Development, Ltd., will buy a preloaded Linux desktop PC for a new server and six new laptops, all preloaded with Linux, for the new employees. Since all the software needed for an intranet server and local e-mail solution comes with Linux, and since StarOffice is downloadable for free, the additional software costs are zero. In addition, the office manager has assured the CEO that those employees currently with Windows machines can keep them (should they want to), and that the new Linux desktops will be compatible.

Figures 5-1 and 5-2 show the present and future setup at Development, Ltd.

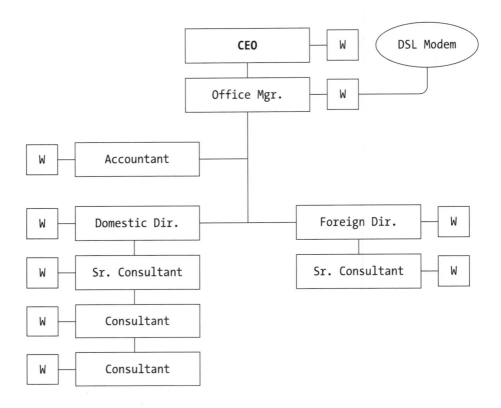

Figure 5-1. The old setup, before expansion

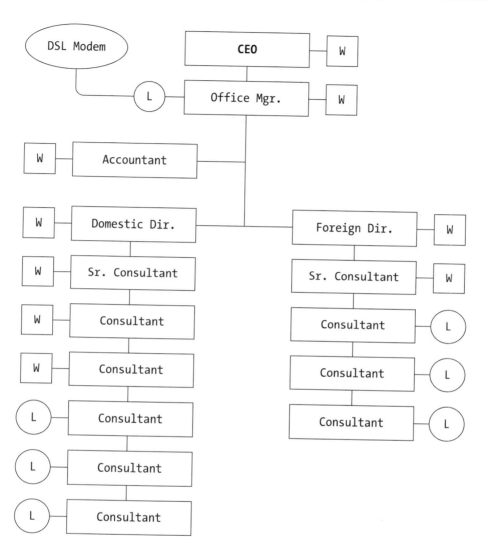

Figure 5-2. The fruits of success: six new employees, six new computers, and a mixed Linux/Windows network

LESSON 5-1.

HARDWARE AND ADDRESSES

This lesson covers hardware connections and computer addresses in a mixed Linux/Windows LAN.

Hardware Connections

IN BRIEF

1. Install two NICs into the Linux server, one for the incoming Internet connection and the other for the workgroup hub or switch.

2. Connect the Linux and Windows workstations to the hub or switch with Ethernet cable.

3. Connect a printer (or printers) to either the server or workstations, designating those machines as printer servers.

4. With increasing numbers of workstations, cascade the hubs or replace them with a switch.

Figure 5-3 presents a diagram of a simple SOHO Linux/Windows LAN.

EXPLAINED

Ethernet is the universal type of network for everything from the SOHO to the enterprise. It's simple to set up, the necessary hardware is inexpensive, and the result is fast communications between computers.

To set up an Ethernet network, you need

- A hub or switch, which acts as the central connection point for all the computers

- Network interface cards (NICs), one connected to every computer

- Ethernet cable to connect the computers to the hub(s) or switch

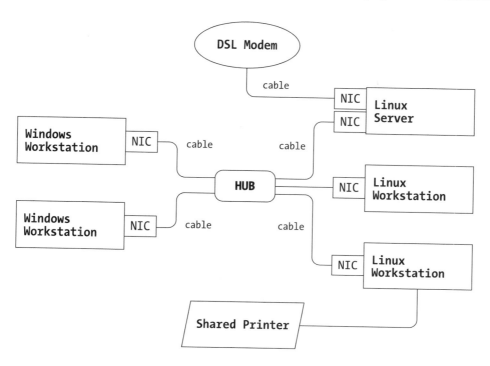

Figure 5-3. Three Linux workstations (one doing double duty as an Internet server, another as a print server) and two Windows workstations, all tied together with a hub

Keeping in mind the example in Figure 5-3, let's start from the outside and move in. Every small business LAN will be connected to the Internet. There are several ways to make such a connection, but a likely method is through an ISP-provided ADSL modem. Service speeds for such lines are now very fast; small business ADSLs can be capable of up to 4Mbps (this speed represents download-ing—uploading will be much slower). Standard Ethernet cable would connect the ISP's modem or router to the Linux server's second NIC.

In the example in Figure 5-3, note that the topmost Linux workstation has two NICs, one of which is connected to the ADSL modem. This workstation acts as an Internet server to the rest of the LAN, eliminating the need for a router (Chapter Four contains connection and configuration details for the server's ADSL line).

Your ISP will probably provide the modem for the incoming Internet line. However, you'll be responsible for providing all the hardware for the LAN itself. Before shopping around, it's a good idea to know exactly what specifications you should be looking for.

- *If possible, you should buy all the hubs, switches, and NICs from the same manufacturer,* and they should be certified by the manufacturer to work in both a Linux and Windows environment. This does not mean that you have to buy expensive hardware—you can find quite inexpensive hardware to fit this specification.

- *The hub or switch.* You should buy a 100Mbps (Fast Ethernet) hub or switch. Hubs are cheaper; switches are faster.

- *The NIC.* It's easy to install a network interface card into a computer, but it's even easier to buy a computer with one preinstalled at the factory. If you have to buy a NIC, make sure that it fits into your computer—you should have a spare PCI slot. Like the hub, the NIC should be 100Mbps. Laptops will need a PC Ethernet card; there are many available.

- *Avoid hardware needing USB ports.* Linux has only scrappy support for USB at this time.

- *The cabling.* Buy standard category 5 twisted pair Ethernet cable. You can buy this cable either with or without connector jacks attached.

Hubs or Switches?

The difference between a hub and a switch is that the different ports of a hub all share the same bandwidth, while the different ports of a switch are assigned their own. What this means practically is that hubs produce slower connections on heavily loaded networks. What's worse, the slowdown will not necessarily have a linear relationship with the amount of traffic; it may get much slower quite suddenly, as traffic appears to increase only moderately.

On the other hand, a hub with only a light and occasionally a moderate load, particularly a 100Mbps hub, can function quite well.

The benefits of a hub over a switch are cost and ease of use. A switch with the same number of ports and similar basic specifications as a hub from the same manufacturer will typically cost two to three times as much. And with a hub, you simply plug in the Ethernet cabling, whereas with many switches there's a certain amount of initial configuration.

Both hubs and switches come in a bewildering variety of sizes (number of ports) and costs. You can find very cheap but perfectly capable hubs with only five to eight ports for US$50 to US$60. A low-end eight-port switch can be had for

US$80. Moving up the ladder, you can buy a 24-port hub from a major manufacturer for about US$500, while a 24-port switch from the same company will run about twice as much. All the examples given are for units capable of 100Mbps. You can mix and cascade switches and hubs (to increase the size of the LAN), although cascading will slow the LAN down, as well as increase the number of connections.

Linux Compatibility

Fortunately, most major (and many minor) brands and models of NIC and associated hardware are now Linux compatible. However, if you have any doubts, and you have trouble finding a company representative, consult the Linux Hardware Database (you can find a link to it at `http://www.linuxleap.org`).

Cabling

Unless you're handy with hand tools and willing to go to some trouble, it's best to buy the cable with connectors attached. This means some advance planning: You need to have a wiring plan before you buy the wire. Ethernet cable can be bought in many different lengths, and some stores will sell custom lengths and attach the connectors for you. Note that there is a limit of 100 meters (328 feet) to any single connection.

Making the Connection

Ideally, the NICs were already in the computers when you loaded Linux. However, if they weren't, turn off the machines and install the NICs and the PC Ethernet cards, if you have laptops. After all the NICs and cards are installed, connect them with the Ethernet cables to the hub or switch.

If the hardware is Linux compatible, it should be detected automatically during a reboot. You can check on this quite simply by using the ifconfig command, as follows:

1. Open a terminal and type **ifconfig**.

2. Press Enter.

This should produce a display something like the one shown in Figure 5-4.

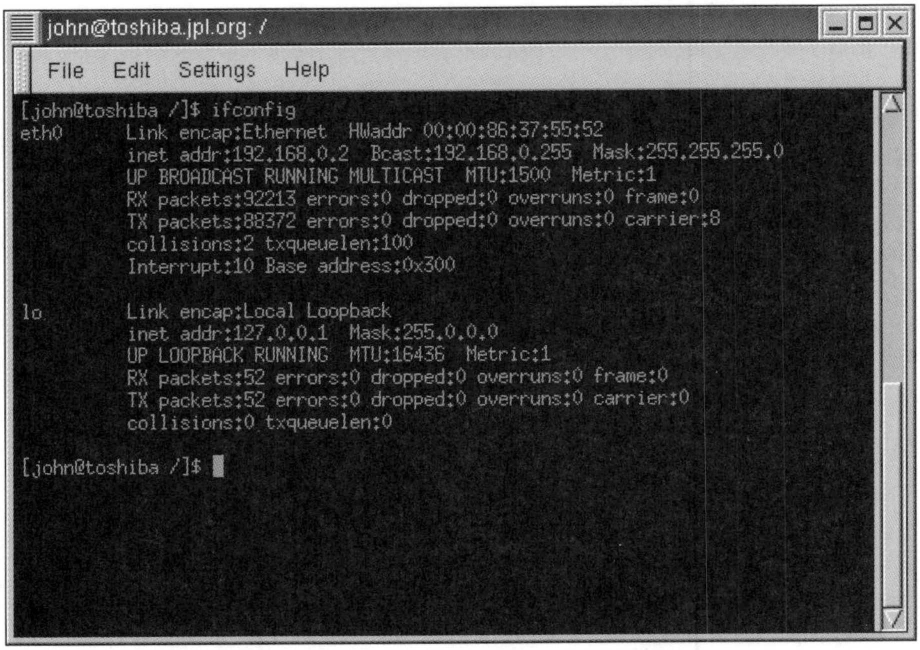

```
john@toshiba.jpl.org: /                                    _ □ ×

  File   Edit   Settings   Help

[john@toshiba /]$ ifconfig
eth0      Link encap:Ethernet  HWaddr 00:00:86:37:55:52
          inet addr:192.168.0.2  Bcast:192.168.0.255  Mask:255.255.255.0
          UP BROADCAST RUNNING MULTICAST  MTU:1500  Metric:1
          RX packets:92213 errors:0 dropped:0 overruns:0 frame:0
          TX packets:88372 errors:0 dropped:0 overruns:0 carrier:8
          collisions:2 txqueuelen:100
          Interrupt:10 Base address:0x300

lo        Link encap:Local Loopback
          inet addr:127.0.0.1  Mask:255.0.0.0
          UP LOOPBACK RUNNING  MTU:16436  Metric:1
          RX packets:52 errors:0 dropped:0 overruns:0 frame:0
          TX packets:52 errors:0 dropped:0 overruns:0 carrier:0
          collisions:0 txqueuelen:0

[john@toshiba /]$ █
```

Figure 5-4. The network interface card showing as eth0

On older and less compatible hardware, special steps may be necessary to enable Linux to detect NICs. Chapter Four presents details on configuring new hardware in Linux.

Computer (IP) Addresses

IN BRIEF

1. Decide on a domain name for your company LAN and hostnames for each computer.

2. Decide on a range of IP addresses. An easy and safe method is to double the maximum expected size of your LAN. One of the standard address ranges for a LAN starts at 192.168.0.1. Therefore, a range of computer addresses for a 20-computer LAN expected to grow to a maximum of 40 would be, when doubled, 192.168.0.1 to 192.168.0.80. This allows for a total of 80 computers on the LAN.

3. Assign each computer on the LAN its own IP address.

EXPLAINED

Names

Each computer on a LAN needs its own unique name and address. Names are divided into hostnames and domain names. Each machine has its own hostname, whereas the entire LAN—and probably the company—will share a domain name. In addition, the LAN's domain name will probably be the same as the company's Web domain name. This is a straightforward convention that promotes simplicity and easy configuration.

Some examples of host and domain names include the following:

ceo.dev.org

ibm1.dev.org

mariann.dev.org

In all these examples, the domain name is dev.org. The hostname examples represent three different ways of deriving hostnames: the first by job function; the second by computer make, model, or number; and the third by the user's name.

NOTE *The dev.org domain name is an example only, for the fictional company Development, Ltd. In fact, such a firm would almost certainly find that all its most obvious choices have already been taken, and it would be forced to devise some abbreviation that would be euphonious, easy to remember, clearly connected to the firm—and available.*

Addresses

People communicate with computers by names, but computers communicate with themselves via Internet Protocol (IP) addresses. It follows that each computer has both kinds of addresses, which are unique to that machine.

IP addresses are written in groups of four decimal numbers, each number being in the range of 0 to 255. The four numbers are separated from each other by dots. Two random examples are

192.168.0.23
142.57.108.143

Special groups of addresses have been reserved for LANs that are not directly connected to the Internet—as in this case, where each computer is indirectly connected through an Internet server (see Chapter Six). A typical small business would use the IP addresses in one of these groups (called a class C private network), which run from 192.168.0.1 to 192.168.255.255.

As an example, in a very small LAN of only five machines, the computer's IP addresses could be as follows:

Computer 1	192.168.0.1
Computer 2	192.168.0.2
Computer 3	192.168.0.3
Computer 4	192.168.0.4
Computer 5	192.168.0.5

The addresses need not start at 1—they could just as easily be 24, 25, 26, 27, and 28. However, it's a good idea to lay as simple and transparent a network foundation as possible.

The computers on a network share several other addresses, which are mathematically determined by their IP addresses. To give some examples, all the IP addresses in the range beginning with 192.168.0.X (such as the five previously listed addresses) would typically share the following other addresses:

Netmask: 255.255.255.0

Network: 192.168.0.0

Broadcast: 192.168.0.255

These are typical addresses for use in a class C private network and are used in this book.

Server Assigned or Client Assigned Addresses?

Should the server be in charge of handing out names and IP addresses to client machines, or should each client be in charge of identifying itself?

On a very small LAN, it's easier if every client identifies itself. In such a case, every computer on the local network, including the server, usually carries a record of every other computer's address. On Linux machines, these records are kept in the /etc/hosts file; on Windows PCs they're kept in the lmhosts or hosts file.

As the LAN grows, it becomes more and more work to keep all of these files on all computers up-to-date. Much of this work can be eliminated by putting the server in charge of assigning addresses to the clients. This is done by running a Dynamic Host Configuration Protocol (DHCP) server.

Each method has its advantages and disadvantages, as shown in Table 5-1.

Table 5-1. Client Assigned versus Server Assigned Addresses

METHOD	ADVANTAGES	DISADVANTAGES
Client assigned	Simplicity. Only hosts or lmhosts files need to be configured, and they're very simple to write. There is no complex server configuration.	Escalating maintenance. Every time a new computer is added to the LAN, configuration files on the server and any other computer it needs to communicate with must be updated. As the LAN or LANs grow, this can become rather impractical.
Server assigned	New computers can be added at any time with little or no configuration necessary. "Guest" computers, for temporary workers, visiting consultants, or clients, can connect immediately and have Internet access through the LAN.	Initial setup on the server is more complex and time consuming.

 NOTE *This book suggests using a server assigned system using DHCP. Many consultants will set up DHCP as a matter of course, because that is the method they've found over time to produce the best results with the least maintenance overhead. It's more flexible, with much less work in the long haul, and server setup is made easier with the latest GUI setup tools and with the prewritten configuration files available for download from the Linux Leap Web site.*

The Scenario

Development, Ltd., has decided on dev.org for their domain name. Hostnames are assigned to each computer based on the place of each employee in the business.

With the latest expansion, the company has 16 computers, and the owner has no intention of letting the company grow larger than that. But to be on the safe side, she has chosen a large pool of addresses (considering the size of the company) to be prepared for any contingency. The company will have 40 IP addresses, for a class C private network, ranging from 192.168.0.1 to 192.168.0.40.

The server will be given the first address in the range: 192.168.0.1. The management group follows, starting with the CEO at 192.168.0.2, the domestic consultants, and finally the foreign consultants.

The result will look like Figure 5-5. The method of coming up with computer hostnames is clear (i.e., the CEO's computer is ceo.dev.org).

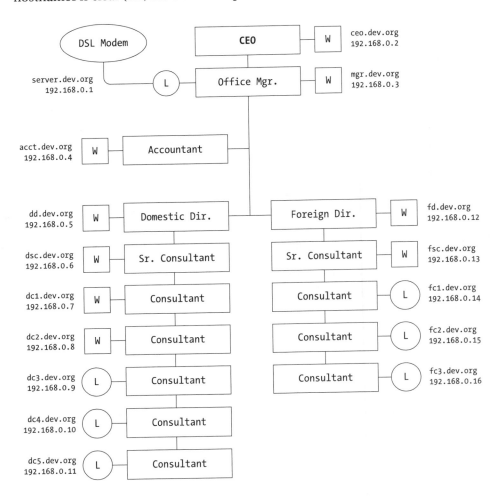

Figure 5-5. Hostnames and static IP addresses

Lesson 5-1 Review

This lesson was devoted to hardware and IP addresses. You learned

- The basics of connecting computers into a LAN with Ethernet cable, NICs, and hubs or switches; the specifications to demand; and purchasing tips

- The difference between a hub and a switch, the advantages and disadvantages of both, and some typical price ranges

- The use of the ifconfig command to check whether Linux has detected your NIC or PC Ethernet card

- Methods of deriving host and domain names

- The most common range of IP addresses to use for a small LAN

- The advantages and disadvantages of client assigned and server assigned addresses

LESSON 5-2.

SETTING UP A DYNAMIC SERVER AND CLIENTS

This lesson shows how to set up a Dynamic Host Configuration Protocol (DHCP) server that will provide both static and dynamic IP addresses to clients on the network. This is the first, and most fundamental, software configuration job you need to accomplish to get the LAN up and running. System administrators will recognize this lesson as enabling TCP/IP networking, which is the foundation for all subsequent network connections.

A DHCP server can be configured to always assign a fixed (static) IP address to a certain computer, or it can be configured to assign one of several addresses chosen from a pool (dynamic) to any computer that requests one. Dynamically assigned addresses represent the lowest long-term maintenance solution, but can be a significant amount of work to set up for Linux client machines permanently on the LAN (see Appendix B for an explanation and instructions). Therefore, this book suggests a mixed approach for the small business or workgroup: Each fixed computer on the LAN is given its own fixed IP address (assigned by the server), while "guest" computers are assigned addresses from a pool.

This scheme ensures a maximum of stability and intercommunication within the LAN, while allowing guest computers to log onto the Internet with minimal client and no server configuration.

This lesson covers server configuration first, and then Linux client and Windows client machines.

Server Configuration

IN BRIEF

1. Use the Network Configurator tool in GNOME to configure the server's hostname, local IP address, and local Ethernet interface.

2. Configure Linux to start the DHCP server upon computer start-up by checking the dhcpd option in the System Services menu of the Setup tool.

3. Download the dhcpd, dhcpd.conf, and dhcpd.leases files from `http://www.linuxleap.org`.

4. Copy the files into their correct directories:

   - /etc/init.d/dhcpd

   - /etc/dhcpd.conf

   - /var/lib/dhcp/dhcpd.leases

5. If needed, edit the dhcpd file to insert the correct Ethernet interface.

6. Determine the MAC addresses of Linux clients with ifconfig, of Windows 98 clients with winipcfg, and of Windows 2000 clients with ipconfig.

7. Edit the dhcpd.conf file, inserting your own client hostnames, MAC addresses, and IP addresses.

8. Start the server with the "./etc/init.d/dhcpd start" command.

EXPLAINED

Configuring Addresses, Hostnames, and Ethernet Interfaces

Before anything else, you should configure the server's hostname and IP addresses, and the local Ethernet interface.

Open the Network Configurator in GNOME by clicking the main menu, navigating to Programs ➤ System ➤ Network Configuration, and entering the root password if necessary. Click the DNS tab and enter the server's hostname and

domain in the appropriate boxes. Enter the domain name alone in the DNS
Search Path box, and finally, add the server's local IP address in the Primary DNS
text box. The result for the scenario company, Development, Ltd., would look like
Figure 5-6. The DNS section of the Network Configurator writes the
/etc/resolv.conf file for those who want to edit this setting manually.

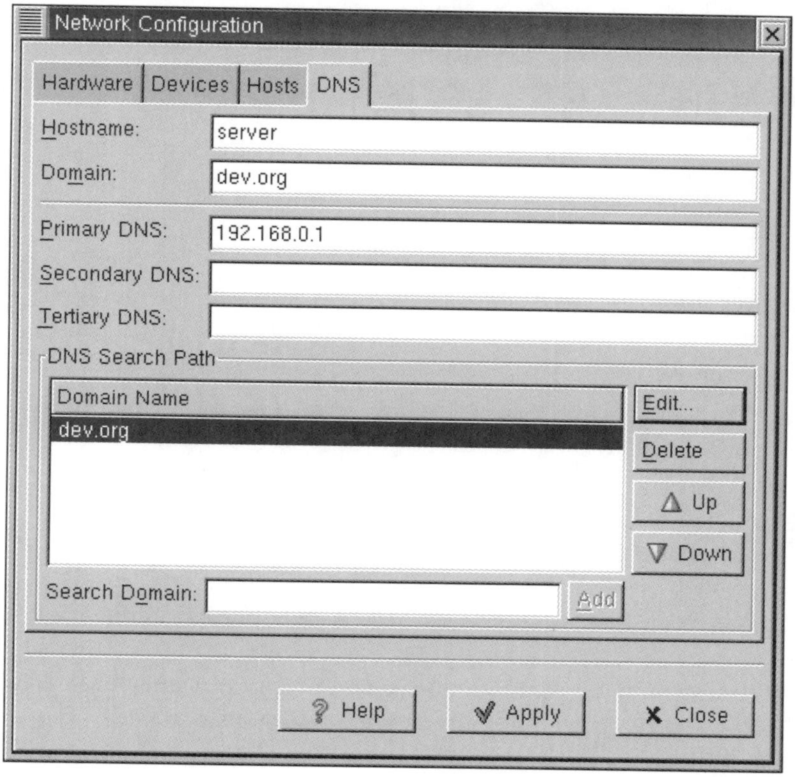

Figure 5-6. Server setup in the DNS window of Network Configurator

Now click the Hosts tab. The /etc/hosts file will serve as a backup identification for the computer on the network. Clicking the Add and Edit buttons allows
the user to enter the server's hostname and local IP address. Only two entries
should appears: The server itself and the localhost entry, which is automatic,
always appear and always must appear. Figure 5-7 shows how this would look on
the scenario company's server.

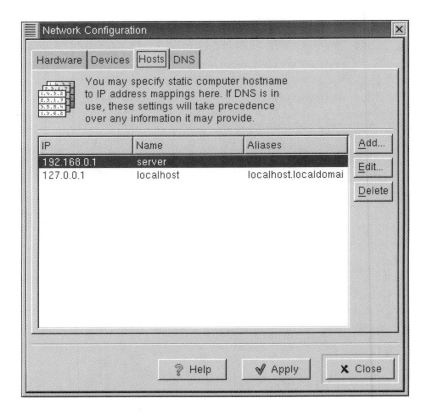

Figure 5-7. The Development, Ltd., server's /etc/hosts file in Network Configurator

Finally, you must configure the local Ethernet interface. On a small business Linux server, there are likely to be two Ethernet interfaces: one for the local network and one for the connection to the ISP. The interfaces will appear as follows:

eth0   The first interface
eth1   The second interface

Click the Devices tab on the Network Configurator. The interface for the local network should have been configured during installation, but if it wasn't, simply add or edit the interface by clicking the appropriate button. Clicking the Edit button brings up the Ethernet Device screen; under the General tab, check the "Activate device when computer starts" box; under the Protocols tab, select TCP/IP; and then click the Edit button. In the TCP/IP Settings screen, select the TCP/IP tab and fill in the information in the Manual IP Address Settings area. This will be the IP address of the server—192.168.0.1, in the example—the standard class C subnet mask, 255.255.255.0, and the default gateway address (the same as the IP address). Figure 5-8 shows the Devices, Protocols, and TCP/IP screens.

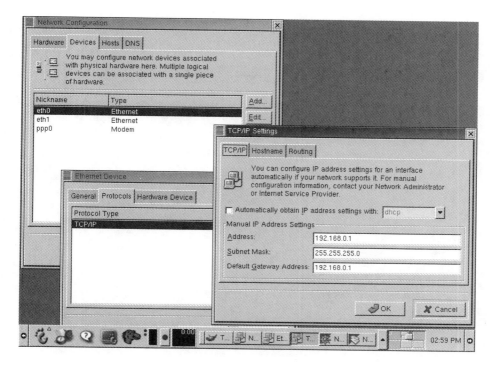

Figure 5-8. Configuring the server's local Ethernet interface

Make a note of your local Ethernet interface; you'll need it a little later.

Configuring the DHCP Server to Start at Boot-Up

The Services part of the Setup tool configures which services are started when the computer boots up. As part of the routine to start the DHCP server, Setup places a start-up file for the server into the /etc/init.d directory. It's necessary to perform this step before copying the identically named file from Linux Leap into that directory; otherwise, the Setup tool will overwrite the file you've just downloaded and copied.

You can start the Setup tool from the main menu by navigating to Programs ➤ System ➤ Text Mode Tool Menu. (Note: You need to be logged in as the root user.) Then open Services by tabbing down to System Services and clicking the Run Tool button.

An alternative way to start the Service tool within GNOME, if you're running as the root user, is to click the terminal icon to open a terminal window, type **ntsysv**, and then press the Enter key.

Make sure the dhcpd box is checked (see Figure 5-9). Tab to the OK button, press the Enter key, and close the terminal window.

Figure 5-9. Configuring the server to start DHCP upon booting

Downloading and Copying the Files

Download from the Linux Leap Web site the three files mentioned previously and copy them to their correct directories on your Linux server:

- /etc/init.d/dhcpd

- /etc/dhcpd.conf

- /var/lib/dhcp/dhcpd.leases

Downloading and Copying Linux Leap Files

The simplest method is to download the files to the directory they belong in on your Linux server. However, that won't be possible if the server's Internet connection is not yet up and running. It may be necessary to copy the files to the server from another machine (possibly a Windows machine) via floppy disks.

Windows-formatted floppy disks work fine in Linux. You can copy files to and from Windows floppies in a Linux terminal using the mcopy command, or you can drag and drop files using either the GMC or Nautilus file manager in GNOME.

One thing to remember: When you use floppy disks within GNOME, you should always unmount the disk before you eject it.

As an example, say you've copied the dhcpd file onto a Windows floppy disk, and you want to transfer the file to the correct directory on your Linux server. You would follow these steps:

1. Insert the floppy disk into the Linux computer.

2. In GNOME, click once on the floppy disk icon on the Panel. This mounts the floppy—the floppy icon will change color and a separate floppy icon will appear on the desktop, indicating that the disk is mounted. Double-clicking the desktop icon opens the file manager, which automatically reads the contents of the floppy disk.

3. Click Tree on the file manager's left panel, find the /etc/init.d directory, and use the mouse to drag and copy the file.

4. Close the file manager and click the floppy disk Panel icon once again. This unmounts the disk.

5. Wait a few moments and then eject the floppy.

Of the three files you download, you may need to edit two. The third file, dhcpd.leases, starts life as a completely empty file and is automatically configured by the program itself. The dynamic server, however, won't start unless this file is present. There are two ways of creating it: You can either download it from the Linux Leap site, as described previously, and copy it into the correct directory, or you can simply type, at a terminal, **touch /var/lib/dhcp/dhcpd.leases** and press the Enter key. This will automatically create an empty dhcpd.leases file.

Editing the dhcpd File

The dhcpd file starts the dynamic server when the computer boots up. There is only one line that you may need to edit. It concerns which Ethernet interface your local network is attached to.

You should have previously made a note of this interface in the section titled "Configuring Addresses, Hostnames, and Ethernet Interfaces." The downloaded dhcpd file is set by default to eth0. This is the first Ethernet interface, and it's the preferred one for the local network.

If, however, you need to edit this setting, open the file with the gedit editor within GNOME by logging in as root, clicking the Start button, and navigating to Programs ➤ Applications ➤ gedit.

Within gedit, click the Open icon and navigate to /etc/init.d/dhcpd. The line you may need to edit is shown in Figure 5-10.

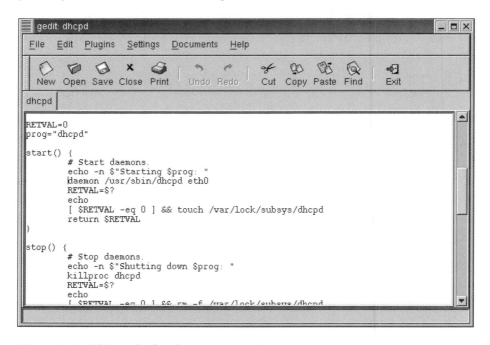

Figure 5-10. Editing the local network interface

Only one small change may need to be made. If your LAN interface is eth1, instead of eth0, change the line:

```
daemon /usr/sbin/dhcpd eth0
```

to

```
daemon /usr/sbin/dhcpd eth1
```

Then save the file and exit the editor.

Determining the MAC Addresses on the LAN

The DHCP server assigns static addresses to computers based on each computer's Media Access Control (MAC) address. This is nothing more nor less than the Ethernet card's unique hardware number. Therefore, the system administrator must determine each machine's MAC address. This is quite simple, but it's performed differently on each OS.

In Linux

Open a terminal and type **ifconfig**. The numbers on the line that starts with eth0, and appear after HWaddr, are the MAC address. They are always six pairs of numbers or numbers and letters, separated by colons. An example is 00:00:86:37:55:52. (See Figure 5-4.)

In Windows 2000

Open a command prompt and type **ipconfig /all**. The MAC address is on the line marked Physical Address. An example is 00-80-C6-F9-0B-66 (see Figure 5-11).

In Windows 98

Click the Start button, select Run, and enter **winipcfg**. Look for the Adapter Address under the correct network interface.

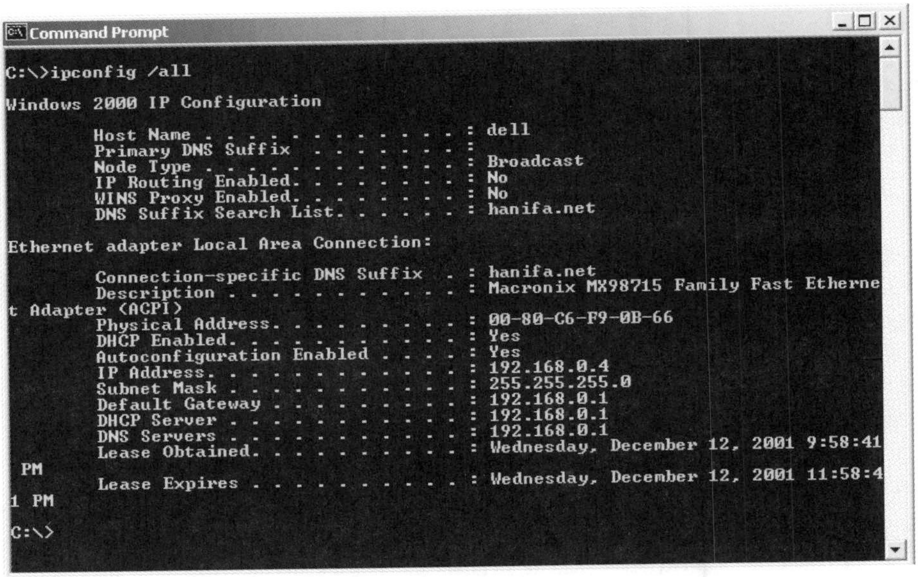

Figure 5-11. Finding Ethernet card addresses in Windows 2000 with ipconfig /all: physical address near middle of screen

Editing the dhcpd.conf File

The main configuration file for the DHCP server is dhcp.conf. It determines the range of addresses to use and which fixed addresses from the range will be assigned to which computers.

The file as downloaded from Linux Leap is configured for a range of IP addresses starting with 192.168.0.1—the server—and going on to 192.168.0.40. The file has 20 prewritten "host" sections, for computers with static addresses. The host and domain names, the MAC addresses, and the IP addresses need to be supplied for each.

If each of the host sections were used—if the LAN had exactly 20 computers with fixed addresses—and the administrator followed a rigid system of address allocation, the result could be as follows:

192.168.0.1	Server
192.168.0.2 to 192.168.0.20	Range of fixed addresses on the LAN
192.168.0.21 to 192.168.0.40	Range available for dynamic addresses

The range of addresses available for dynamic allocation can be expanded to take advantage of unused addresses in the static range. Thus, in the Development, Ltd., scenario, with only 16 computers in the firm, 23 addresses from the range of .17 to .40 could be available for dynamic allocations to guest machines or other additions to the LAN.

NOTE *Of course, you can modify the prewritten /etc/dhcpd.conf file to suit any range of addresses you like. The IP and other addresses suggested here are typical for a modest class C private network. Note, however, that there are strong relationships between IP, network, netmask, and broadcast addresses. Those readers who are interested in learning more may with profit turn to The Linux Networking HOWTO (*http://www.linuxports.com/howto/networking/*).*

The file can be edited in gedit within GNOME. If the standard IP address range is acceptable, only the sections in capital letters and capital Xs need to be edited. (Note: Unused sections should be deleted from the file.) Figure 5-12 shows an example of the first part of this file, edited to reflect the Development, Ltd., scenario. In this example, the company's domain name has been entered, as well as the host and domain names of the first three client computers, their MAC addresses, and their complete IP addresses.

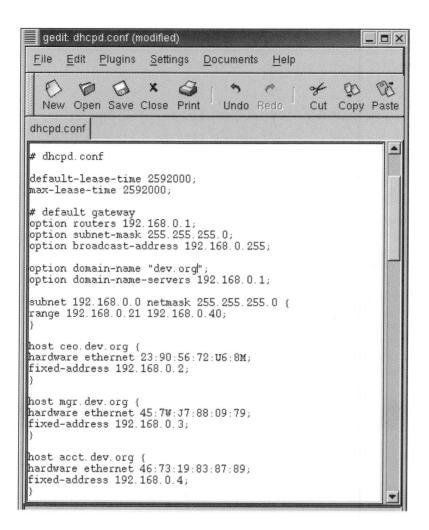

Figure 5-12. Inserting names and MAC and IP addresses in dhcpd.conf

Starting the Server

This is the simplest step of all. Log in at a terminal as root, type **/etc/init.d/dhcpd restart**, and press the Enter key. The server should start up, giving you an OK message.

TIP *It is seldom necessary to reboot a Linux server to start a new or reconfigured program or service. Scripts to start most services are in the /etc/init.d directory. You can start, stop, and restart most servers in the same way as the DHCP server.*

Linux Client Configuration

Although much of the following configuration will already have been done during installation, it's a good idea to do a postinstallation check and update and correct settings as necessary.

IN BRIEF

1. From within GNOME, open the Network Configurator, and from within DNS, enter the client's hostname, primary DNS, and domain.

2. Within Hosts, enter the server's IP address and name.

3. Go to Devices ➤ Protocols ➤ TCP/IP and configure the interface to automatically obtain IP address settings with DHCP.

EXPLAINED

You can completely configure a Linux desktop's network settings from within the Network Configurator program in GNOME.

Entering the Client's Hostname, Primary DNS, and Domain

Open the program by clicking Start and navigating to Programs ➤ System ➤ Network Configuration. Enter the root password if prompted.

Make sure that the client computer's hostname is entered in the DNS window (e.g., ceo). Beneath it, next to Domain, enter the LAN's domain name (e.g., dev.org). Enter the server's IP address next to Primary DNS, and finally, under DNS Search Path enter the domain name again. This will look very similar to Figure 5-6. Enter the server's hostname and IP, and enable DHCP.

Next, under Hosts, enter the local server's hostname and IP address, using the Add and Edit buttons as necessary. This will look exactly the same as Figure 5-7.

Finally, under Interfaces, select the Ethernet interface and click the Edit button to reach the Ethernet Device window. Check the "Activate device when computer starts" button. Then click the Protocols tab and the Edit button to reach the TCP/IP window. Check the "Automatically obtain IP address settings with

DHCP" box. You can leave all other boxes blank. Figure 5-13 shows an example. Note the difference between this TCP/IP window and the one shown in Figure 5-8 for the server.

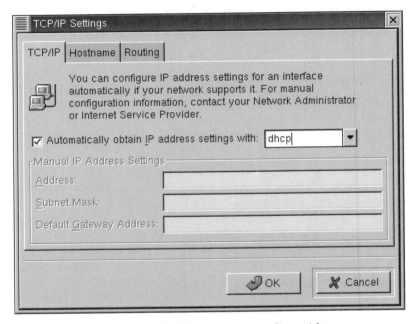

Figure 5-13. Configuring DHCP on the Linux client side

Windows 2000 Client Configuration

Windows 2000 defaults to DHCP, which reduces configuration time in many cases to near zero. Also, Windows configuration is so familiar to so many users that it's covered here only in the "In Brief" section.

Windows 98 is still in common enough use to warrant a separate section.

IN BRIEF

1. Click the Start button and navigate to Settings ➤ Network and Dial-up Connections.

2. Right-click the Local Area Connection icon and choose Properties from the pop-up window.

3. Click Internet Protocol (TCP/IP) and the Properties button. Your screen should now resemble Figure 5-14.

4. As in Figure 5-14, check the "Obtain an IP address automatically" and "Obtain DNS server address automatically" options.

5. Exit by clicking the OK buttons.

6. Click the Start button again and navigate to Settings ➤ Control Panel.

7. Double-click the System icon, choose the Network Identification tab, and click the Properties button.

8. Type in the computer's hostname in the Computer Name box and its domain name in the Workgroup box.

9. Exit again by clicking the OK buttons.

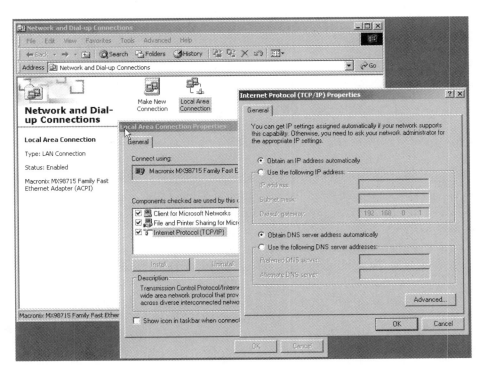

Figure 5-14. Configuring a dynamic address client in Windows 2000

Windows 98 Client Configuration

IN BRIEF

1. Click the Start button and navigate to Settings ➤ Control Panel.

2. Double-click the Network icon. Select the line that begins with "TCP/IP" and continues with a description of your Ethernet network card, and click the Properties button.

3. Check the "Obtain an IP address automatically" option.

4. Exit to the main Network window by clicking the OK button. Choose the Identification tab and enter the computer's hostname in the Computer Name box and its domain name in the Workgroup box.

5. Exit by clicking the OK buttons.

Testing the Connection

At this stage, the client computers can talk to the server only with IP addresses, not names. To test this fundamental level of networking, use the ping command. This small program sends a tiny packet of information that asks for an *echo*, or, in other words, a return receipt. This is a command line–only program, both in Linux and Windows, and all it needs is the IP address of the machine you're trying to ping.

From a terminal in your Linux Server, type **ping *(IP address of client)***. As an example, to test the connection to a client named ceo.dev.org with an IP address of 192.168.0.2, you would type **ping 192.168.0.2** and press the Enter key.

If successful, ping will produce an apparently endless series of connection messages. Stop the program by simultaneously holding down the Ctrl and c keys. If unsuccessful, ping will return a Destination Host Unreachable error message, which may have to be stopped with the Ctrl+c key combination.

 TIP *The ping test works exactly the same way in Linux and Windows clients. In Windows, open a command prompt and enter the ping command with the IP address of your server.*

Lesson 5-2 Review

This lesson was devoted to setting up a dynamic IP address server and clients. You learned

- How to configure a Linux DHCP server's Ethernet interface

- How to configure the server to start at boot-up

- Which files need to be downloaded from Linux Leap and where they need to be copied

- Why you may need to edit the dhcpd and dhcpd.conf files, and how to do so

- How to start the server without rebooting

- How to configure a Linux client by entering its server's name and address, and how to configure the client for DHCP

- How to configure DHCP assigned addresses in both Windows 2000 and Windows 98

- How to use the ping command to test network connectivity from either Linux or Windows

LESSON 5-3.

SETTING UP A DOMAIN NAME SYSTEM SERVER FOR THE LAN

Why a domain name system (DNS) server for a small firm's LAN? Because, although it is more work up front, it greatly increases the LAN's flexibility. It enables maximum communication—including e-mail—between all computers on the LAN and makes Web and e-mail serving to the Internet very simple to implement. It also increases LAN stability and reduces maintenance.

What a DNS Server Does

A DNS server resolves computer hostnames to IP addresses (and vice versa). When any computer on the network tries to get in touch with another computer by using its hostname, the DNS server matches the name with the IP address, thus enabling the communication to take place. The server does not just resolve host-names on the local LAN: When it's unable to find a computer locally, it directs enquiries to "root servers" on the Internet, and it then "caches" the results in memory, so that when a computer on the LAN needs to resolve the same address again, the correct IP address comes from the local DNS server. This can greatly increase response time.

Thus, a local DNS server acts as a nameserver for the company's domain on the LAN. However, this can also extend to the Internet. In order to be registered, every domain needs two nameservers to match up the domain's IP address with its name. Although a firm does not need to host its own nameservers, it does give the firm more control.

Traditionally, setting up DNS meant a great deal of work with several text configuration files of abstruse design. Fortunately, GNOME's BIND Configuration Tool greatly simplifies this job for small firms.

The files to be configured are several "zone" files in /var/named/ and one general configuration file, /etc/dhcpd.conf. The zone files (all end in ".zone") match local computer names with addresses (forward master zones) and addresses with names (reverse master zones). In addition, one file, /var/named/named.ca, directs queries that can't be resolved locally to the Internet's root servers.

A small firm's administrator does not need to touch one of these files with a text editor. The administrator can configure them all from the BIND Configuration Tool. ("BIND" is an abbreviation for Berkeley Internet Name Domain, the actual name of the server program.) Usage of this tool will be a mystery to the uninitiated. Some scanty help is provided in the Red Hat Customization Guide, which is available on the documentation CD and on the Red Hat Web site. However, short of a lengthy tutorial, the best way to show how the tool works is to give an example. The Development, Ltd., scenario will be used.

Configuring a DNS Server for Development, Ltd.

The following operations take place on the scenario company's Linux server. You can access the configuration tool by clicking the Start button and navigating to Programs ➤ System ➤ DNS Configure DNS.

Configuring the Forward Master Zone for dev.org

To configure the forward master zone for dev.org, click the Add button, check the Forward Master Zone option, and enter the domain name **dev.org**.

This procedure creates the forward master zone file for the local domain. To be of use, every computer on the network must be listed in it. First, however, identify the LAN's nameserver by selecting dev.org under Records and clicking the Edit button.

In the Settings window, click the Add button and type in the fully qualified domain name (FQDN)—the hostname plus the domain name—of your server. In Development, Ltd.'s case, it is **server.dev.org**. Click the OK button, and enter the server's IP address at the bottom of the window—for the scenario, **192.168.0.1** (see Figure 5-15). Click the OK button to return to the main Master Zone window.

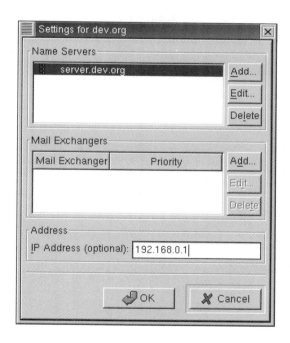

Figure 5-15. Setting up dev.org's nameserver on server.dev.org

Now the tedious part: Each computer has to be entered under Records. Start by clicking the Add button, selecting Host as the type of record resource, and typing in the first client machine's hostname and IP address (see Figure 5-16).

Figure 5-16. Adding a host record—the scenario company's first client name and address

You need to add each client computer in this way. When you've finished, the hostname and IP address of each machine will show up in the Records pane, as shown in Figure 5-17. Exit this window by clicking the OK button.

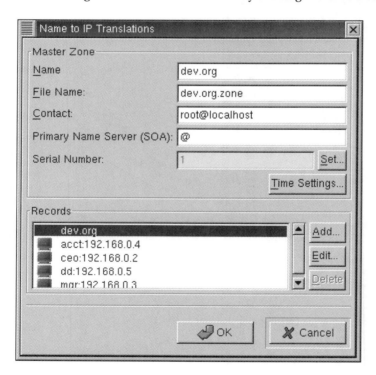

Figure 5-17. Each client appearing under Records

Configuring the Reverse Master Zone for dev.org

Now you must create the reverse master zone file. Go back to the very first window and click the Add button. This time, choose Reverse Master Zone and enter the first three sections (octets) of the server's IP address. For the scenario, the administrator would enter **192.168.0**. Click the OK button.

In the IP to Name Translations window that appears, click the Add button to add the local nameserver. Simply type in the FQDN of the server—in the scenario, this is **server.dev.org.** Note that in this box you must include a period (or "full stop" for British, Irish, and Indian readers) after the domain name.

Next, you must add every computer on the LAN, including the server, to the Reverse Address Table, much as you added them earlier. Click the Add button next to the bottom panel and enter the last "octet" of each machine's IP address, along with its FQDN. Note that here, also, a period must be added to the end of the name.

When you've finished, the window will look something like Figure 5-18.

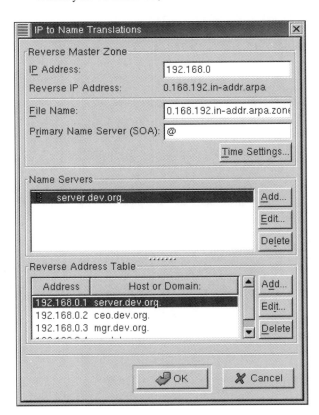

Figure 5-18. The IP to Name Translations window for the scenario. Each machine on the LAN appears in the Reverse Address Table.

Closing the configuration tool by clicking the X in the upper right-hand corner will automatically write all the configuration files to disk.

Client Configuration

The client configuration for DNS is very simple, and it's covered in this section in brief for all three types of client in the scenario.

Linux Clients

IN BRIEF

1. Using the Network Configurator tool, make sure that in the DNS window the local server's IP address is entered in the Primary DNS box and the domain name is entered under DNS Search Path.

2. In the Hosts window, make sure that the server's hostname and IP address are entered.

Windows 2000 Clients

IN BRIEF

1. Click the Start button and navigate to Settings ➤ Network and Dial-up Connections.

2. Right-click Local Area Connection and choose Properties.

3. Select Internet Protocol and click the Properties button.

4. Check the Use the Following DNS Server Addresses option, and enter the local server's IP address.

Windows 98 Clients

IN BRIEF

1. Click the Start button and navigate to Settings ➤ Control Panel.

2. Double-click the Network icon.

3. Under the DNS Configuration tab, check Enable and enter the client machine's hostname and domain.

4. In the same screen, add the local server's IP address under DNS Server Search Order (see Figure 5-19).

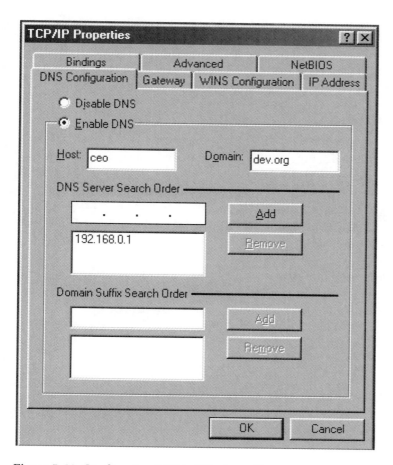

Figure 5-19. Configuring DNS in Windows 98

Starting DNS

You should configure BIND to start at system boot. To do so, start the Setup tool at a terminal and enter the System Services section. Check the "named" entry. To restart BIND at any time, type **/etc/init.d/named restart**.

Testing the Connection

With DNS working, all the computers should be able to resolve each other's names into IP addresses and vice versa. To test this, use the same program you used in the previous lesson, the ping program, but try it using the hostnames of the computers on the LAN.

For instance, from a terminal in your Linux server, type **ping** *(hostname of client)*. As an example, to test the connection to a client named ceo.dev.org, you would type **ping ceo** and press the Enter key.

This procedure should work from and to any machine on the LAN, including Linux to Windows and Windows to Linux.

Lesson 5-3 Review

This lesson was devoted to setting up BIND, the domain name server. You learned

- What a name resolver is, and why it needs to be used

- How to use the BIND Configuration Tool to configure the forward and reverse master zone files

- Client configuration for DNS

- How to configure the BIND program to start at system boot-up

- How to restart and test DNS

What's to Come

The next chapter of the book builds on the foundation presented in this chapter.
Topics covered are

- Setting up an Internet server for the LAN

- Setting up a file server

- Setting up a print server

- Setting up a local e-mail server

- Setting up a local Web and database server

# CHAPTER SIX

Linux As an Internet, File/Print, E-mail, Web, and Application Server

This chapter continues where the last left off: in setting up practical uses for the Linux server on the LAN. As the "Reality Byte" suggests, there are many of them. This chapter covers the setup and configuration of

- An Internet server for the LAN

- A file and print server

- A local e-mail server

- A local Web and database server

This chapter includes a good deal of material—the section·on sharing files is particularly long—and for the reader's benefit, the material is separated into six lessons, all with at least one review:

- Lesson 6-1. Setting Up an Internet Server for the LAN

- Lesson 6-2. Setting Up a File Server

- Lesson 6-3. Setting Up a Print Server

- Lesson 6-4. Setting Up an Internal E-mail Server

- Lesson 6-5. Setting Up a Local Web and Database Server

- Lesson 6-6. Adopting Postgres

The same scenario used in the previous chapter is continued here.

Reality Byte:

LINUX AS A BUSINESS SERVER IN IRELAND, FROM A SYSTEM ADMINISTRATOR'S VIEWPOINT

Before I joined TradeSignals.com (http://www.tradesignals.com) in June 1998, the company was well on its way to becoming a purely Windows shop. All the computers in the building (shared with two other companies) ran either Windows 9*x* or Windows NT and there was no mention of UNIX anywhere.

During that summer, I helped convince my boss that UNIX, and specifically Linux, was the way to go for further development of our Web site. I also convinced him to let me use Linux on my desktop machine, something I really needed if I was to be more productive.

At the time, we were using an NT server and an ISDN line owned by a sister company for our e-mail addresses and Internet connectivity. I applied for 16 IP addresses to cope with any future expansion, but we were refused and were allocated 8 addresses instead. Thankfully, I was aware of the IP masquerading (NAT) facilities of Linux and convinced my boss that it was a viable way of getting all our machines on the Internet.

Originally, the NT machine was going to handle e-mail services for the company, but there would be trouble if the NT machine was behind a masqueraded gateway/firewall. At the time, I didn't know Sendmail very well, but after a weekend in Galway at Intersocs '98 I saw it was simplicity itself to configure Sendmail.

After I figured out how to get Samba and Sendmail working, our Web site mirror machine became

- An Internet server

- A mail server

- A Samba/NFS file server

- A DNS server

- A database server

The machine had 32MB RAM originally, but I upgraded to 64MB. The mail server has now been happily working for 101 days.

Linux has helped us work better in the following ways:

- I'm amazed at what a 64MB Linux box can do. It's been very stable, and I don't remember the last time it crashed.

- The group permissions in UNIX allow me to give access to only certain people to the Web server files. This is possible in NT as well, but in UNIX permissions are a lot more visible to the user.

- Using Linux as my desktop OS gives me access to virtual desktops, The GIMP, Netscape, and the powerful text manipulation tools and stability of UNIX.

- Linux allows the company to become familiar with UNIX concepts required if we move to larger, "Enterprise Class" UNIX systems, such as AIX or Solaris.

- Linux is free.

However, it took some time for me to figure out how Sendmail, Samba, and BIND were configured. Now that I know how, I not only understand the basic facilities of the services offered, but I also have some insight into some of the neat things they can do. I've taken advantage of this knowledge several times, and it's something I won't forget.

About TradeSignals.com

Trade Signals Corporation Ltd. was founded in 1997. The company's mission is to bring cutting-edge systematic trading systems and analysis to professional and private futures investors using the Internet as a cost-efficient delivery mechanism.

About the Author

Donncha O Caoimh is a graduate of the Cork Institute of Technology.

 NOTE *Most of this chapter is concerned with configuration issues, so, where it is not explicitly stated, it's assumed that the user is logged in as the root user (the system administrator).*

LESSON 6-1.

SETTING UP AN INTERNET SERVER FOR THE LAN

Linux allows a firm to use its LAN server as an Internet server for the company, which enables every computer to share a single Internet connection. This is a job usually done by a separate piece of hardware called a *router.* Linux does the job by itself through Network Address Translation (NAT).

The advantages of NAT are twofold:

1.   It saves the company money, both by eliminating the need for a router and by eliminating the need for multiple Internet connections.

2.   It automatically provides a basic level of firewall security.

This lesson shows how to set up NAT for a small office, thus enabling Internet access across the LAN. This lesson covers the server setup first and then the client setup, for both Linux and Windows machines. Clients are covered in brief only—their setup is straightforward. Chapter Four covered setting up the server's DSL connection.

Server Configuration

IN BRIEF

1.   Download the rc.local file and copy it into its correct location: /etc/rc.d/rc.local.

2.   Edit the file if necessary.

3.   Check the iptables option and uncheck the ipchains option in the Services window of the Setup tool.

EXPLAINED

The rc.local file is the last file to be read during the computer's start-up. At the end of this file, you can insert the commands to start NAT, or you can simply download the file from Linux Leap (http://www.linuxleap.org) and copy it into the correct directory (using the copying techniques from the previous chapter).

The file is set to identify your second Ethernet card (eth1) as the card connected to your ISP. If this isn't the case—if in fact eth0 is connected to your ISP—you will have to edit this file.

To edit the file, use the gedit program, as in the previous chapter, and simply change "eth1" to "eth0" near the end of the second-to-last line. The correct place in the download file is shown in Figure 6-1.

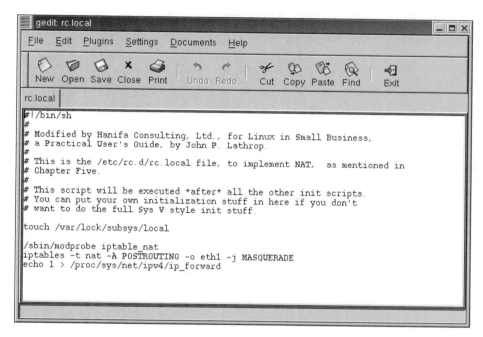

Figure 6-1. Editing the Ethernet interface in the rc.local file in gedit

Next, you need to check the iptables option within the Services part of the Setup tool. As mentioned in the previous chapter, you can start this tool from the main menu by navigating to Programs ➤ System ➤ Text Mode Tool Menu (when logged in as root) or by opening a terminal window and typing **ntsysv** (see Figure 6-2).

 NOTE *The iptables option must be checked for NAT to work, but ipchains, which appears a few entries above iptables within the Services Setup tool, must* not *be checked. Ipchains is an older implementation of NAT, but it is incompatible with the newer implementation, iptables, and if checked will prevent it from working.*

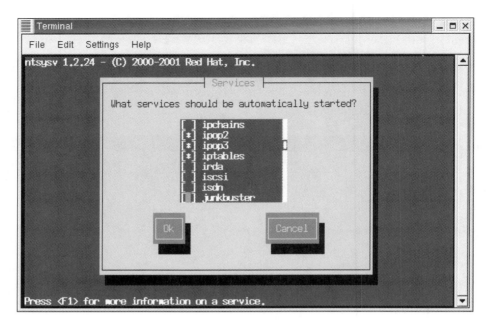

Figure 6-2. Check iptables to start at boot, but not ipchains

Finally, on the server machine, check that in the DNS window of Network Configurator you have indeed entered your server's IP address in the Primary DNS box, its correct hostname and domain, and its domain name under DNS Search Path. You probably did this earlier when you set up the DNS, but it's just as well to check.

 TIP *The DNS section of Network Configurator writes your /etc/resolv.conf file, but some ISPs, when they first connect during server boot-up, will rewrite this file. This issue was addressed in Chapter Four. To solve this problem, download from the Linux Leap Web site* (http://www.linuxleap.org) *the file /sbin/ifup and install it in the /sbin directory.*

Linux Client Setup

IN BRIEF

There should be nothing more to be done. Just make sure that in the DNS window of the Network Configurator, the server's IP address is entered in the Primary DNS box, and the LAN's domain name is entered under DNS Search Path.

Windows 2000 Client Setup

IN BRIEF

1. Click the Start button and navigate to Settings ➤ Network and Dial-up Connections.

2. Right-click the Local Area Connection icon and choose Properties from the pop-up window. Click Internet Protocol (TCP/IP) and the Properties button.

3. Click the Advanced button, and under "Default gateways," click the Add button and enter your local server's IP address (see Figure 6-3).

4. Exit by clicking the OK buttons.

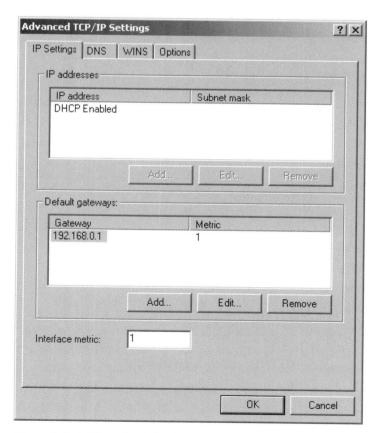

Figure 6-3. Adding the default gateway (the local server) in a Windows 2000 client

Windows 98 Client Configuration

IN BRIEF

1. Click the Start button and navigate to Settings ➤ Control Panel. Double-click the Network icon.

2. Select the line that begins with TCP/IP and continues with a description of your Ethernet network card, and then click the Properties button.

3. Click the Gateway tab and add the local server's IP address (see Figure 6-4).

4. Exit by clicking the OK buttons.

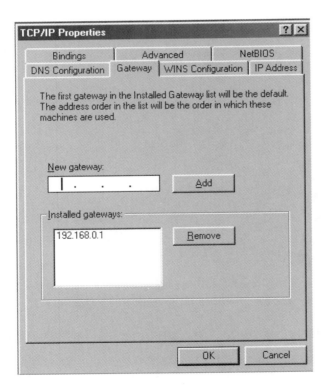

Figure 6-4. Making your local server your gateway in Windows 98

Testing the Connection

Test NAT by testing your computers' Internet connections on the Web.

First test out the server, either within GNOME by opening Netscape and trying to connect to a Web site, or at the command line by using Lynx, a text-only Web browser.

When you're sure that it's working (and if the server does not have a live Internet connection, it's doubtful that the clients will), try out the Linux clients the same way. Finally, try the Windows clients, using either Netscape or Internet Explorer.

Lesson 6-1 Review

This lesson was devoted to setting up an Internet server for the LAN, using Network Address Translation (NAT). You learned

- The advantages of using NAT

- How to configure a Linux Internet server for NAT, using a downloaded Linux Leap configuration file and the Setup and Network Configurator tools

- How to use Network Configurator to set up a Linux client for NAT

- How to set up Windows 2000 and Windows 98 clients for NAT

- How to test the connection at the server and the clients

LESSON 6-2.

SETTING UP A FILE SERVER

Linux can act as a drag-and-drop file server for both Linux and Windows machines on the LAN. Setting it up is not a purely technical job. First, the administrator needs to decide on the system architecture—that is, who is sharing what, from where. Then the administrator must create users, groups, and shared directories, and set permissions.

Thus this lesson covers, in a brief, practical way, the interesting subject of groups, users, and permissions. This book relies largely on the Development, Ltd., scenario to show how users, groups, and shared directories should be created and configured. This part of the lesson is preceded by a special "Background" section to give the reader the necessary grounding in the concepts and tools involved.

A Linux server relies on two completely different programs to connect in a familiar, drag-and-drop way to the Linux and the Windows client machines on the LAN. It relies on the Network File System (NFS) to connect to the Linux clients and on Samba for connections to the Windows machines. Setting up both programs is covered in this lesson, with the aid of downloaded configuration files from Linux Leap (http://www.linuxleap.org).

This lesson is divided into four sections:

- The Design Stage

- Users, Groups, and Permissions

- Connecting Linux Clients to the Server with NFS

- Connecting Windows Clients to the Server with Samba

Due to the length of these sections, a section review, instead of a lesson review, will appear after the first two sections and after the last two sections.

The Design Stage

IN BRIEF

1. Decide on what you want the file server to do. Exactly why are client machines accessing the server?

2. Divide users into groups, depending on how they share access to the server.

3. Decide on a directory structure for the server.

EXPLAINED

System administrators scan save themselves a tremendous amount of time and trouble if they give some thought to the kind of file sharing needed before attempting to create or configure anything. The first rule is always to ask the first and most important question: *What do you want it to do?*

It's at this point that a flowchart or company diagram comes in very handy, and the reader is asked to look back at Figure 5-5 in the previous chapter. Figure 5-5 is a hierarchical diagram of Development, Ltd., showing each employee and how he or she fits into the corporate chain.

Although it is quite possible to set up a LAN in which every computer can drag and drop files to and from every other computer, it's generally not considered an optimal solution, except for the very smallest local networks. The reason this is not done is partly for security and partly for simplicity. A computer should be able to access only the computers it needs to access. In a small firm or workgroup, there are three common reasons to access a server:

- To back up files

- To collaborate with other users by sharing files

- To access publicly available files

Designing File Sharing in the Development, Ltd., Scenario

What do you want it to do?

In order to answer that question, you may ask others these questions: "How do we want people to work?" and "What will people use the server for?"

In the case of Development, Ltd., the CEO and the office manager—the de facto system administrator—have decided on the following file sharing setup.

- All employees need their own local home directory, on their own computer, where they can work on their own files and create their own subdirectories as they like. This, in fact, is not file sharing at all, but basic privacy, simplicity, and good use of resources.

- There has to be a backup for each user's work on the server.

- In terms of collaboration, there are three basic groups in the company:

  Management, consisting of the CEO, the office manager, and the part-time accountant. Management does not exist in a void, and so all three members of the management team will automatically have access to the shared directories of the other two groups.

Domestic consultants, headed by the domestic director, with a senior consultant and five consultants below her.

Foreign consultants, headed by the foreign director, with a senior consultant and three consultants below him.

- Each of the three basic groups will have a single shared directory on the server.

- There will be one directory shared publicly by everyone.

All of these directories will be created under the server's /home directory. So, the directory structure under /home will look like Figure 6-5. This figure shows that the server will have a backup directory for each user. For example, the backup for the CEO is /home/ceo, and the backup for domestic consultant 5 is /home/dc5. The three shared directories in Figure 6-5 are in capital letters: /home/MGMT, /home/DOMESTIC, and /home/FOREIGN. The publicly accessible directory is /home/PUBLIC.

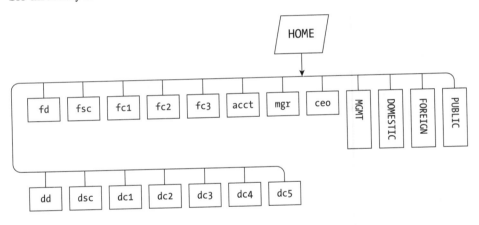

Figure 6-5. Server shared directory structure for Development, Ltd.

Users, Groups, and Permissions

BACKGROUND

Before you create users and directories, it's important to have a basic understanding of users, groups, and permissions, for it is these three concepts in combination that determine how files and directories are shared.

NOTE *The information in the following sections is germane for a Linux server sharing files with Linux clients. The complications—and security benefits—of users, groups, and permissions aren't necessary for Windows clients; Windows PCs communicate with the Linux server in a different, and simpler, manner.*

However, for the purpose of this lesson, assume that the administrator is setting up the server to be able to handle a LAN where every client is a Linux PC—instead of only the six latest, as in the scenario. Although this is more work now, it means that the office will be able to adopt more Linux PCs easily in the future. And the Windows machines will not be adversely affected.

Users and Groups

During installation, when you create a user account for your Linux machine, you also automatically create a home directory for that user and a special group to which that user belongs.

For instance, Robert installs Linux on his PC and, when prompted during the installation, creates the user robert. This automatically creates the directory /home/robert and it also automatically creates a group to which Robert (and so far, only Robert) belongs.

Users and groups have both names and numbers. The numbers are called the user ID (UID) and group ID (GID). By default, Red Hat Linux gives the first user a UID and GID of 500, the second user gets 501, the third user gets 502, and so on.

See Table 6-1 for an example of how this ID convention works.

Table 6-1. Examples of User and Group Names and ID Numbers

USER NAME	GROUP NAME	UID	GID
root	root	0	0
firstuser	firstuser	500	500
seconduser	seconduser	501	501
thirduser	thirduser	502	501

This ID convention is fine on a single, non-networked PC, on which each user will want his or her files to be secure and private. However, on a LAN with backup directories and shared directories, identical UIDs must be created on the server and client, and all users that belong to the same group must share the same GID.

Permissions

In Linux, directories aren't automatically shared by all users. Instead, they have certain "permissions" that enable them and their contents to be shared in certain ways with certain users.

There are three types of directory (and file) permissions:

- *Read permission (r).* The permission to read a file or directory.

- *Write permission (w).* The permission to create or delete files in a directory.

- *Execute permission (x).* The permission to execute a file.

In addition, these permissions are granted (or withheld) to three user categories:

- The user who owns the directory. For example, the user Miranda owns /home/miranda.

- Members of the directory's group.

- Anyone else.

Some examples will make this clearer. A user's home directory will always give complete permissions (r,w,x) to the owner—that is, the user John will always have total permissions for his home directory /home/john/. Home directories are always private; it follows that no one else (except for the root user) can access that directory.

If you type **ls -l** and press the Enter key in the /home directory, you will see exactly what permissions the home directories have. In the preceding example, you would see this:

```
drwx------    2    john    john    4096  Jul  27  13:08  john
```

Starting from the left, this means that john is a directory (d), and that the user (john) has r,w,x permissions. The next six dashes mean that neither other members of John's group nor anyone else has any permissions for this directory at all. The name, repeated twice, identifies first the directory's user and then the directory's group.

Figure 6-6 shows more clearly the design and meaning of the first ten elements of the ls -l readout.

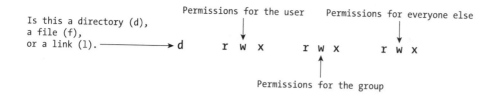

Figure 6-6. The format of permissions shown by the ls -l command

To give another example, if this directory gave complete permissions to the user and to the group, but no permissions to any other user, the first ten elements would read as follows:

```
drwxrwx---
```

If this directory gave complete permissions to the user, the group, and everyone else, it would read as follows:

```
drwxrwxrwx
```

If the directory gave complete permissions to the user, but only read and write permissions to the group and everyone else, it would read as follows:

```
drwxrw-rw-
```

The following is another example with the user and group:

```
drwxr-----    2    john    accounting   4096  Jul  27  13:08  john
```

This directory belongs to the user john and the group accounting. John has complete permissions in this directory, but other members of the accounting group have only read permissions, and people outside of the group have no permissions at all.

Here's one more example, this time with a user and group:

```
drwxrw-rw-    2    pam    management    4096 Aug 12 14:00 pam
```

Pam has complete permissions in this directory, and other members of the management group have read and write permissions. In fact, all other users also have read and write permissions.

From these examples, you can establish certain general rules of directory administration.

- For backups on the server, it's most straightforward to give users' accounts the same name and UID on both server and client machines.

- For different users to share directories (that are not, however, shared by everyone), it's necessary that their shared directories belong to that group, and that the directories have correct permissions set for that group.

- The simplest way to create directories that can be shared by everyone is to create them with read and write permissions for everyone.

Tools

The tools used for adding directories, users, groups, and so on are traditionally command-line tools used at a terminal. There are graphical tools for this purpose, but they come and go—the future of some is uncertain. For this reason, this book presents five commands used most commonly by system administrators. Examples of their use are given in the scenario.

- *mkdir.* This command creates a directory.

- *groupadd.* This command adds groups and is often used with the -g option, which allows the administrator to set the GID. Typical usage is

```
groupadd -g X groupname
```

where X is the GID and groupname is the name of the group.

- *useradd.* This command adds users, and you can use it with the -g and the -u options, which set the group and user ID, respectively. In addition, the -G option adds additional groups—a user can belong to multiple groups simultaneously. An example of usage is

```
useradd -g X, -u Y -G group1,group2,group3
```

where X is the GID and Y is the UID.

- *chgrp.* This command changes a file or directory's group. An example of usage is

```
chgrp X filename
```

where X is the GID or group name and `filename` is the name of the file or directory.

- *chmod.* This command changes the file or directory's permissions—the user's permissions (u), the group's permissions (g), or the permissions of other users (o) or all users (a). The following examples provide you with an idea of this command's typical usage.

This example gives the file or directory's group both read and write access:

```
chmod g=rw DIRECTORYNAME
```

This example withdraws all permissions for all but the directory's user and group:

```
chmod o=   DIRECTORYNAME
```

This example gives complete permissions to all users:

```
chmod a=rwx DIRECTORYNAME
```

 NOTE *Other very useful commands are usermod, to modify a user account, and groupmod, to modify a group. Sometimes you just need to delete—for this kind of situation you can use userdel to delete a user and groupdel to delete a group.*

The Scenario:
Implementing Directory Sharing at Development, Ltd.

IN BRIEF

1. Make a plan for group and user IDs.

2. Create shared groups on the server.

3. Add users on the server.

4. Recreate users on the client machines.

5. Create shared directories on the server.

6. Create public directories, if any.

EXPLAINED

Making a Plan for Group and User IDs

It makes sense to coordinate user and group IDs as much as possible. Numbers below 500 are generally reserved, while you can choose numbers above 500 according to the plan you prefer.

For the scenario, the administrator decided to parcel out group IDs as follows:

Management	600
Domestic	700
Foreign	800

GID/UID coordination will be achieved by including each user's ID within his or her groups. The CEO, the first member of the management group, will have UID 601, while the domestic director, the first member of the domestic group, will have UID 701.

Creating Shared Groups on the Server

Create the groups using the groupadd command with the -g option to assign specific GIDs.

The administrator would type **groupadd -g 600 management** and press the Enter key. The other two groups can be added similarly:

```
groupadd -g 700 domestic
groupadd -g 800 foreign
```

The three groups have now been added to the server with assigned GIDs.

Adding Users on the Server

Add the users with the useradd command and the -g and -u options to ensure each user belongs to the correct group and has a user ID that you can recreate on the client machines.

The administrator would type **useradd -g 600 -G 700,800 -u 601 ceo** and press the Enter key. This adds the user ceo to the server, along with the backup directory /home/ceo. The CEO has the UID 601 and belongs to the management group. In addition, this user also belongs to the domestic and foreign groups. Note that you can enter the group either as the name or the assigned numeric ID—it makes no difference.

This is a tedious job, but it only has to be done once. On a small company or workgroup such as this, with only 15 workstations, it's not especially onerous. The following is every line that you would have to enter on the server to add every user in this workgroup.

First, for the management group:

```
useradd -g 600 -G 700,800 -u 601 ceo
useradd -g 600 -G 700,800 -u 602 mgr
useradd -g 600 -G 700,800 -u 603 acct
```

Second, for the domestic group:

```
useradd -g 700 -u 701 dd
useradd -g 700 -u 702 dsc
useradd -g 700 -u 703 dc1
useradd -g 700 -u 704 dc2
useradd -g 700 -u 705 dc3
useradd -g 700 -u 706 dc4
useradd -g 700 -u 707 dc5
```

Third, for the foreign group:

```
useradd -g 800 -u 801 fd
useradd -g 800 -u 802 fsc
useradd -g 800 -u 803 fc1
useradd -g 800 -u 804 fc2
useradd -g 800 -u 805 fc3
```

Keep records! When you've finished, correct directories, users, and groups are set up for backups on the server.

Recreating Users on the Client Machines

On a Windows client, the administrator must only make sure that an identically named user is created, and he or she must also make a note of the password, which is necessary for file sharing under Samba.

But on a Linux client PC, both the group(s) and the user must be recreated exactly as he or she was on the server. As an example, on the CEO's Linux workstation (the CEO is experimenting with Linux and has a dual-boot Linux/Windows PC), the administrator first creates the management group as follows:

```
groupadd -g 600 management
```

Then the administrator creates the domestic and foreign groups. Next, the administrator creates the CEO's user account:

```
useradd -g 600 -G 700,800 -u 601 ceo
```

Thus, the CEO's information is recreated exactly on her client Linux PC.

There is one additional client step. Since a Linux user cannot log in without a password, a password must be created for the user ceo. The CEO can do this herself, for there is no need in Linux for an accompanying password on the server. (However, few administrators would want the CEO—or any user—to create her own password. Typically, the administrator would jealously guard root access "superuser privileges" on all machines on the LAN and insist that the administrator alone assign all passwords.)

The administrator types **passwd ceo**, presses the Enter key, and enters the password when prompted.

Here's another Linux client example. On the third domestic consultant's workstation, the administrator creates the domestic group as follows:

```
groupadd -g  700 domestic
```

and then creates the consultant's user account:

```
useradd -g domestic -u 705 dc3
```

and finally adds a password for the account:

```
passwd dc3
```

When the administrator is finished, correct directories, users, and groups are set up for every Linux client machine.

Creating Shared Directories on the Server

There are three shared directories, one each shared by management, domestic consultants, and foreign consultants. Creating shared directories is a three-step process.

First, the administrator creates each directory on the server as root, using the mkdir command:

```
mkdir /home/MGMT
```

Pressing Enter creates the /home/MGMT directory. The administrator repeats this process for /home/DOMESTIC and /home/FOREIGN.

The next step is to change each directory's group to the group whose files will share it, with the chgrp command, as follows:

```
chgrp management /home/MGMT
```

Pressing Enter applies the management group ownership to the /home/MGMT directory. The administrator then repeats this step, using the correct group, with the other shared directories.

Finally, the correct permissions need to be set for each shared directory using the chmod command:

```
chmod g=rwx /home/MGMT
```

and

```
chmod o=   /home/MGMT
```

The first chmod command changes permissions to r,w,x for the group, and the second withdraws all permissions for all other users (≡ followed by nothing). These steps must be repeated for each shared directory.

Creating Public Directories

To create a public directory for all users, /home/PUBLIC/, use mkdir. This directory's group owner is not important—simply use the chmod command to set all permissions for all users, as follows:

```
chmod a=rwx /home/PUBLIC
```

At the end of this whole process, the administrator will have created a total of 19 directories under /home on the server. The readout of the ls -l command would look like Figure 6-7.

```
[root@server home]# ls -l
total 76
drwx------    3 acct     manageme     4096 Nov 22 11:18 acct
drwx------    3 ceo      manageme     4096 Nov 22 11:18 ceo
drwx------    3 dc1      domestic     4096 Nov 22 11:19 dc1
drwx------    3 dc2      domestic     4096 Nov 22 11:19 dc2
drwx------    3 dc3      domestic     4096 Nov 22 11:20 dc3
drwx------    3 dc4      domestic     4096 Nov 22 11:20 dc4
drwx------    3 dc5      domestic     4096 Nov 22 11:20 dc5
drwx------    3 dd       domestic     4096 Nov 22 11:19 dd
drwxrwx---    2 root     domestic     4096 Nov 22 11:29 DOMESTIC
drwx------    3 dsc      domestic     4096 Nov 22 11:19 dsc
drwx------    3 fc1      foreign      4096 Nov 22 11:21 fc1
drwx------    3 fc2      foreign      4096 Nov 22 11:21 fc2
drwx------    3 fc3      foreign      4096 Nov 22 11:22 fc3
drwx------    3 fd       foreign      4096 Nov 22 11:20 fd
drwxrwx---    2 root     foreign      4096 Nov 22 11:30 FOREIGN
drwx------    3 fsc      foreign      4096 Nov 22 11:21 fsc
drwxrwx---    2 root     manageme     4096 Nov 22 11:29 MGMT
drwx------    3 mgr      manageme     4096 Nov 22 11:18 mgr
drwxrwxrwx    2 root     root         4096 Nov 22 11:33 PUBLIC
[root@server home]# 
```

Figure 6-7. Result of the ls -l command on Development, Ltd.'s server

Section Review

The previous two sections were devoted to the first two steps in setting up a Linux file server: the design stage and users, groups, and permissions. You learned

- The importance of planning before creating users, groups, and directories

- Typical reasons to access a server in a small firm

- The necessity of dividing users into groups and of deciding on a directory structure according to groups

- The relationship between users, groups, and permissions

- How to read directory permissions from the ls -l command

- Common command-line tools for creating and manipulating users, groups, directories, and permissions

- How to implement all of the previous entries in this list on the scenario company's Linux server

Connecting Linux Clients to the Server with NFS

IN BRIEF

1. Download the server's exports file, /etc/exports, from the Linux Leap Web site and turn on NFS, nfslock, and portmap on both the client and server.

2. Create the mount point on the clients.

3. Mount the server shares from the Linux clients.

4. Make mounting shares automatic with fstab and netfs.

EXPLAINED

The Network File System (NFS) is a method of "exporting" directories from one Linux computer to another, so that they can be easily accessed not only from the command line, but also from any GUI file manager. Setting up NFS is quite simple.

First, download the /etc/exports file from the Linux Leap Web site (http://www.linuxleap.org), and copy it into the /etc directory on the Linux server. This file is only one line long:

```
/home 192.168.0.0/255.255.255.0(rw,no_root_squash)
```

but it is extremely sensitive to such minor errors as having a single space in the wrong place. The Linux Leap export file configures the server to "export" all the directories under /home. That means that each Linux client machine will be able to see the home directories, but it will only be able to access those for which it has correct permissions.

Next, using the System Services menu of the Setup tool, ensure that the following services are configured to start at boot-up (on both the Linux server and Linux client machines):

- nfs

- nfslock

- portmap

Finally, start the services by rebooting the server and the clients.

NOTE *The exports file from the Linux Leap Web site is written for a LAN with a network address of 192.168.0.0 and a netmask of 255.255.255.0. This is standard for a small LAN, but if your addresses are different, you will have to edit the file—simply replace the addresses with your own. The gedit text editor within GNOME is an excellent tool for this purpose.*

Note also that the Linux Leap exports file exports the contents of the /home directory. If you want it to export a different directory, you will need to edit this as well.

Creating the Mount Point on the Client

The next step is to create the mount point on the client PCs, which will be used to mount the /home directory on the server. The *mount point* is a directory like any other, and it's created with the mkdir command. It can be anywhere within the directory structure, and it can have any name you like. In the scenario, the mount point is /SERVER and you create it by logging in as the root user, typing **mkdir /SERVER**, and pressing the Enter key.

Mounting the Server Shares from the Linux Clients

To mount the server's NFS share, type as the root user on one of the Linux clients **mount SERVERNAME:/home /MOUNTPOINT**.

An example of this on a Linux client machine in the scenario is

```
mount server.dev.org:/home /SERVER
```

You can test this example in the scenario by starting GNOME on any of the Linux clients (after you mount the server's NFS share) and opening the file manager—in this case, the GMC file manager. Figure 6-8 shows what the file manager could look like when opened on the dc5 Linux client machine.

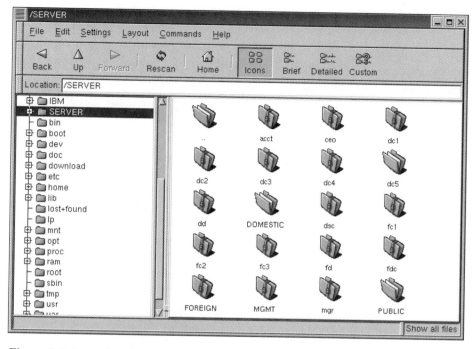

Figure 6-8. Accessing the server from the dc5 Linux client PC

In the left-hand panel, you can see that the /SERVER directory is selected—this is the mount point for the server's /home directories, and those in fact are visible on the right. By looking at the icons, you can see which directories are open to this client machine, belonging to domestic consultant 5 on staff. The open file directories are as follows:

- dc5, the user's backup directory on the server

- The DOMESTIC directory, which is the group the user belongs to

- The PUBLIC directory, which is open to all

The dc5 user can drag and drop files from his or her home directory to and from any of the three shared directories. All other directories are closed to this user, as you can see from the directory icons showing strapped and sealed folders.

Making It Automatic

There is one more step to perform if the user does not want to manually mount the server's share every time he or she starts up the computer. You can automate the process by making sure that the netfs script is run at boot time (again, through the Setup tool) and by adding a line similar to the following at the end of the /etc/fstab file:

```
server.dev.org:/home   /SERVER   nfs   rw,hard,intr   0 0
```

As you can see, the file begins with the hostname of the server and the directory to be shared, and then includes the mount point on the client.

With these two changes, the server's /home directory should be automatically mounted every time the Linux client machine starts.

Connecting Windows Clients to the Server with Samba

Downloading the Linux Leap smb.conf file onto the server, making one small change (inserting the domain name of your LAN), and recreating Windows users and passwords in Samba will enable Windows clients to drag and drop files to and from their home directories and the public directory on the Linux server.

IN BRIEF

1. Download the server's Samba configuration file, /etc/samba/smb.conf, from the Linux Leap Web site, and insert your own domain name.

2. Recreate the Windows clients' user names and passwords on the server as Samba users and passwords.

3. Turn Samba on.

EXPLAINED

The Samba program, running on the server, allows Windows to see shared directories just as if the server were another Windows machine. These shared directories can then be mapped to drives, simplifying further the process of opening, saving, copying, and moving shared files.

The default Samba configuration file, smb.conf, is long and complex. Fortunately, it needs very little modification to be run "out of the box." You can download a slightly modified version from the Linux Leap Web site (http://www.linuxleap.org). This version reflects the needs of the Development, Ltd., scenario, with the exception that the FOREIGN, DOMESTIC, and MGMT shared directories are disabled, by "commenting them out."

The Linux Leap version of smb.conf enables the following shared directories:

- Home directories

- A public directory in /home/PUBLIC

The configuration file has two main sections: Global Settings and Share Definitions. The Linux Leap modifications include the following modifications to the standard Red Hat 7.2 smb.conf file in the Share Definitions section:

- The [homes] section is commented out (replaced by [backup] section).

- The [pchome] section has changed to [backup] and has been enabled.

- The [public] section is enabled for the /home/PUBLIC directory.

- The [Foreign] section, for members of the foreign group, has been disabled.

- The [Domestic] section, for members of the domestic group, has been disabled.

- The [Management] section, for members of the management group, has been disabled.

Customizing the smb.conf File

First, rename your original /etc/samba/smb.conf file to smb.conf.old. Then download the smb.conf file from Linux Leap and copy it into the /etc/samba directory.

Open the file in GNOME using gedit. Replace MYGROUP with the name of your domain. Figure 6-9 shows the file edited for the Development, Ltd., scenario's domain name.

Scrolling down through the file will reveal the entries for the backup, public, foreign, domestic, and management sections. Only the backup and public sections are enabled by default—to enable the other sections, simply delete the semicolon (;) at the head of each line. You can easily customize these sections to suit many different environments.

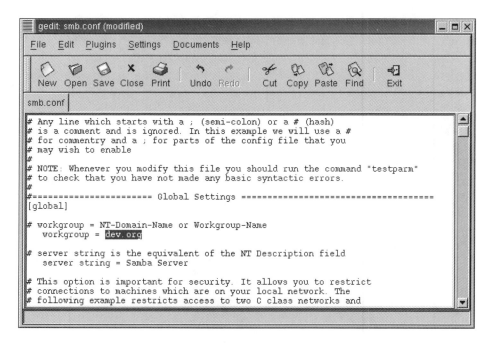

Figure 6-9. Inserting your own domain name in the Samba configuration file

Creating Samba Users and Passwords

Windows users and passwords have to be recreated as Samba users and passwords on the server. And Samba users can only be created if the Linux user already exists.

Fortunately, you've already ensured that both Linux and Windows users are identical. This leaves only Samba to configure.

Staying with the Development, Ltd., scenario, to create the Samba user fc3 with her password, the administrator types **smbadduser fc3:fc3** in a terminal on the server and presses the Enter key. At the prompt for a password, the administrator enters the same password as that user's password on the Windows client.

This procedure recreates the Windows user and password as a Samba user and password on the server. You do not have to perform these steps for every client on the LAN—only the Windows clients.

Turning Samba On

You can use the Setup tool to make sure that Samba starts automatically at system boot. To manually start, or restart, Samba at a terminal type **/etc/init.d/smb start** or **/etc/init.d/smb restart** and press Enter.

There is no special configuration necessary in Windows, other than what you already did in Chapter Five for setting up TCP/IP networking. Double-clicking the My Network Places icon in Windows 2000 and then double-clicking Computers Near Me will reveal the folders representing other computers on the LAN. (In Windows 98, just click Network Neighborhood.)

Clicking the folder representing the Linux server will reveal shared and backup directories. In Figure 6-10, you can see exactly what, for instance, the domestic director would see on her Windows client. Her backup directory on the server, /home/dd, is represented as the backup folder. She can save and drag and drop files to and from it as she wishes. She also has complete access to the public folder and the Domestic folders, which represent the server directories /home/PUBLIC and /home/DOMESTIC, respectively.

However, although both the Foreign and Management folders appear in her server window, she cannot access them, because she does not belong to either of those groups.

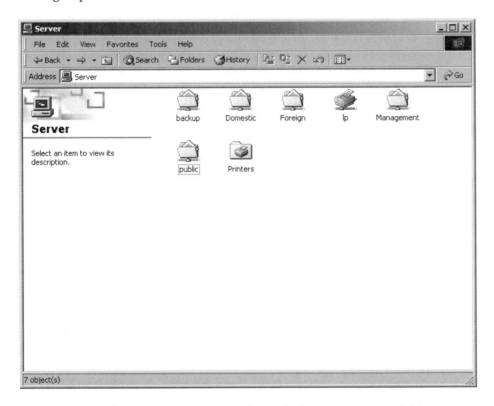

Figure 6-10. Backup and shared directories on the Linux server available on a Windows client

Using NETFS to Remount Shared Directories

When the server and the Linux clients start up, they may not start all services in the best order, and certain shares may not be automatically mounted. If this is the case, simply rerun the /etc/init.d/netfs script. This automatically unmounts, and then remounts, all NFS and Samba shares. To do so, type **/etc/init.d/netfs** and press the Enter key.

Section Review

The last two sections were devoted to the final steps necessary to set up a Linux file server in a heterogeneous network environment: connecting the clients to the server. You learned

- NFS is necessary to connect a Linux client to a Linux server for drag-and-drop file sharing

- How to create client mount points and how to mount server shares on them

- How to make mounting NFS shares automatic by configuring fstab and setting netfs to start at boot-up

- Samba is necessary to connect a Windows client to a Linux server for drag-and-drop file sharing

- How to configure the smb.conf file (downloadable from Linux Leap)

- How to start Samba on the server

- How to automatically remount all shares from the server and Linux workstations

LESSON 6-3.

SETTING UP A PRINT SERVER

This lesson covers setting up either a Linux or a Windows print server on a mixed Linux/Windows LAN.

In a LAN such as the one used by Development, Ltd., shared printers can be connected either to the Linux server (a Linux print server) or to any of the Windows desktops (a Windows print server). This lesson covers the two different configurations separately.

A Linux Print Server

IN BRIEF

1. Configure the printer using the Printer Configuration tool in GNOME, using Queue Type: Local Printer.

2. Make sure that Samba is running on the Linux print server.

3. Add the printer to the Windows desktops from the Printers window.

4. Add the printer to the Linux desktops using the Printer Configuration tool in GNOME, using Queue Type: UNIX Printer.

EXPLAINED

Until fairly recently, printing (certainly non-PostScript printing) was poorly supported in Linux. Drivers for many printers either didn't exist or were buggy, and printing, when it worked, was often very slow. That has changed. Although printer support is still not as good as it is in Windows, you can use a Linux computer with most printers to provide an acceptable print server.

A Linux server uses the Samba program to share a printer with Windows desktops, just as it does to share files. It does this without any modification to the Linux Leap Samba configuration file, smb.conf (which you can download from http://www.linuxleap.org).

First, configure the printer attached to the Linux server. Do this with the Printer Configuration tool in GNOME.

1. On the Linux server, click the Start button and navigate to Programs ➤ System ➤ Printer Configuration.

2. Click the New icon on the toolbar, and then click the Next button. Enter a name in the Queue Name box. The Queue Name simply identifies the printer. The name can be as simple as an abbreviation of the printer's manufacturer and model (e.g., hp).

3. Select Local Printer under Queue Type, and click Next. Accept the next screen as is and click Next again.

4. Choose your printer driver—you'll have to continue clicking the arrow symbols until you reach a down-pointing arrow to find the actual driver. After you select your driver, click Next and finish out the screens.

5. Click the Apply icon on the toolbar and test the printer via the menu bar.

Second, follow the steps as you would for a Linux file server to get Samba running:

1. Download smb.conf and copy it into the /etc directory.

2. Using smbadduser, add Samba users and passwords to the Linux server, recreating the users and passwords shared by both the Linux server and the Windows workstations.

3. Start Samba by typing **/etc/init.d/smb start** in a terminal, and configure it to start at boot-up with the Setup program.

Third, add the printer on each Windows computer, in the same way you would add any Windows network printer.

Finally, add the printer to the Linux workstations. Use the Printer Configuration tool, as you did on the server, but for the Queue Type, choose UNIX Printer. In the next screen, type in the FQDN or IP address of the server and the queue, usually **lp** (see Figure 6-11). (Note: This queue is not the same as the "queue name" mentioned previously. Your server's queue will probably be lp. The numbering scheme for multiple printers and their queues is as follows: lp, lp0, lp1, and so on.) Remember to choose the identical print driver as on the server.

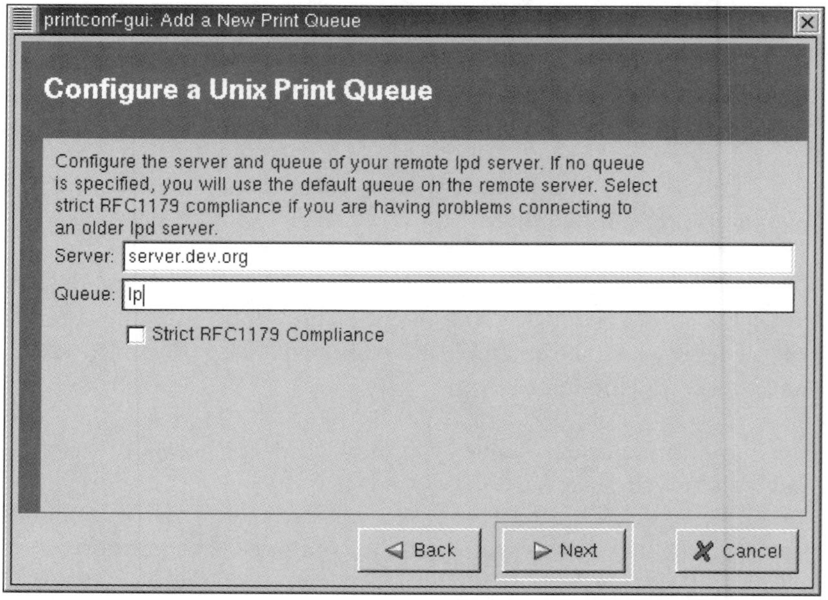

Figure 6-11. Connecting to a Linux print server from a Linux client

A Windows Print Server

IN BRIEF

1. Configure the printer as you would any Windows local printer.

2. Add the printer to the Windows desktops from the Printers window.

3. Make sure that Samba is running on the Linux workstations.

4. Add the printer to the Linux desktops using the Printer Configuration tool in GNOME, using Queue Type: Windows Printer.

EXPLAINED

You can connect a printer to any Windows machine on a mixed Linux/Windows LAN, and any other Windows PC on the LAN can use that printer. In addition, as long as the Linux workstations are configured with static IP addresses (or as long as the LAN is running its own domain name server), the Linux PCs, too, can use the Windows printer.

First, configure the Windows printer as you would any local printer attached to a Windows system.

Second, add the printer to the other Windows desktops, as you would any Windows network printer.

Third, make sure that Samba is running on the Linux workstations, as in the previous section, "A Linux Print Server."

Finally, use the Printer Configuration tool in GNOME to add the printer to the Linux workstations:

1. Click the Start button and navigate to Programs ➤ System ➤ Printer Configuration.

2. Click the New icon on the toolbar, and under Queue Type, choose Windows Printer. Enter an appropriate queue name as previously explained in the section "A Linux Print Server."

3. In the next window, fill in the Share box by using the Windows PC's hostname (the host-only part of the hostname) and the printer name, using the following format:

```
//hostname/printername
```

4. Enter the Windows machine user's name and his or her password.

5. Under Host IP, enter either the Windows print server's IP address or the FQDN.

6. Enter the LAN's domain name in the Workgroup box.

Figure 6-12 shows how this would look for the scenario.

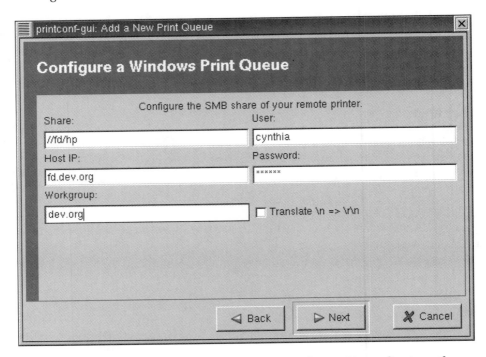

Figure 6-12. Connecting to a Windows print server from a Linux client; see the section "The Scenario" that follows.

The Scenario

Development, Ltd., has two printers. The main printer is an IBM connected to the Linux server. However, the foreign consulting group churns out a lot of paper (proposals, management review drafts, and so on), so they have their own printer, a Hewlett Packard that is attached to the foreign director's personal workstation.

The foreign director works on a Windows PC, and so the Linux workstations in her group have a setup in their Printer Configuration tool that looks like Figure 6-12. Notice that the share is //fd/hp. This corresponds to the foreign director's computer hostname, followed by the Windows name of the director's local printer, hp. The director's name and password is entered in the appropriate fields, as is the LAN's domain name under Workgroup.

Lesson 6-3 Review

In this lesson, you learned

- How to set up a Linux print server in a heterogeneous LAN using the GNOME Printer Configuration tool for both the Linux clients and Linux server

- How to set up a Windows print server in a heterogeneous LAN using the Printer Configuration tool for the Linux client machines

LESSON 6-4.

SETTING UP AN INTERNAL E-MAIL SERVER

This lesson covers setting up an internal e-mail server for the LAN with Sendmail.

Nowadays, e-mail is possibly the most common method for a company's employees to share data, and it follows that every employee should have an e-mail account. But as a small business grows, one of the first things it runs out of is e-mail accounts (the "mailboxes") assigned to it by its ISP. More can often be purchased, but since you can create unlimited internal (within the firm) e-mail accounts for no cost, it often makes more sense to assign ISP-provided Internet e-mail to those employees who need it for company business, while providing all employees with internal accounts.

This lesson is presented in three sections. The first section covers the Linux e-mail server, and the next two sections cover client setup: Netscape Communicator on Linux and Outlook on Windows. Outlook is covered only in brief.

 NOTE *These instructions will also lay the groundwork for setting up an Internet e-mail server for the company. The few additional steps to take to ensure complete Internet e-mail broadcasting and access are presented in the next chapter.*

Setting Up a Linux E-mail Server

IN BRIEF

1. Download the sendmail.mc file from the Linux Leap Web site and use it to generate the Sendmail configuration file, /etc/sendmail.cf.

2. Add your domain name to the /etc/mail/local-host-names file.

3. Make sure that sendmail, xinetd, and ipop3 are configured to start at boot, in Setup.

4. Restart sendmail and xinetd.

EXPLAINED

Sendmail is the most common mail transport agent (MTA) in use. It's the "upstream" server that accepts e-mail from clients and sends it to other servers for eventual delivery. IPOP3 is the "downstream" server that accesses and downloads e-mail to its recipients—this server is started automatically when needed by xinetd.

The only one of these programs that needs any special configuration is Sendmail. It's a pity that /etc/sendmail.cf—the Sendmail configuration file—is probably the most horribly complicated configuration file in existence for any computer program in common use. Luckily, there is no need to configure it manually. You can download /etc/mail/sendmail.mc from the Linux Leap Web site (http://www.linuxleap.org) and, without changing a line, use it to automatically configure sendmail.cf.

First, download /etc/mail/sendmail.mc from Linux Leap and copy it to /etc/mail/ on the server.

Next, at a terminal, type **m4 /etc/mail/sendmail.mc > /etc/sendmail.cf** and press the Enter key. This automatically generates the Sendmail configuration file.

Although Sendmail is now configured to work internally on the LAN, each user's local e-mail address will have to include the server's FQDN (e.g., mariann@server.dev.org). To avoid this, use gedit to add your domain name to the server's /etc/mail/local-host-names file. This is a very simple file, with only one line of comment. In the case of the Development, Ltd., scenario, with the company's domain added, it would look like this:

```
# local-host-names - include all aliases for your machine here.
dev.org
```

The preceding example e-mail address can now be shortened to mariann@dev.org.

Finally, open the Setup tool in a terminal, and within System Services, check the options sendmail, xinetd, and ipop3. Checking these options will ensure that they're all present and that sendmail and xinetd both start automatically at system boot.

Now restart sendmail and xinetd. You can do this by rebooting the server or by typing **/etc/init.d/sendmail start** and **/etc/init.d/xinetd start** in a terminal.

Configuring Netscape Communicator 4.78 in Linux

IN BRIEF

1. Configure the e-mail address to include the server's domain name.

2. Configure the incoming and outgoing mail servers with the server's IP address.

EXPLAINED

The Netscape Communicator e-mail client on Linux client machines must be configured to reflect the local e-mail server.

First, click Edit and Preferences in Netscape and open the Identity window. Enter the user's name and his or her e-mail address using this format: **username@domainname**.

Figure 6-13 shows an example from the scenario. In this example, the user's name is pam and the mail server for the LAN is dev.org.

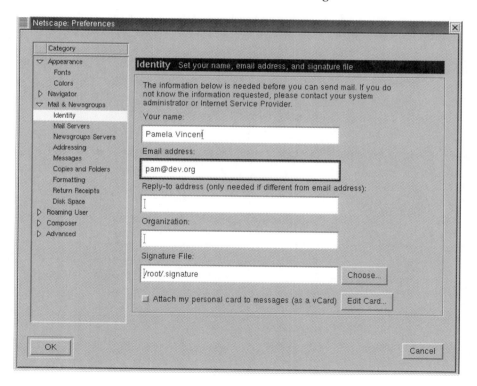

Figure 6-13. Setting the name and e-mail address in Netscape on a Linux client

The next step is to configure the incoming (POP) and outgoing (SMTP) mail servers. Click Mail Servers in the left pane, select the Incoming Mail Server, and click the Edit button.

Configure the POP server name to reflect the user's name, followed by the at sign (@) and then the mail server's IP address. Next, in the Outgoing Mail (SMTP) Server box, enter just the mail server's IP address. When you've finished, both the POP and the SMTP server entries should look like the ones shown in Figure 6-14.

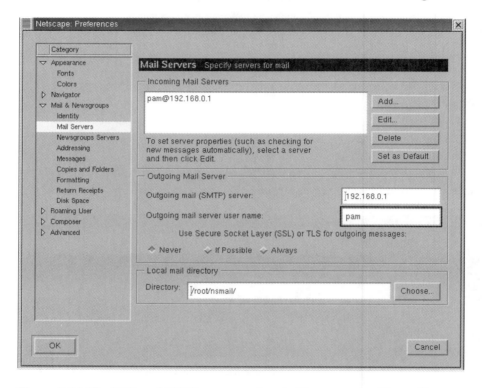

Figure 6-14. The POP and SMTP server settings in Netscape on a Linux client

 NOTE *For users of Mozilla and Netscape 6.1, the server settings for local mail follow the Microsoft Outlook example in the next section—only enter the IP address of the server.*

Configuring Microsoft Outlook in Windows

IN BRIEF

1. In the Properties window of the user's Outlook Internet Account, enter the e-mail address as in the preceding section, using the form **username@domainname**.

2. Under the Servers tab, enter the mail server's IP address in both the POP3 and the SMTP boxes (see Figure 6-15).

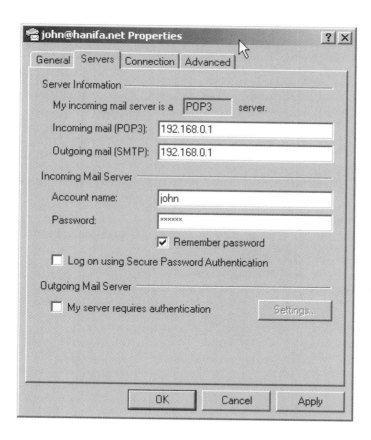

Figure 6-15. The POP and SMTP server settings in Microsoft Outlook on a Windows client

Lesson 6-4 Review

In this lesson, you learned

- How to set up a Linux internal e-mail server for the LAN, using Sendmail and the sendmail.mc configuration file from Linux Leap

- How to set up both Netscape and Microsoft Outlook for receiving internal e-mail

LESSON 6-5.

SETTING UP A LOCAL WEB AND DATABASE SERVER

A Web server can be used to serve up HTML pages on a company intranet to good purpose. A company Web site can be used to disseminate to employees information such as company news, personal contact information, or company policies and procedures. An intranet can also be used as a convenient download point for templates, invoices, and other files. However, the type of information likely to be of most use to the company's bottom line—namely, clients, prospects, and sales—really needs to be in a database to be most useful, particularly to different types of users, such as accounting, sales, and management, who need to query the database in somewhat different ways for their own purposes.

For this reason and others, an intranet Web site is increasingly used for and seen as a front end for a company's database.

This lesson is divided into two main parts. The first, brief section is devoted to the Apache Web server, and the second, longer section is devoted to databases, especially PostgreSQL, a proven open source SQL database with a growing user base, and its Web-based and open source GUI tools.

The Apache Web Server

The Apache Web server comes configured and set to start at system boot, right out of the box.

Apache is to the Web what Sendmail is to e-mail: ubiquitous. As of February 2001, according to the Netcraft Web Server Survey, 60 percent of all Web sites were using the Apache server. And Apache, like Sendmail, works as well on a small LAN as it does in an enterprise.

By default in Red Hat 7.2, Apache is up and running as soon as the server boots up. To test this, open any browser anywhere on the network and type

http://HOSTNAME.DOMAINNAME, where hostname.domainname is the name of the server running Apache. As an example, in the scenario, to test whether or not the Web server is running, the system administrator opens any browser on any platform on the LAN and enters **http://server.dev.org**. Immediately, the Apache test page should appear.

 NOTE *If DNS is working properly on your system, just typing in your server's hostname should bring up the test Web page.*

Starting and Stopping the Program

If for some reason the server has not been set to start up automatically, you can configure it to start at system boot with the Setup program. Open it in a terminal and enter System Services. The program to check is httpd, which stands for "http daemon"—the Apache server.

 NOTE *Anyone reading Linux or UNIX system administration books will frequently come across references to* daemons. *The word as used in computers means a server or process that runs in the background, performing an operation either at predefined intervals or in response to some request—for example, serving up a Web page upon demand. Its derivation is sometimes explained as coming from "demon," although why a computer term should be coined from an obsolete spelling of a word still in common usage is not immediately clear. Suggestions that the term was derived from Greek mythology are unconvincing. Alternately, it is defined in the Telecom Glossary as an abbreviation for "disk and execution monitor,* a procedure that is invoked without being called explicitly whenever an alteration, an addition, or a deletion or other event occurs." This definition may be closer to the mark.*

You can stop, start, or restart the httpd program at will at a terminal by typing **/etc/init.d/httpd restart** with **restart** substituted by **stop** or **start**, depending on the action you desire.

Default Directories and the Apache Configuration Tool

In the Red Hat 7.2 distribution, the home directory where the index.html file is located is /var/www/html. The /var/www directory comes complete with subdirectories already created for CGI scripts and icons.

Red Hat also has a GUI Apache configuration tool in GNOME. You can access it by clicking the Start button and navigating to Programs ➤ System ➤ Apache Configuration.

The Apache Configuration Tool is somewhat similar to the BIND Configuration Tool, in that it's an excellent GUI tool for someone who already has at least a working knowledge of Apache configuration. The opening screen is shown in Figure 6-16. The Apache tool, however, does come complete with good HTML Help files, which are accessible from within the program.

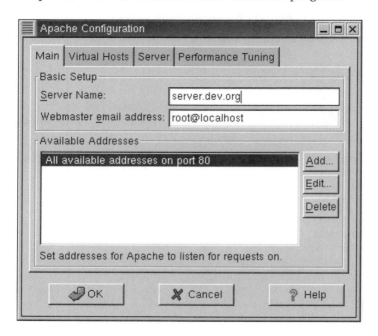

Figure 6-16. The opening screen of the Apache Configuration Tool, with the server name set to the scenario's Web server

Databases for Linux

There is an embarrassment of riches for Linux in the database market. As you would expect for an operating system known primarily as a server, most of the databases available for Linux are Structured Query Language (SQL) products designed to be networked on the client-server model. This is good, in that SQL databases are by nature networkable, scalable, and stable. They will grow with the firm, remaining reliable as the LAN grows, and they'll even be there, ready to go, if the company decides to host its own e-commerce Web site. However, their virtues carry a corresponding liability: Because their natural character is that of an enterprise-level database, they are neither easy to learn nor simple to administer.

Fortunately, this is beginning to change. This part of the book introduces several examples of GUI administration and development tools for PostgreSQL—one of the leading open source databases for Linux—and also demonstrates a GUI method of transferring existing databases, a necessity for widespread adoption.

Available Database Products

At the enterprise level, both Oracle and IBM have now ported their flagship prod-ucts to Linux. But how many small businesses are going to be running DB2 or Oracle? Smaller firms will neither need these enterprise-strength solutions nor be able to afford them. Lower down the range, the programs become open source and, of course, free. The two most popular open source solutions are MySQL and PostgreSQL (or Postgres, as I'll call it from here forward, since its full name lacks both euphony and clarity of pronunciation). Both products are more than robust enough for most small business. Of the two, the latter has a reputation for being somewhat more stable and feature-rich. Postgres has also recently gained signifi-cant commercial support from Red Hat, which has renamed its product the Red Hat Database.

This book advocates the use of open source databases for small businesses, not from an evangelical attitude, but from a practical standpoint. Open source databases have all the benefits—and drawbacks—of Linux itself. Their benefits are overwhelming: They're free and under constant development. Their draw-back—difficulty of use—is being addressed, and GUI tools exist to develop and administer Linux-based databases from within Microsoft Windows. These tools are introduced in the next lesson.

Installing Postgres

You need to install the Postgres database both on the Linux server and on any Linux workstations that will need to access the database. Several installation methods are available. You can buy Red Hat's version of the product (which comes with a good deal of documentation for the system administrator, several CDs, and installation support) and install it from the CD. Or, since it comes with the Red Hat distribution itself, you can just choose to install it automatically when you load Linux on your server.

IN BRIEF

1. When you install Red Hat on the server, choose to install everything, as recommended earlier. This will automatically install the Red Hat Database (Postgres).

2. Download and install the/etc/init.d/postgresql file from the Linux Leap Web site.

3. Start the database server.

4. Download and install the /var/lib/pgsql/data/pg_hba.conf file from the Linux Leap Web site.

5. Log in as postgres and create users.

6. Create an initial database.

IN DETAIL

Installing Postgres During Initial Linux Installation from the Red Hat Linux CDs

Postgres comes in several packages, and correct installation is automatic if you just choose to install everything. If you choose to perform a custom installation, make sure to check every Postgres package for inclusion. This is especially important for the server.

> **NOTE** *If you have to install Postgres after Linux installation, and you want to use the GNOME RPM GUI tool, the packages are under Applications/ Databases and Development/Libraries. The packages are divided among both installation CDs, so you will have to install the database from both.*

Downloading and Installing the Start-up File from Linux Leap

By default, networking is turned off in the Postgres start-up file. Turning it on involves a very small, but very picky, adjustment to the start-up file on the server. The user can either edit it him- or herself, or just download the file from the Linux Leap Web site. The file is /etc/rc.d/init.d/postgresql.

Should the user care to edit this file by hand, then they should insert `-o "-i"` in the following line (as all one line) as shown here:

```
su -l postgres -s /bin/sh -c "/usr/bin/pg_ctl -D $PGDATA -p /usr/bin/postmaster
-o "-i" start>/dev/null 2>&1" </dev/null
```

For many, it is simpler just to download the file and copy it into the correct directory on the server.

Starting the Database Server

You'll want the server to start automatically at system boot. Check the postgresql option in the System Services section of the Setup tool, and then reboot the computer. The computer will both start the server and, since this is the first start-up for the database, create a number of directories and files that Postgres relies on for operation.

If you later want to stop, or restart, the server, you can do so from the command line by typing **/etc/init.d/postgresql start** (or **stop** or **restart**) and pressing the Enter key.

Downloading and Installing the Host Access Control File

You cannot copy the second file to be downloaded to the correct directory until the database is started for the first time; until then, the correct directory is not yet created. The Host Access Control File sets permissions—which clients can connect to which databases. Initially, no access whatsoever is created. The Linux Leap file allows all clients to connect to all databases. If the system administrator wants to restrict certain databases to certain users, the notes within the file itself are very clear and contain useful examples.

Download /var/lib/pgsql/data/pg_hba.conf from the Linux Leap Web site (http://www.linuxleap.org) and install it into the correct directory on the server.

NOTE *The pg_hba.conf file supplied by Linux Leap will work for LANs on the 192.168.0.X class C standard IP address. If your address is different, you'll need to edit that line.*

Logging In as Postgres and Creating Users

Access to the database is denied to the root user; it's restricted to special users whose names and accounts must be created. To start this process off, an initial user is automatically created at installation with the name of postgres. The system administrator will probably find it convenient to administer the database under their normal logon name, and they will want to create user accounts, under their own names, for those in the firm who need to access the database.

To create database user accounts, log in first as root, and then log in as postgres with the su command:

```
su postgres
```

Now create users with the "createuser *(username)*" command. For example, from the scenario, the system administrator, Pam, wants to clone her own normal logon name for convenient access to the database. She types **createuser pam**.

Immediately she is given two prompts: Should the new user be allowed to create databases, and should they be allowed to create new users? Since this account is for the system administrator's use, she answers Yes to both questions.

Nearly every employee in the small firm will eventually need access to the database, so she creates more database user names that are clones of the user names already in use. She uses the same createuser command in each case, but denies anyone else the ability to create new database users and restricts the ability to create new databases to management and senior consultants.

Access to individual databases can be restricted to certain users via the Host Access Control file.

Creating an Initial Database

An initial database is automatically created, but it should not be used. Its name is template1, and as its name suggests, it's used as a template for the system files needed by all databases. Any user who has been given database creation privileges can create a new database with the "createdb *(name)*" command. Again, from the scenario, Pam decides to create the company database and name it devel. At a terminal, she enters **createdb devel** and presses the Enter key.

Lesson 6-5 Review

In this lesson, you learned

- Some of the database products available for Linux, and why it's a good idea to consider using an open source SQL database for the firm

- How to install Postgres and configure it for the system administrator and for other users

- How to create the initial (so far empty) company database

LESSON 6-6.

ADOPTING POSTGRES

Most companies will have to rely on user-friendly front ends. These front ends can be written especially for the firm or used off-the-shelf. There are three off-the-shelf products currently available for Postgres: pgAdmin, PgAccess, and phpPgAdmin.

Each of these programs has advantages and disadvantages, which are summarized in Table 6-2.

Table 6-2. Postgres Front-End Comparison

PRODUCT	ADVANTAGES	DISADVANTAGES
pgAdmin	Able to develop, administer, and output query results.	Only works in Windows clients, not Linux.
PgAccess	Drag and drop, works in both Windows and Linux.	Still at the beta stage, so it's buggy and lacking features.
phpPgAdmin	Good administrative tool, and it's Web-based, so it's cross-platform.	Orientation toward data structures rather than function ensures a murky learning experience for the new user.

Of the tools in Table 6-2, the most capable is, ironically, the one that only runs in Windows: pgAdmin. This is not necessarily a major drawback, since most firms will rely, at least initially, on Linux for their servers rather than their desktops. pgAdmin is capable not only of administering, developing, and querying Postgres databases on Linux servers, but it's also capable of converting databases from other formats to Postgres. This capability is helpful, since unless the firm has just opened its doors for business, it will already have a database of some kind that it will need to convert to the new system.

PgAccess is at the time of this writing a technology demonstrator, rather than a production tool. Further development, however, could certainly take it to the head of the pack.

phpPgAdmin is an administrative tool designed with the professional SQL administrator in mind, rather than the new user. However, its Web-based format makes it totally cross-platform. Although it's doubtful that a program written in PHP will ever have the drag-and-drop functionality of PgAccess, its ease of development can guarantee a high degree of customization for a firm's database front end.

How a Small Business Can Adopt Postgres

A firm has two basic approaches to take: rely completely on local staff or rely to some degree on consultants. The second approach has several possible permutations. Just a few are as follows:

- Bring in consulting trainers to train local staff on installation and maintenance, and then rely on the GUI tools already available—for Windows and for the Web—for database development and management.

- The same approach as the previous list entry, but either hire a consultant or train local staff to build a customized front end for database development and management, perhaps using PHP.

- Buy the whole package from Red Hat: Rely on their help for installation and initial support, pay them to build the front end, and have them train your staff.

These are only a few possibilities. Migrating to an open source SQL database is not a step to be taken lightly. But it pays dividends, and it can be made, if not painless, at least only slightly uncomfortable during the changeover period.

All three front ends mentioned previously are briefly introduced in the following sections.

Installing and Using pgAdmin

The installation and use of pgAdmin is complicated by the fact that it's available in two versions: I and II. The first version is officially discontinued by the development team, but is still available; the second version is undergoing development.

Version II is much easier to install and configure, has a better interface, and relies less on other programs to work correctly than version I. On the other hand, the Migration Wizard tool from version I has yet to be included—it's the last component to be rewritten—and this is an invaluable tool to migrate a firm's current database to Postgres.

For this reason, I've chosen to present both versions. By sometime in 2002 the Migration Wizard will have been rewritten, and then the user will only have to download and install version II.

Installation for both pgAdmin I and II is covered in brief only. Through the scenario, you'll learn how to use the first version to convert Microsoft Access databases and how to use the second version to develop queries.

pgAdmin I

INSTALLATION IN BRIEF

1. From within Windows, open the pgAdmin I Web site at `http://gborg.postgresql.org/project/pgadmin`. Download the pgAdmin I program from the Downloads page.

2. Download and install Microsoft MDAC and any other required packages (on a recent version of Windows 2000, these should already be on your system). Install pgAdmin I.

3. Click the Start button and navigate to Settings ➤ Control Panel ➤ Administrative Tools ➤ Data Sources (ODBC).

4. Under User DNS add PostgreSQL if it is not already on the list.

5. In the PostgreSQL Driver Setup window, enter the name of the PostgreSQL database you have created (**devel** in the scenario), the hostname of the server, and a valid user's name and password (see Figure 6-17).

6. Click the DataSource button and configure the Advanced Options window as shown in Figure 6-18. Click the OK buttons to save your configuration.

7. Start pgAdmin from the menu, and enter PostgreSQL as the data source and a valid user name and password.

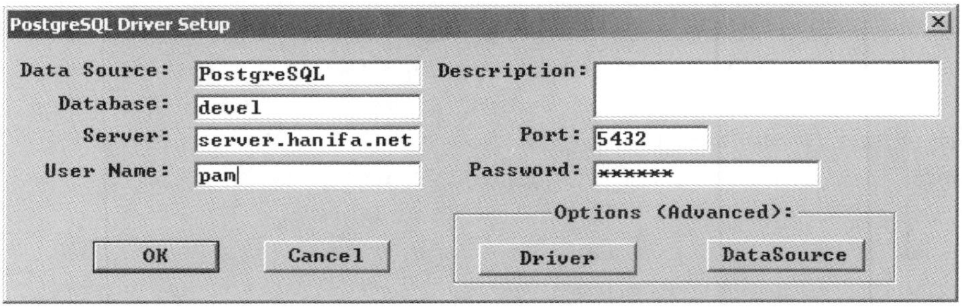

Figure 6-17. Entering the database name, server hostname, and user's name and password in the PostgreSQL Driver Setup window

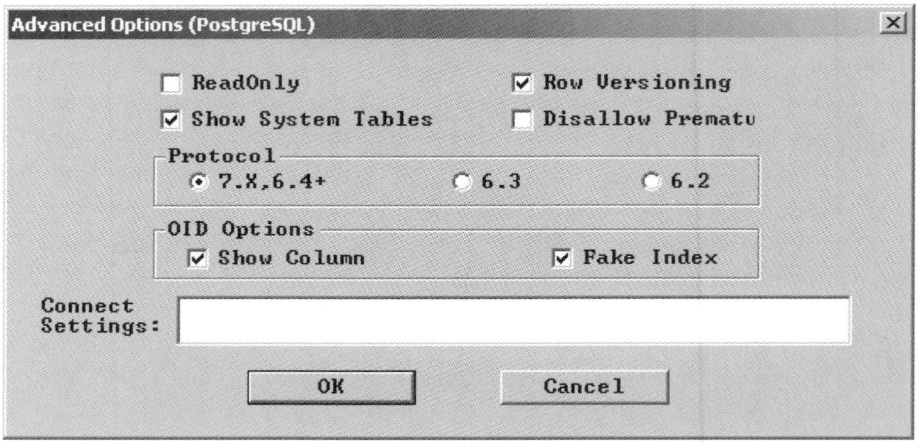

Figure 6-18. Configuring the Advanced Options window

The Scenario: Converting a Microsoft Access Database to Postgres at Development, Ltd.

Development, Ltd., has been using Access for some time. They're delighted with its ease of use, but less than content with its performance, especially as the company grows. And they know it's unsuitable for their Web site. However, the system administrator has no intention of burning her bridges, and she intends to adopt the use of Postgres gradually, only after a period of testing.

The firm has two Microsoft Access databases it wants to nondestructively convert to Postgres. Since databases are converted table by table, the system administrator decides to migrate all the tables from both Access databases to her new "devel" Postgres database.

IN BRIEF

1. Create the Postgres database.

2. In pgAdmin, choose the Tools menu and open Migration.

3. Choose the database to migrate.

EXPLAINED

The Postgres database has to be made first, before the existing database, Access or otherwise, can be converted. You do this with the createdb command, as described in the previous lesson (in the scenario, the sysadmin has already created devel).

The sysadmin starts pgAdmin, and in the left panel chooses the Tools menu and clicks the Migration key icon. She clicks the small button to the right of the .mdb line and browses the system for the databases to convert. She enters her user name and her password and clicks the Next button.

The next several screens allow the user to choose which tables and indexes to migrate. The sysadmin chooses them all, and in the end she clicks the "Migrate db" button. The database migration wizard takes it from there.

To check her work, the sysadmin chooses the Schema menu and clicks Databases and Tables. Figure 6-19 shows the result of the conversion. The Postgres devel database now contains the following former Access tables:

1994 sales

divisions

employees

projects

training type

vendors

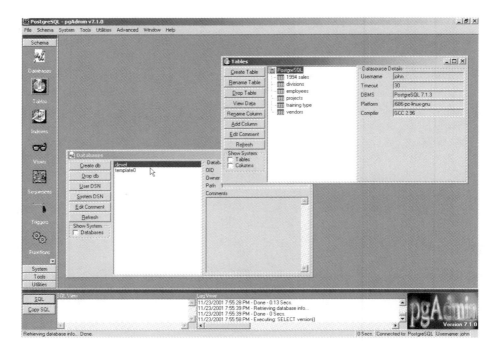

Figure 6-19. Checking the conversion of database tables from Access to Postgres

pgAdmin II

INSTALLATION IN BRIEF

1. From within Windows, open the pgAdmin II Web site at
    http://pgadmin.postgresql.org. Download and install the pgAdmin II
    program from the Downloads page.

2. Start pgAdmin II from the menu. Use the far left toolbar button to
    connect to the Linux database server, and enter the server name and a
    valid user name and password.

The Scenario:
Creating a Query in pgAdmin II at Development, Ltd.

You can create queries in standard SQL or via the SQL Wizard. Most users coming from the Windows world will prefer the latter. In this scenario, the CEO wants to recreate a query she has done before in Access: She wants to know how many sales were over US$20,000 and which of her consultants made those sales.

IN BRIEF

1. In the left panel of the pgAdmin II screen, expand Databases and select the database to be queried.

2. On the toolbar, click the "three-eyed monster" query icon, and then click the Wizard button.

3. Choose the tables to include; the shared fields to join, the join type, and operator; which columns to include in the query; selection criteria; and data sort order.

4. Execute the query.

5. Export the results to the screen, ASCII text, an Excel spreadsheet, or to HTML.

EXPLAINED

The left panel of the screen allows the user to select the database to be queried and to examine the data in the database's tables by right-clicking a table and choosing View Data (see Figure 6-20). Clicking the query icon (the three-eyed monster) on the toolbar brings up an SQL window in which to enter a standard SQL query. However, clicking the Wizard button allows users with an unsteady command of SQL syntax to create queries in a somewhat more easy-to-use environment.

The wizard introduces several screens that walk the user through query creation. The first prompts for table selection. In the case of the scenario, where the CEO wants to know which contracts were worth more than US$20,000 and which consultants brought them in, she chooses the 1994 sales and the employees tables by selecting them one by one and pressing the button to add them to the right panel (see Figure 6-21). The next screen prompts for the shared fields to join; both tables share an Employee ID field, so she chooses that and accepts the default join type of Inner Join and = operator.

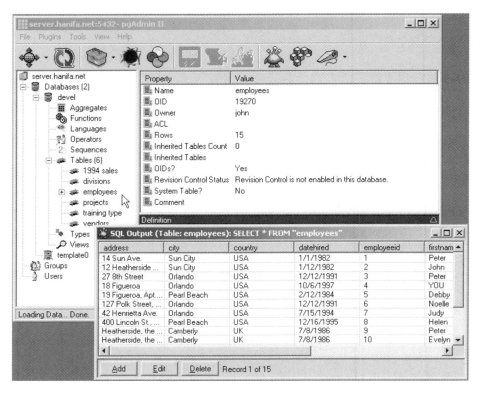

Figure 6-20. Viewing a table's data in pgAdmin II

Figure 6-21. Choosing tables in pgAdmin II's SQL Wizard

She decides to include the Sales and First Name and Last Name columns in her query, and in the following screen she chooses the selection criteria to be on sales greater than or equal to $20,000 (see Figure 6-22). Finally, she decides to sort her data by sales and descending, in order to have the larger amounts listed first.

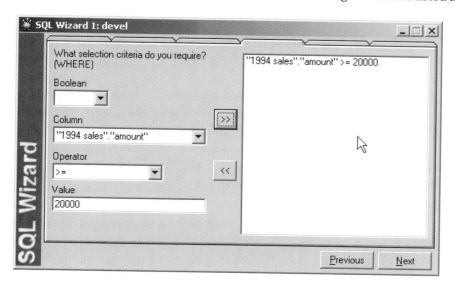

Figure 6-22. Choosing selection criteria in pgAdmin II's SQL Wizard

She first executes the query to the screen, so she can see if it works (it does). Pleased with her success, she executes it next to an Excel spreadsheet to print out, and then in HTML to e-mail to the consultants involved.

PgAccess

Whereas pgAdmin runs only in Windows, PgAccess is a GUI administration and development tool for Postgres that runs in both Linux and Windows. It comes as part of the Postgres package in Red Hat Linux 7.2, and it's also part of the package of their separate database product.

As of this writing, PgAccess is more of a technology demonstrator than a production tool. It is still a work in progress, very much in beta stage—many features are missing, and many of those present are buggy. However, it's a drag-and-drop tool, and for that reason it should be comfortingly familiar to those Windows users who only require limited functionality.

Installation in Linux is automatic if all the Postgres packages are selected during the initial installation. Installation in Windows is more problematic, as it requires several additional files to be present. You can find more information on installing PgAccess in Windows at the program's home page: `http://ns.flex.ro/pgaccess`.

Opening Databases in PgAccess

Once again using the Development, Ltd., scenario, the CEO starts the program (this time from within Linux) by clicking the Start button and using the Run command **pgaccess**. She opens up the devel database by clicking Database on the menu bar and selecting Open. In the Open Database window, she enters the hostname of the database server, the database name, and her own user name and password. The list of database tables appears, confirming that devel is open and running in PgAccess.

Creating Queries in PgAccess

Clicking the Queries tab and the New button brings the CEO to the Query Builder screen. She names her query "sales," and she checks the "Save this query as a view" box. At this point she has the choice of either writing a SQL query or choosing the Visual Query Designer. Since she comes from the Windows world, she chooses the Designer.

The Visual Query Designer strongly demonstrates the drag-and-drop potential of PgAccess. The query performed uses several screens, as in the prior pgAdmin example, but it can be performed largely with the mouse in PgAccess, much as in Microsoft Access. The Visual Query Designer interface is in fact reminiscent of the program's namesake, as shown in Figure 6-23.

Here, however, you come to a serious limitation of this program, for although you have a good query with an identical result to the one performed earlier, printing the information as a report or sending it via e-mail is a major hassle. To sum up, PgAccess is an excellent technology demonstrator, but it still has a ways to go.

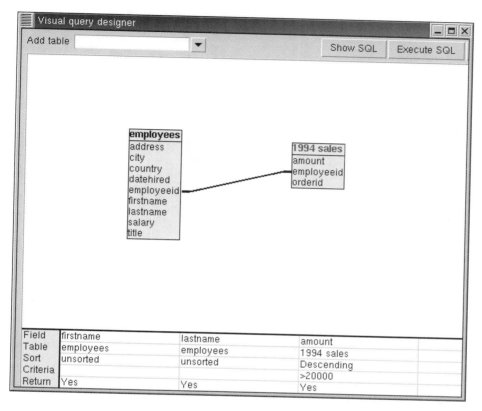

Figure 6-23. The sales query in PgAccess' Visual Query Designer

phpPgAdmin

phpPgAdmin is, as its name implies, a Postgres administration program. It's completely Web-based, and therefore it's totally cross-platform. PHP is a server-side, HTML-embedded scripting language that's easy to use and capable of developing very customized front ends for Postgres databases.

You can download the phpPgAdmin program from SourceForge at `http://phppgadmin.sourceforge.net`. Once it's installed on the Linux server, you can access the program from any browser anywhere on the network. PhpPgAdmin's design is centered on data structures, rather than on database functions, and as a result the program is more oriented toward professional SQL administrators than new users to the SQL world. However, you can clearly see some of its capabilities from the view in Figure 6-24.

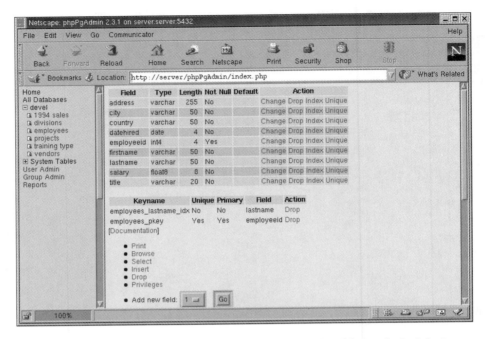

Figure 6-24. A view of table structures for the employee's table in phpPgAdmin

Lesson 6-6 Review

This lesson was devoted to Postgres adoption. You learned

- The three front ends currently available for Postgres and their strengths and weaknesses

- How to install pgAdmin and how to use it to convert Access databases and run queries

- How to run a query in PgAccess

What's to Come

The next chapter offers a short discussion of the next steps in a company's network evolution:

- Putting up a company Web site

- Establishing company e-mail on the Internet

- Building a firewall

# CHAPTER SEVEN

Serving a Web Site and Mail to the Internet

Turning an intranet and local e-mail server into an Internet Web and mail server is not a difficult technical task. There are, however, serious technical and business issues to consider, which together will determine how, and even whether, a small firm should host its own Web site.

This chapter is presented in two lessons. The first lesson focuses on whether or not a small company should self-host its own Web site, and the second focuses on some of the technical issues involved. A chapter review and concluding notes are included at the end.

LESSON 7-1.
SELF-HOSTING OR CONTRACTING OUT?

Should a small firm host its own Web site? Much depends on the firm's resources. Cost, as always, is a serious element of the equation, especially since these days the yearly cost of a single static IP address can be more than the yearly fee charged by a Web site hosting company. However, you must take both the many costs, direct and indirect, and the basic technical issues into account when making a decision.

Type of Site and Expected Traffic

Perhaps the first questions to ask relate to what kind of site the firm wants or needs, and how heavy its traffic is likely to be.

Also, how much in-house technical expertise does the company have? Is it willing to hire more? How much additional IT infrastructure is it willing to buy?

You may arrange a suitable questionnaire in many different formats. One format that resembles a decision tree is as follows:

- Will the site be static and without an e-commerce component? If so, from a complexity standpoint, a small firm could very likely handle the creation and maintenance of its site without hiring additional personnel. If not, the firm should consider hiring additional personnel or a consultant.

- Is the traffic likely to be medium or low? If traffic is expected to be low, additional IT resources may not be needed. If traffic rises to even a moderate amount, however, a dedicated server will have to be installed, probably with its own dedicated line.

- If the traffic likely to be high? If so, a much more powerful server is likely to be required, along with a more robust IT infrastructure. Does the firm have the personnel on hand to maintain this setup?

A simple static site, without either a database back end or an e-commerce element, is well within the resources of many small firms to build, maintain, and possibly to host, depending on the amount of traffic expected. Many commercial packages are available for both Windows and Linux that allow an employee with basic design and computer skills to put together a fairly decent corporate site.

However, an e-commerce component raises the complexity level dramatically. It's true that e-commerce packages are now available that allow a developer to build an entire site, complete with standard e-commerce pages, as well as specialized product and service pages linked to industrial-strength databases, all via point and click. However, the casual user who buys one of these packages and expects to put together a working site in a few days is in for a surprise. It takes training and some skill to put together even a fairly simple e-commerce site, and when it's allied with a SQL database, it's probably time to call in a consultant.

The question of traffic has an impact on the hardware required, the Internet connection required, and the staff needed to service it all. A computer that hums along quite nicely, acting as a file and print server, a database server, an internal Web and e-mail server, and an Internet server for a small office can suddenly grind to a complete halt when asked to serve even a very low-traffic Web site to the Internet. And the relationship between increased "hits" and the degradation of service is not necessarily linear: After a certain point, a relatively small increase in traffic can result in dramatically lowered response times from the server.

Buying a serious server, hiring a consultant, and installing a T1 line will definitely prove to be more expensive than contracting the job out to a Web hosting firm. That, in fact, is the secret of hosting firms' success.

Security

Oddly enough, security is probably the last consideration that a small firm should take into account when deciding whether to host their site themselves or contract it out. A small company running a simple mail and static Web server can implement a simple but effective firewall easily and is unlikely to be the target of a serious, industrial-strength hacker attack.

The three primary types of security attack are as follows:

- Viruses

- Denial of service attacks

- Other targeted attacks with malicious intent

The vast majority of viruses are designed and written to affect Microsoft Windows machines. Such viruses are unable to attack a Linux server. However, a virus attached to an e-mail (not uncommon in the Windows world) and sent to a workstation on a LAN using Microsoft Outlook may well make it through the server and infect the Windows workstation (it won't affect Linux workstations on the same LAN using Netscape or Evolution as their mail clients).

Viruses are simply part of computing life. The fixes are to run the latest antivirus Windows software from firms such as Symantec and to keep abreast of software fixes to Microsoft products. A useful site to visit for this is `http://windowsupdate.microsoft.com`.

Denial of service attacks and other targeted attacks are aimed toward a specific Web site or static IP address or server. It's the nature of such attacks that those aimed at large, well-known sites get the most publicity. This doesn't mean that a small firm won't be targeted by a cruising, criminal hacker. It means that you have to make breaking into your site irritatingly hard enough to not be worth their trouble. A safe irritation level can be reached with a basic mix of security procedures and a simple but effective firewall.

Security is not the best reason for a small firm to consider contracting out its Web site. The best reason is cost: the cost associated with design, equipment, and staff.

LESSON 7-2.

ADMINISTRATIVE AND TECHNICAL ISSUES

There are a few administrative and technical issues to consider when you prepare a server to publish either a Web site or e-mail to the Internet. This chapter assumes a server setup similar to that presented in Chapters Five and Six.

A Static Address

A static address is the first prerequisite. It's not difficult to obtain. Most large ISPs will provide static addresses, although at a higher cost than their normal dynamic addresses. And it's worth noting, as mentioned previously, that the yearly cost of a single static address, even from a very reasonable ISP, is likely to be more than the yearly fee charged by a Web hosting company.

The setup for a static address is identical to that of a dynamic address and is covered in detail in Chapter Four. The static address from the ISP will not show up on any of the LAN workstations, either Linux or Windows. What will show up is the server's local IP address, which in the scenario presented in Chapter Five is 192.168.0.1. (For DSL connections, an important point to remember is that the static address given to you by your ISP is still provided by a DHCP server, and as a result your local /sbin/ifup file will, by default, let your /etc/resolv.conf file be overwritten with the ISP's static address. A good way to keep this from happening is to download and install /sbin/ifup from the Linux Leap Web site.)

Registering a Domain Name

A domain name is the second prerequisite. You'll find life simpler, from a technical point of view, if the name of your company is the same as the domain name of the company LAN and the company Web site. These days, especially for new firms, acquiring a domain name and deciding on a company name are inextricably linked.

Acquiring a domain name for your company is a three-stage process:

1. Decide on a suitable name.

2. Use whois or a similar tool to find out if the domain name you want is available. If it isn't available, go back to step 1. If it is available, proceed to step 3.

3. Actually register the name with an accredited registrar.
   You can find a list of these firms at the InterNIC Web site
   (http://www.internic.net/alpha.html).

Although you can use the whois command at the command line of a Linux server, to immediately tell if your desired name is taken or not, you can find a better interface at the InterNIC Web site or the sites of many registrars.

You may notice that your ISP, which offers, among many other services, to register your domain name, is not on the InterNIC list of accredited registrars. That's because many firms that offer registration services act as subcontractors and register your domain name through an accredited registrar for you.

Obtaining or Creating a Nameserver

A nameserver is the third prerequisite, although it's frequently a hidden one for those who want their own domain but aren't interested in self-hosting their Web site. This is because a Web hosting company or ISP that both registers your domain and hosts your site will take care of the nameserver requirement, thus relieving you of yet another small but irritating technical hurdle.

However, if you want to host your own site, you'll need not just one, but two nameservers, both of them linked to your static address. The easiest way to accomplish this is to have your ISP or Web registration company do it for you, although it's far more likely that an ISP will do it, rather than a pure registration firm. This is a business request, and many an ISPs' customer service representatives will not know what you're talking about—you'll probably have to get in touch with your ISP's business department and perhaps with their technical support department as well.

It's possible, of course, to host your own nameservers, although the necessity for two means that two machines on your network must be set up as servers. You can do this through the BIND Configuration Tool in GNOME, which you can access through Start ➤ Programs ➤ System ➤ bindconf. The steps you need to perform are as follows:

1. Open Bindconf.

2. Select the name of your local server and click the Edit button.

3. Click Add and choose Nameserver next to Add Record Resource.

4. Enter the domain name of your server and your static IP address.

Not every small business will be running two servers, and it's probably more reliable to have your ISP handle the nameserver requirement for you. There are companies that specialize in doing only this, for a fee.

E-mail Relaying

The Sendmail setup in Chapter Six is sufficient for e-mail within the LAN. Very few steps are required to make the identical setup work well for sending and receiving company e-mail on the Internet.

Once you've performed the steps in the previous sections—obtaining a static address, registering your domain, and setting up nameservers—all that remains is to configure Sendmail to relay mail sent internally to outside addresses on the

Internet. You do this by adding a single line to the /etc/mail/access file. (Note: This step assumes the use of the Linux Leap sendmail.mc file.)

Either the domain name or the subdomain of the LAN (which is now also the company's registered domain name, with two nameservers linking the domain name to the firm's static IP address) must appear in the file. The following is an example from the scenario. The first three lines are standard. The fourth line allows the relay of mail from the firm's domain—in this case, dev.org, with a subdomain of 192.168.0—to the Internet.

The /etc/mail/access File, Which Allows the Relay of Mail to the Internet from dev.org

```
locahost.localdomain    RELAY
localhost               RELAY
127.0.0.1               RELAY
192.168.0               RELAY
```

Security

Good security does not depend solely on a firewall. In fact, there are at least four considerations to take into account:

- Physical security

- Passwords

- Surplus communications programs

- The firewall

Physical Security

Physical security is so obvious that it can easily be overlooked—and in the case of passwords, it frequently is. How often have you seen a workstation adorned with a post-it note, on which is written an obvious password? Another breach of physical security would be the system administrator taking a coffee break with his or her computer left on and the screen showing a root prompt. In a small firm this might not seem at first like a serious security breach, but how long would it take a naïve coworker, trying innocently to access some information in the administrator's absence, to seriously harm the server's configuration or even destroy data? The answer must be as speculative as the question, but it could be "Not long."

Passwords

Passwords are the first line of defense against both unauthorized people looking for confidential information and criminal computer hackers trying to remotely trash a system. Unfortunately, good password practice is extremely difficult to enforce. In general, people aren't interested in memorizing, at regular and frequent intervals, passwords that have been chosen specifically for their lack of mnemonic or associative character. It remains the duty of every system administrator to insist, as much as practicable, on a rigorous password policy.

Surplus Communications Programs

One of the simplest ways to enhance system security is to turn off Internet communications programs that you don't need to run. Such programs represent potential security holes and should be closed off. You can use the Setup tool to make sure these programs are not started at system boot. Some examples of programs that should probably not be started, for the company in the scenario, are

Finger

Ipop2

Ntalk

Talk

Tftp

The Firewall

Finally, the firewall. The main purpose of a firewall is to block unwanted intrusions from the Internet to the LAN. Many firewall programs and solutions are available.

In the open source world, the latest Linux firewall program for the 2.4 series of kernels is called Netfilter, or iptables. This program takes the place of the older ipchains. It isn't, however, implemented by default in Red Hat Linux 7.2—the older ipchains is suggested during the installation routine. In order to implement iptables, you must use the setup program to first turn off the older program, and then turn on iptables. Finish the process by rebooting the machine.

Iptables is an industrial-strength, highly configurable and flexible firewall tool. It is also highly complex. The firewall script suggested here is just that: a suggestion. For most small firms, and certainly for a firm using NAT and a LAN resembling the scenario, it should be adequate.

The design of this firewall is simple and rests on these assumptions:

- Unneeded communications programs have been turned off.

- The LAN's Internet server has two NICs, one for the Internet and one for the LAN. The LAN is sharing the Internet connection via NAT (this is the Development, Ltd., scenario).

- The Internet NIC is on eth1, and the LAN NIC is on eth0.

- The server is running an external Web site and thus needs port 80 (the standard HTTP port) open.

- The server is running Sendmail and relaying mail to the Internet, and thus needs port 25 (the standard Sendmail port) open.

The firewall is designed to do the following:

- Masquerade the LAN. This is exactly the same script used in Chapter Six.

- Reject intrusions on the Telnet port, while allowing Telnet within the LAN and outgoing Telnet.

- Reject intrusions on the FTP port, while allowing FTP within the LAN and outgoing FTP.

The entire firewall code, including the code for NAT (also called *masquerading*), is only four lines long. I've appended this code to the /etc/rc.d/rc.local file introduced in Chapter Six. You can download it from the Linux Leap Web site (http://www.linuxleap.org). Please note that this code is extremely susceptible to spacing errors—leaving out the space after the numeral 1 in the second line, for instance, will disable NAT.

The code, and a brief explanation, follows:

Firewall Code for the Development, Ltd., Scenario

```
iptables -A POSTROUTING -t nat -o eth1 -j MASQUERADE
echo 1 > /proc/sys/net/ipv4/ip_forward
iptables -A INPUT -p tcp -destination-port telnet -I eth1 -J DROP
ptables -A INPUT -p tcp -destination-port ftp -I eth1 -J DROP
```

The first two lines masquerade packets going out on the Internet connection, eth1.

The third line drops all tcp packets coming in on eth1 and aimed at your Telnet destination port.

The fourth line drops all tcp packets coming in on eth1 and aimed at your FTP destination port.

Note that if your Internet port is eth0, you'll have to change the port numbers accordingly.

Chapter Review

This chapter was devoted to the business and technical issues involved in self-hosting a Web site and e-mail. You learned

- The decision whether or not to self-host a Web site must be made taking into account cost and technical issues, which are likely to be related.

- A decision tree can be helpful in both asking the right questions and finding the correct answers.

- The technical issues involved in self-hosting include acquiring a static address, registering a domain name, and either acquiring or running two nameservers.

- LAN-based e-mail can be expanded to Internet e-mail with the addition of a single line to the /etc/mail/access file.

- LAN security depends on several considerations, of which a firewall is only one.

- How to configure a simple but effective firewall for a LAN similar to the scenario's.

Conclusions on Self-Hosting a Web Site and E-mail

For a small firm, the greatest advantage of self-hosting undoubtedly comes from e-mail. For a relatively small cost, a company can have as many e-mail addresses as it likes, not only just within the firm, but Internet-wide. If a firm has 100 employees and wants Internet e-mail for even half of them, this is undoubtedly the way to go.

E-mail by itself can easily justify the expense of a static address, domain registration, and the expense or administrative hassle of two nameservers.

However, self-hosting a Web site is a different matter entirely. Although some initial expense can be put toward the cost of e-mail, the remaining cost equation is clear. For a small firm with a limited IT budget and limited IT manpower resources, it generally makes financial sense to self-host a Web site only if the site is simple in design and can expect very low traffic. The more complex the design and higher the traffic, the more financial sense it makes to contract the job out to one of the hundreds of firms that are competing to do it.

What's to Come

The next chapter discusses Linux as a workstation solution. For the past several years, Linux has been advancing steadily as a server solution, but its penetration into the desktop side of the market has been slight. That's now beginning to change. In certain—generally the most standard—office desktop roles, Linux has become a stealthy competitor. It's making quiet inroads, often unannounced. But a company that wants to capitalize on cost advantages is well advised to look at Linux seriously as a desktop alternative, particularly in the mixed Linux/Windows LAN environment.

CHAPTER EIGHT

Linux As a Workstation Solution

Linux on the desktop is a subject that has had its ups and downs in the press, in venture capital boardrooms, and on the beer- and Coke-cluttered workplaces where software developers congregate. However, in the marketplace—which is the only workspace that counts—Linux adoption on the desktop has continued to increase. It continues to increase in business, government, and education; in the Americas, Europe, and Asia; and in the developing world. It continues to gain acceptance because for most office uses it's as good as Microsoft Office and Windows. It continues to improve. And it costs far, far less.

This chapter's title refers to a "workstation solution." The term "workstation" sometimes refers to desktop machines more powerful than most, typically used for applications requiring an unusual amount of processing power and memory. The term can also, however, refer to a secretary's or salesperson's thin client—that is their "workstation," too. In this book, the terms "workstation" and "desktop" are used interchangeably to mean any computer used largely for office applications.

By office applications, I mean the kind of work that most computers are still used for in the home and office: the typical business tasks of word processing, organizing and crunching numbers, and trying to sell someone something (an idea or a product) with a snappy presentation. E-mail, of course, has taken over our lives, both in the home and office, and must be included. And, to be practical, you must know how to exchange files with Microsoft applications and how to work with them—it's far from a pure Linux world yet. Finally, most of us are now managed by our calendars, and that application too must be included.

This chapter is organized into ten lessons:

- Lesson 8-1. Setting Up E-mail and the Web Browser

- Lesson 8-2. Installing and Setting Up Office Applications

- Lesson 8-3. Setting Up a Linux Workstation Printer

- Lesson 8-4. Word Processing in StarOffice Writer

- Lesson 8-5. Creating Spreadsheets in StarOffice Calc

- Lesson 8-6. Creating Presentations in StarOffice Impress

This book is written for the new Linux user, but not for the new computer user. It is expected that the reader will have a working prior knowledge of most or all of these kinds of programs, most likely in either Microsoft Office or Corel Office. Therefore, in each lesson a table summarizes the similarities between two office suites, Microsoft Office and StarOffice, especially in the most basic tasks. The rest of the lesson is devoted to clarifying, sometimes in a step-by-step fashion, certain commonly used features that work somewhat differently between the two suites. Exercises are occasionally included for those readers who want to practice certain procedures. Cumulative lesson reviews follow Lesson 8-3, Lesson 8-8, and Lesson 8-10.

Reality Byte:

IF IT'S GOOD ENOUGH FOR SCOTLAND YARD . . .

Users are protesting against Microsoft's changes in licensing terms—with some vowing to abandon its products for good.

The Central Scotland Police is just one of the many organizations angered by changes to Microsoft's licensing model, which will leave them paying more for software.

Chief Inspector Stewart Marshall said the force had moved more than 1,000 users to Sun Microsystems' StarOffice suite—saving almost a quarter of a million pounds in the process.

"We saw how Microsoft was moving with licensing and how much it was going to cost," the chief inspector said. He added that he would recommend any organization looking to reduce its overheads to consider StarOffice as an alternative. "The aim in the foreseeable future at the Yard is to do away with Microsoft [products] altogether."

Other large users are seeking ways of reducing software costs. A local council, which does not want to be named, has saved £170,000 by moving 260 desktops onto StarOffice.

From Maggie Holland at Computing UK, 3/8/2001

LESSON 8-1.

SETTING UP E-MAIL AND THE WEB BROWSER

Netscape is probably the most commonly used e-mail client and Web browser in Linux. This lesson shows how to configure Netscape to send and receive e-mail, and how to customize the Web browser to enhance the appearance of Web pages.

Before starting, however, you should make a note of the names of your incoming and outgoing mail servers, and your logon or user names. You can glean this information from two sources: your e-mail service provider or the e-mail client you were using before you installed Linux.

For Microsoft Outlook users, you can look up these settings by selecting Tools ➤ Services from Outlook's menu bar. Highlight the correct e-mail profile, and click the Properties button and Servers tab.

....

Which Netscape (or Mozilla)?

Red Hat 7.2 includes one version of Netscape—4.78—and also Mozilla. In addition, you can download Netscape 6.2 from Netscape's Web site. Which one should you use? And what is Mozilla, anyway? Although most people have heard of Netscape—many are using it as their primary Web browser—few Microsoft users have probably heard of Mozilla. It's the open source version of Netscape, and it's very similar to Netscape 6.2.

So, there are three browser/e-mail clients available in Linux that look and feel similar to their Windows counterparts. They are

- Netscape 4.78

- Netscape 6.2

- Mozilla

Of these, only Netscape 4.78 is suitable for company deployment as of mid-2001. Netscape 6.2 is still beta software (although at a very refined state), and Mozilla is also still under development.

This book is written around Red Hat 7.2, and in that version both Netscape 4.78 and Mozilla are included. However, Netscape 6.2 can be easily downloaded for free from the Netscape site. The program installs in Linux with no difficulty, and you can use it alongside the older version.

The great benefit of Mozilla and Netscape 6.2 is that they both allow several POP e-mail accounts, whereas Netscape 4.78 only supports one POP account at a time. These days, more and more people have several e-mail accounts, and it's increasingly necessary to run an e-mail program with that capability.

Because Netscape 4.78 is still most users' preferred e-mail client for Linux, this section covers its basic setup. However, to recognize its probable future replacement, setting up Mozilla/Netscape 6.2 is also covered in Lesson 8-9.

Configuring Netscape Communicator E-mail

To start Netscape, click once on the Netscape icon on the panel. The Web browser will open. To configure your e-mail, click Edit on the menu bar, and then click Preferences, the last item in the drop-down menu.

 NOTE *The examples in this lesson assume that the user's e-mail account is with their ISP, or another commercial POP3 e-mail account provider. Browser-based e-mail is handled in exactly the same way in Linux as it is in Windows—through the Web browser. Configuring the e-mail client for a local mail server (the firm's own mail server, should it have one) is covered in Chapter Six, Lesson 6-4.*

The left column in the Preferences window is a collapsible menu tree. Click Mail & Newsgroups to expand that section, and then click Identity (see Figure 8-1). Please note that the examples here are imaginary: The famous German writer Erich Maria Remarque died in 1970, well before there were CompuServe mail accounts.

In the "Your name" box, type in your name as you want it to appear when someone else receives a message from you. Beneath that, under "Email address," type in your actual e-mail address. If you would like a "virtual card" attached to your e-mail messages, click the Edit Card button toward the bottom of the screen, and fill in the blanks.

Next, in the left column, click the Mail Servers menu item. This is where you'll configure your incoming and outgoing mail servers.

Incoming and outgoing e-mail uses different protocols, and as a result everyone with an e-mail account has two servers—one for receiving and one for sending mail. In addition, there are two different types of incoming servers: POP and IMAP. Most people now use POP. The configuration process for both is almost identical.

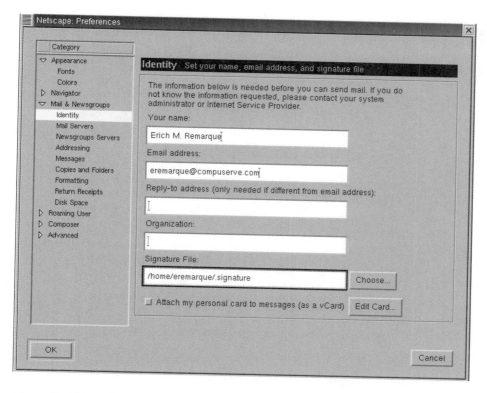

Figure 8-1. E-mail identity configuration in Netscape

Under Incoming Mail Servers, highlight the POP entry, and click the Edit button. If you have a POP server, fill in the server name and your user name, and check the "Remember password" box (see Figure 8-2). You also have the choice of automatically checking for incoming mail every 10 minutes and automatically downloading any mail present on your server.

If you have an IMAP incoming mail server, click the button next to Server Type and choose IMAP. The basic entries here are the same, but there are more entries under the IMAP and Advanced tabs. If you have an IMAP server, it's likely that you also have a corporate e-mail account—ask your system administrator for the correct settings.

Click the OK button to return to the Mail Servers window. Your POP server name should now appear under Incoming Mail Servers. In the box next to "Outgoing mail (SMTP) server," enter your SMTP server name. Below it type in your user name (see Figure 8-3). Click the OK button, and you're ready to send and receive e-mail.

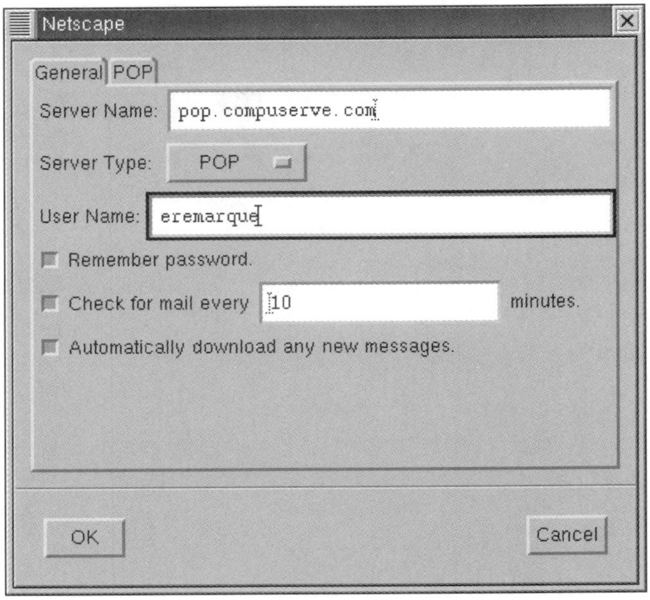

Figure 8-2. Setting up the incoming (POP) e-mail server

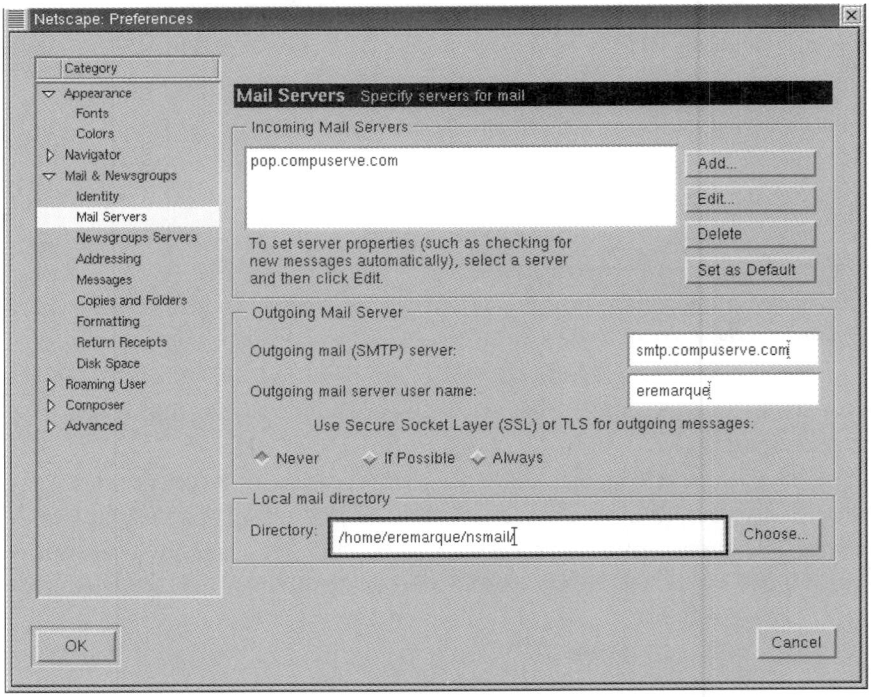

Figure 8-3. Setting up the outgoing (SMTP) mail server

The first time you check your e-mail, by clicking the mail icon at the bottom right-hand corner of the main Netscape window, you will be prompted for your password. Since you checked the Remember Password box, you won't be asked for it again.

Importing Address Books

Most new Linux users will be coming from a Windows environment and will want to import their e-mail address books from Windows to Linux. If they were using Netscape in Windows, the process will be painless. If, however, they were using Outlook (the more likely scenario), the process is easy but not exactly straightforward.

First, check in Netscape in Linux that you're running version 4.78. (This step isn't necessary if you're running Red Hat 7.2.) Do this by opening Netscape, clicking Help on the menu bar, and selecting the About Communicator menu item. The first line of the resulting page should read "Netscape Communicator 4.78." If it's any number less than 7.7, you must upgrade it. This simple task is described in Chapter Nine of this book.

Now turn to the e-mail client in your Windows computer. If it's Netscape, simply open the address book, and select File ➤ Export from the menu bar. Choose .ldif as the file type, and name your file "address.ldif". Now, skip to the chapter section titled "To Linux Netscape."

If you're using Outlook, the procedure is more complex. You must first export your Outlook Contacts address list as a .csv file, then import it into Netscape within Windows, and next export it as an .ldif file. Finally, import that file into Netscape in Linux. Here's the procedure step by step.

From Windows Outlook:

1. Select File ➤ Import and Export.

2. Choose Export to a File and click the Next button.

3. Choose Comma Separated Values (Windows) and click Next.

4. Select the Contacts folder, and then click Next again.

5. Type in the filename **address.csv**, and save it where you like.

6. Click the Finish button, and close Outlook.

From Windows Netscape:

1. Open Netscape's address book by selecting Communicator ➤ Address Book.

2. Select File ➤ Import.

3. Choose Text File, and then click Next.

4. Click the Browse button and open the address.csv file you saved previously.

5. Choose the values you want to import, and click the Import button. The names and addresses will show up in your Netscape address book.

6. Now choose File ➤ Export and export your address book. Choose .ldif as the file type, and name the file address.ldif.

To Linux Netscape, open Netscape's address book and import the .ldif file you just created. Job done.

One last note on addresses: If you want the names to appear last name first, click Edit on the menu bar and navigate to Preferences ➤ Addressing. Near the bottom of the window, choose "Show names using last name, first name."

Configuring Netscape Navigator

Netscape Navigator is a very standard Web browser in common use by millions of people. There is no need for comprehensive instructions, especially since most of the default cache and other settings are perfectly acceptable for nearly all users.

However, you may discover once you start surfing that the fonts displayed aren't to your taste. They may look too small or perhaps just very rough. If so, changing them is a simple matter. The following selections work on a variety of monitors, but you can experiment as you like.

1. Select Edit ➤ Preferences.

2. In the menu tree, under Appearance, choose Fonts.

3. In the Fonts window that opens, make the following selections:

   Variable Width Font: Helvetica (Adobe), Size: 12

   Fixed Width Font: Lucida Typewriter (B&H), Size: 12

   Use my default fonts, overriding document-specified fonts.

4. Click the OK button.

After e-mail and a Web browser, the second most important thing on most computers is an office application package. In the next lesson, you will install one.

LESSON 8-2.

INSTALLING AND SETTING UP OFFICE APPLICATIONS

Several office application suites are available for Linux, but one stands out: Sun Microsystems' StarOffice.

All major distributions, including Red Hat 7.2, ship at least one version of their product with the StarOffice application suite. The suite includes a word processor, a spreadsheet and a presentation program, as well as other, less important modules. Its design is similar enough to Microsoft Office to make working in it completely intuitive for Windows users, and its import and export filters are the best in the business. Sun is supporting it strongly, as is the open source community.

However, although you can download StarOffice for free from Sun's Web site, it's not distributed under any of the major free software licenses. It's distributed under a special Sun license for "internal use." It may be argued that from a practical standpoint, or from the standpoint of an end user or administrator who has no personal interest in customizing the software of a program that runs to millions of lines of code, there's little difference between a program that is downloadable for internal use for free and a program distributed under the Free Software Foundation's GPL.

The open source/free software movement would not agree. They would point out, quite accurately, that a program that's not susceptible to user modification, with the distribution of those modifications, cannot benefit from the attentions— the debugging attentions, for instance—of programmers worldwide.

That criticism no longer applies to StarOffice. Sun *has* released their source code for StarOffice to OpenOffice.org. This is an open source initiative to rewrite and improve StarOffice, and release the result under the GPL. Sun meanwhile will incorporate the new code into a new version of StarOffice (already available in beta), which they will make available, with some proprietary code, under their current license.

The OpenOffice mission statement is short and to the point: "To create, as a community, the leading international office suite that will run on all major platforms and provide access to all functionality and data through open-component based APIs and an XML-based file format."

One day all of us may run their software, and OpenOffice will have become what Microsoft Office is today. In the meantime, Linux users have a working alternative to Microsoft Office, one that works in a familiar way, is feature-rich and file compatible, is bundled with many distributions, can be downloaded for free, and can be legally distributed internally. It is StarOffice.

....

Reality Byte:

A GOVERNMENT CPA'S TAKE ON STAROFFICE

Here's my perspective: I work as a CPA for my federal government employer. Because I work with the personal records of U.S. citizens, security is fairly tight—well, supposedly, considering the 50 "I LUV U" e-mails I got just like everybody else.

My accountant's work papers consist mainly of Excel spreadsheets pasted as tables into Word documents, with surrounding text. I have a thorough knowledge of day-to-day work using office productivity software, rather than a geek's understanding of the internals. My skills are duplicated by thousands if not millions of office workers worldwide. My evaluation of StarOffice carries this context.

From what I can see after two weeks of reasonable use, StarOffice Writer and StarOffice Calc are every bit as clean and usable as their Microsoft Office counterparts. Editing text is a snap, as is putting together spreadsheets quickly. I miss the "Group Mode" of Quattro Pro, but there are workarounds I've learned from not having this handy mode in Excel, either. My caveat is that I use spreadsheets as an accountant, with lots of date functions, plenty of interest and time value work, formatting en route to a word processing document, and little else. I haven't probed the depths of all the functions; if major parts essential to what mathematicians do are missing, I'm sure someone will let me know. As it stands, the average office worker doing financial or managerial accounting, working up projections of business-type data, performing "what-if" analysis, writing correspondence, and so on will feel right at home.

I had some trouble moving some of my documents. Specifically, Quattro Pro native spreadsheets didn't want to cross. My attempts to have Quattro Pro save the documents in Excel 97 format, to be read by the StarOffice filter, proved unsuccessful. I ended up saving them as Quattro native and having Excel convert them. As a test, I saved some of the documents and some StarOffice Writer files in Microsoft format, which Microsoft Office picked up without complaint.

Printing is not a problem. I print to an HP LaserJet 1100, and in all cases printed text looks exactly like screen text, with no hint of roughness even on larger font sizes. Screen fonts are smooth and easy to read, free of the "blotchy look" of earlier StarOffice releases. I'm very impressed.

Those are the major applications I use. The presentation software appears to work, although I haven't used it on an actual presentation yet. Designing test pages revealed no surprises. I could use a friendly interface for entering data into the address book; otherwise, it's useful for creating form letters and reports. I have never used the graphics program, as I prefer to use The GIMP.

Finally I'm able to recommend an alternative to Office for many users. In my opinion, many people who feel they need Microsoft Office to work productively can move to StarOffice with little trouble. I was surprised at how quickly I was able to work productively with this program, and all this without the high cost, the restrictive licensing arrangements, and the hassle of working with proprietary software. At last I have an answer when someone asks me, "Does Microsoft Office run on it?"

Tim Hanson, a CPA working for the government,
is a daily user of office productivity software.

Downloading and Installing StarOffice

You can download StarOffice for free from the Linux Leap Web site (http://www.linuxleap.org). The butterfly symbol will take you straight to the correct Web page at Sun. Registration is necessary but only takes a minute. The download instructions are clear and, as you would expect from Sun Microsystems, the servers are open, reliable, and fast.

What's to Come in StarOffice

The biggest gripe with StarOffice is the time it takes to load. The reason it takes so long is that StarOffice loads many application components when it first starts, rather than on demand, when they are needed. This not only takes time, it also takes memory.

Sun has announced that its next version of StarOffice, which should be out in early 2002, will launch components separately, thereby saving both time during initial start-up and RAM.

Sun is also including the ability to save files in a new file specification based on XML that is designed to make exporting and importing files to other formats even easier (the current format will also be retained). Several other improvements will be included, including a new user help interface, better printing, and internationalization, but topping the list for many users will be a set of filters for Microsoft XP.

NOTE *If you purchase a retail version of Red Hat Linux 7.2, StarOffice is included gratis on a separate CD. Specific installation instructions are given. Follow them. Skip to the chapter section "Adding StarOffice to Your Application Menu."*

You have the choice of downloading the program in one file or in several. One file is, of course, the simpler choice, but you should consider the speed and reliability of your own Internet connection. The single file version is 97.62MB. Over a DSL connection, this will only take a few minutes to download, but over a dial-up modem connection, it could take hours, increasing the likelihood of the line dropping. On a slow connection, you're likely to waste less time by downloading the smaller files one by one.

Once you've downloaded the program, click Run on the Start menu, find your downloaded file with the Browse button, and then run the program (see Figure 8-4).

 NOTE *If you're not running as the root user, you may have to open a terminal and enter the following command to make the file executable:* ***chmod + x so*.***

Figure 8-4. Running the downloaded StarOffice installation file

The StarOffice installation program is very straightforward. You're asked to agree to the license terms, and then you're prompted to enter various user data, such as your company name. This is not for Sun's use, but rather for automatically filling in certain fields in StarOffice templates. You're given three different installation types to choose from: standard, custom, and minimum. Most users will choose standard. All that's left is to choose which installation directory you prefer.

Adding StarOffice to Your Application Menu

Although some distributions have a StarOffice menu item preinstalled, Red Hat does not. Follow this procedure to insert a StarOffice menu item in the Programs submenu:

1. As the root user, open the Menu Editor by opening the main menu and navigating to Programs ➤ Settings ➤ Menu Editor.

2. In the Menu Editor, click Applications in the collapsible menu, and then click New Item on the menu bar.

3. In the Name box, type in the program name, and in the Command box type in the complete directory address and the executable command. (Note that your directory path may not be the same as the one illustrated. Your executable command, however, will be the same: soffice.)

4. Click the Icon button and choose an icon from the list.

The result should look something like Figure 8-5. The icon shown may or may not be available for you, but there are many suitable icons to choose from.

New menu items are by default placed at the bottom of their submenus. However, you can reposition your latest addition by clicking the Move Up arrow on the menu bar.

When you've finished, click the Save button, close the Menu Editor and, navigating to the StarOffice 5.2 menu item, open the StarOffice productivity suite.

 TIP *Save yourself some time and hassle by copying this menu item to the desktop. Simply open the menu to the StarOffice icon and drag it onto the desktop while holding the left mouse button down. An instant desktop program launcher.*

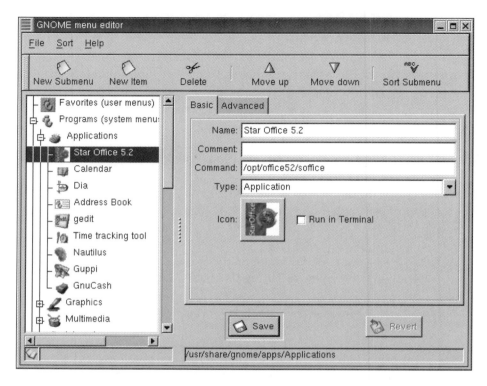

Figure 8-5. Adding a StarOffice menu item using the Menu Editor

Initial StarOffice Configuration

When you start it the first time, StarOffice initiates an automated Internet setup program. This is where it comes in handy to have previously configured your mail settings in Netscape. Of course, you don't have to use StarOffice for e-mail—most users probably will not. But it's not a bad idea to let it configure itself, so click the Next button, select Netscape when prompted, and check the "Apply all settings automatically" option. Click Next two more times, and then click the OK button. This automatically copies your e-mail settings from Netscape to the e-mail client in StarOffice. If you ever do want to use it for that purpose, the program will at least be configured.

You may want to eliminate the welcome "tips" that, if not disabled, will clutter the bottom of your screen every time you open the program. Simply check the "Don't display tips" box, and click the X next to the welcome screen.

The two most important initial configurations are when to automatically save files, and setting up a printer. It's best to set up a printer in StarOffice *after* you set up a Linux-wide printer, which is covered in the next lesson. Printer setup in StarOffice appears there.

Configure StarOffice's save file behavior by selecting Tools ➤ Options. Expand the General menu on the left and click Save.

In this menu you can choose how often you want StarOffice to automatically save your work, and whether or not you want to be prompted to save. You can adjust the number of steps you can "undo." Most interesting, you can configure what you want to be restored (opened) every time you reopen the program. As shown in Figure 8-6, StarOffice has the capability to automatically reopen not only every document you were working on last, but also every document you had open. This can be a great time saver for people who keep multiple documents open at a time.

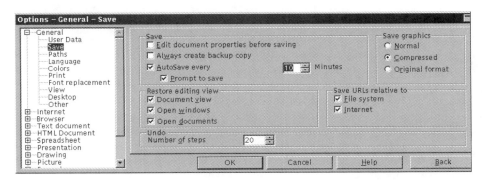

Figure 8-6. Configuring the Save, Undo, and Restore behavior in StarOffice

Configure the save features to your taste and click OK.

LESSON 8-3.

SETTING UP A LINUX WORKSTATION PRINTER

Setting up a printer is straightforward in Linux, but you must first know what kind of printer you need to set up. There are a total of five possibilities, depending on whether or not you are on a LAN, what kind of LAN it is, and what sort of printer you're printing to. Chapter Six covers print setup in LANs. This lesson covers setting up a Linux workstation to print to a local printer—a printer directly connected to either the computer's parallel or USB port.

Open the main menu, and navigate to Programs ➤ System ➤ Printer Configuration. The printer configuration program opens. Click New on the menu bar, and then click Next.

Type in a queue name to identify this printer—many LANs will have several. Check the Local Printer circle, and then click the Next button. The following screen can usually be accepted as is, so click Next again.

In the Select a Print Driver window, it's necessary to not only choose which model of printer you have, but also to select which driver you want to use. Figure 8-7 gives an example: An HP 2000C printer has been chosen, along with the second of three printer drivers for that machine. If your printer isn't listed, choose a similar one by the same manufacturer. Figure 8-8 shows the printer configuration program with two printers set up and configured; the default in this case is the local.

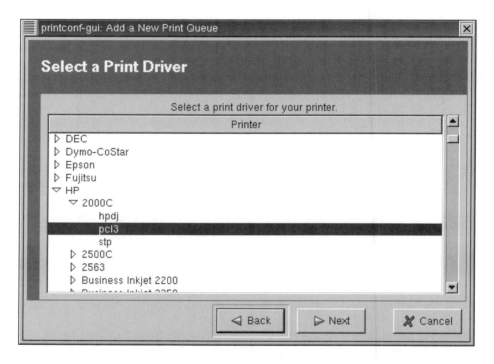

Figure 8-7. Choosing a printer driver

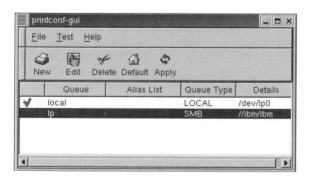

Figure 8-8. Two printers set up, one on the LAN and one on the local system

Before you test your printer setup, click Apply on the toolbar. Then click Test on the menu bar and try printing a PostScript test page. If it doesn't work, the most likely cause is a bad hardware connection. The next most likely cause is a poor printer driver—try another one if you have to.

Setting Up a Printer in StarOffice

Start up StarOffice either by clicking the menu item, or, if you have made one, by clicking the desktop icon. In the StarOffice desktop window, click the icon for Printer Setup.

In the Printer Installation Window, choose the Generic Printer under Installed Printers by selecting it and clicking the Configure button. If it doesn't work, or if its performance is not acceptable, you can choose another printer from the list under Existing Printer Drivers.

The Printer Properties window has three tabs from which to choose various settings. Under Device, make sure you select Resolution and choose the correct value for your printer (see Figure 8-9).

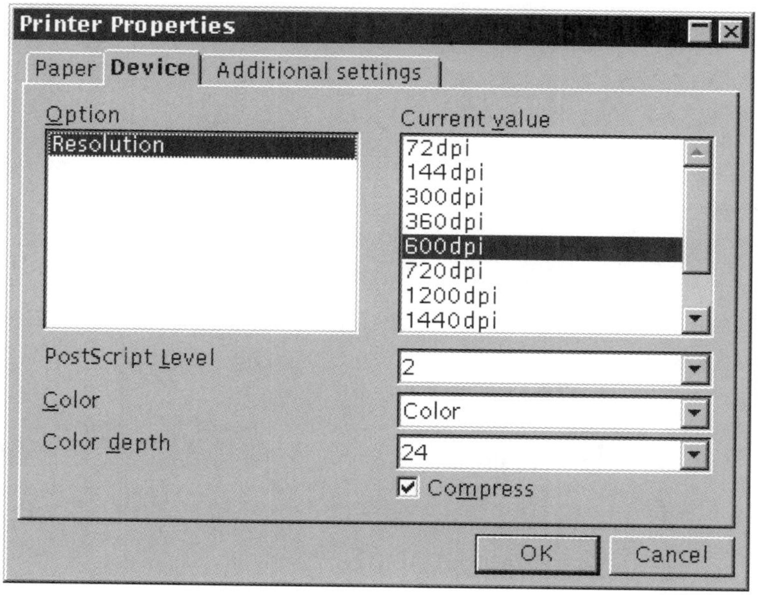

Figure 8-9. Setting printer properties in StarOffice

When you've finished configuring the printer, click the Connect button. In the Connect window, accept the default command and click OK.

Check your work by clicking the Test Page button.

Lesson Review

The preceding three lessons were devoted to setting up e-mail and Web browsing in Netscape, to installing and setting up the StarOffice application suite, and to installing and setting up printing, first for Linux as a whole and then for StarOffice in particular. You learned

- How to configure Netscape Communicator with your POP or IMAP e-mail account information

- How to transfer an address book from either Netscape or Outlook in Windows to Netscape in Linux

- How to change the fonts in Navigator, if you should find it necessary

- Why StarOffice is the market leader in Linux office application suites, what its license terms are, and what the future may bring with OpenOffice

- How to download the StarOffice installation file for free from Sun Microsystems and install the program on your computer

- How to configure StarOffice's Internet settings and save, undo, and restore file behavior

- How to use the Printer Configuration tool to set up and configure a local printer—one attached directly to the computer

- How to set up and configure a printer in StarOffice

LESSON 8-4.

WORD PROCESSING IN STAROFFICE WRITER

The oldest computer office application is the word processor. E-mail may now, in many offices, be the most used application, but the successor to the typewriter is still with us and is almost certainly here to stay.

Fortunately, the basics of the GUI, Windows-style word processor are almost exactly the same across platforms and across word processing packages. Table 8-1 shows some of the similarities between StarOffice Writer and Microsoft Word.

Table 8-1. Similarities between StarOffice Writer and Microsoft Word

FUNCTION AND PROCEDURE IN STAROFFICE WRITER	FUNCTION AND PROCEDURE IN MICROSOFT WORD		
	Menu Bar	Toolbar	Keyboard and Mouse
Opening a document	Identical	Identical	NA
Saving a document	Identical	Identical	NA
Starting a new document	Similar	Different	NA
Printing a document	Identical	Identical	NA
Inserting text	NA	NA	Identical
Deleting text	NA	NA	Identical
Cutting, copying, and pasting	Identical	Identical	Identical
Formatting: bold, italic, underline	Similar	Identical	Similar
Formatting: bullets, numbering	Similar	Identical	Similar
Formatting: alignment	Similar	Identical	NA
Changing font color	Similar	Identical	NA
Setting tabs	Similar	Identical	NA
Spell checking	Identical	Identical	NA
Changing fonts	Similar	Identical	Similar
Finding and replacing	NA	Identical	NA
Undoing mistakes	Similar	Identical	NA

This table could go on and on—but there's no need to extend it. A competent operator will take one look at StarOffice Writer and realize that he or she can immediately get up and running on basic functions and find most others through exploring menus. The following sections introduce some commonly used features that work somewhat differently or need some clarification.

Getting Help

The StarOffice Writer Help is very robust, but its initial display may disappoint users, perhaps to the point of not exploring Help further. This would be a pity, because it has many useful features.

When you click Help on the menu bar, the initial display window may be very small and poorly shaped, and the text awkwardly large. If that's the case, simply pull the sides of the window with the mouse to make it larger, and then click the Reduce button (the icon with a magnifying glass and minus sign).

 NOTE *The Help feature works the same way in all StarOffice applications.*

For a quick Help tutorial, click Tips on Using Help.

Revising Documents

You can make revision marks in documents—the familiar underline for additions and strikethrough for deletions—by choosing Edit ➤ Changes ➤ Show. In addition, you are able to merge multiple versions of a revised document by choosing Edit ➤ Changes ➤ Merge Document.

Inserting Graphics and Drawings

Inserting graphics and producing simple drawings for insertion into text are the most common graphic jobs within a word processor. Unlike other word processors, the icons for inserting graphics and drawings in StarOffice are on a third, vertical toolbar, which extends down the left-hand side of the screen (StarOffice calls it the main toolbar).

The Insert icon, at the top of the main toolbar, extends out horizontally when you click the icon and hold down the mouse button (see Figure 8-10). Keep holding the button down, and slowly pass the mouse over each icon on the horizontal bar. A variety of objects for insertion appear, among them graphics. The user may select graphics from a variety of formats, from whatever directory they prefer, on any mounted drive.

Figure 8-10. The Insert icon on the main toolbar, horizontally extended

Drawings within text are produced by activating the Show Draw Functions icon in the same way (see Figure 8-11). The normal drawing functions within a text document are lines, rectangles, ellipses, polygons, free form, text, and so on. Included also are "Callouts."

Figure 8-11. The Show Draw Functions icon on the main toolbar, horizontally extended

Figure 8-12 gives a simple example of how these two features can work. Using the Insert icon, a graphic has been inserted in the text (this chapter's Figure 8-21). Next, using Callouts from Show Draw Functions, two callouts have been placed below the text and just above the graphic. Some modifications have been made: The lines have been widened, and arrows have been placed at the end of the lines. Text has been inserted into each callout to make its meaning clearer.

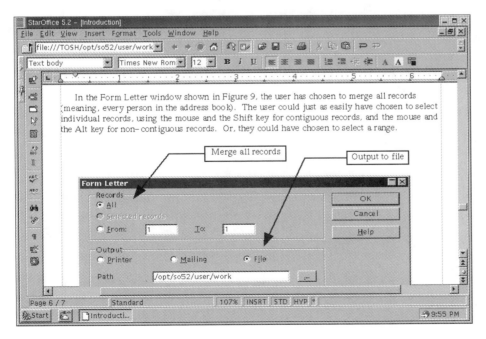

Figure 8-12. An alternative to a caption: callouts inserted to clarify a graphic

Address Books, Templates, and Mail Merge

Merging data from an address database into modified templates in order to produce multiple-submission form letters (mail merge) is one of the most common and effective ways to take advantage of the labor-saving features of modern word processors. The technique is used in the office for billing clients, sending out promotional materials, and so on.

First, you enter data into an address book, then choose or modify a suitable template, and finally merge the data. In the sections that follow, each feature and step is covered in order: using the address book, opening and customizing templates, and merging.

Using the Address Book

To open the address book, click Edit on the menu bar, and then click Address Book. The address book database will open as shown in Figure 8-13. Note that four fictional addresses are included to give the new user an idea of the data to be entered.

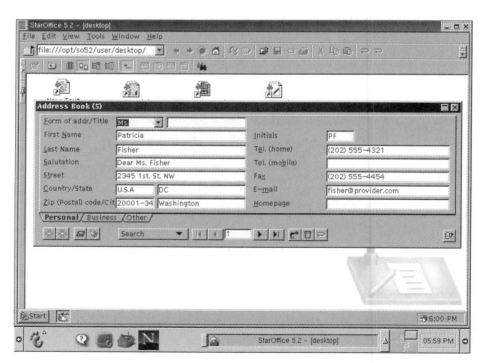

Figure 8-13. The address book opened to the entry of the fictional Ms. Fisher

Each record has three sections, which you can access through the tabs at the lower left, labeled: Personal, Business, and Other. These labels reflect the content of each section; the user can modify fields in the last section, Other.

The user may use the buttons at the bottom of the address book to scroll through the records one by one or to jump to the last or first record. There are also buttons for adding a new record, deleting a record, and undoing the last action.

Hands On:

ADDING A RECORD TO THE ADDRESS BOOK

Add a real record of your own—a friend, business associate, or client—to the address book database.

1. Open the address book by clicking Edit on the menu bar, and then clicking Address Book.

2. Click the New button (see Figure 8-14).

Figure 8-14. The Add New Record button

3. Enter your data into the new record, tabbing from field to field.

Your new record will appear as the last in the list—number 5.

Opening Templates

A template is a preformatted document that you can use over and over again to create identically formatted documents. Templates save time, and the time saved is not one-off, but rather it's accrued every time a template is used or modified. Templates are too valuable a tool not to be used in business correspondence.

You're using templates whether you know it or not—every time you open a new, blank text document, you have in fact opened the standard template. There are many other templates from which to choose, from faxes to invoices to press releases. And, of course, it's possible to create your own, either by altering a pre-made template or by creating one from scratch based on a document of your own.

To view the various templates offered, click the StarOffice Start button and navigate to More ➤ From Template, or click File on the menu bar and choose New ➤ From Template. Once the New Template window opens, select Business Correspondence in the left pane and Contemporary Letter in the right. Click the More button to enable a preview of the template selected (see Figure 8-15).

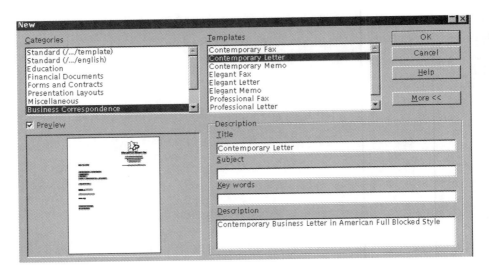

Figure 8-15. A Contemporary Business Letter template selected and Preview enabled

Open the template by clicking the OK button. The address book will appear at the top of the page, over the template. Close the address book by clicking on the hide button—a small up arrow—at the lower left-hand corner of the address book. The open template should look similar to Figure 8-16.

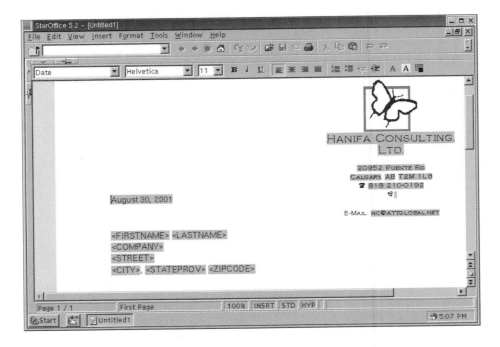

Figure 8-16. The Contemporary Business Letter template opened in a document editing window

The text entries in gray surrounds are actually fields—you can confirm this by holding your mouse over the FIRSTNAME entry. A pop-up informs you that it is in fact the FIRSTNAME field from the address book.

Notice that your personal information—company name and so on—has been automatically inserted. This information comes from the user data you entered during StarOffice installation, but it can always be changed. To do so, just click Tools on the menu bar and navigate to Options ➤ General ➤ User Data.

The Contemporary Business Letter is a good template, useful for business correspondence, but it was formatted in Germany (StarOffice was a German software package before it was bought by Sun Microsystems), and you may want to modify it to more closely fit either your idea of what a business letter should look like, or to look more like the template you have used up to now.

Customizing Templates

You can copy and paste fields in the familiar way in StarOffice. As an example, move the date field from the upper left-hand corner to the far right, on the last line of the address. Follow this procedure:

1. Select the Date field with your mouse.

2. Click the Cut icon (the pair of scissors) on the toolbar, and position your cursor directly after the ZIPCODE field.

3. Tab several times, almost to the right margin, and click the familiar Paste icon on the toolbar.

You may not want a subject entry at all in the letter—it's more a memo feature than a straight business letter feature. You delete a field in exactly the same way as you delete text: Select it and press the Delete key. To replace a field with text, select the field and type in the text.

You can easily insert additional fields from the address book. First, remember to place your cursor where you want the new field to appear. Then, click Insert on the menu bar and navigate to Fields ➤ Other. This brings up the Fields window. Click the Database tab and the "Form letter field" option in the left panel, and expand the Address Book/address menu under "Database selection" on the right (see Figure 8-17). You may now choose which additional fields from the address book you would like to insert in the template. In this example, select the very first field, PREFIX, and click the Insert button. Make sure there is a single space between fields; otherwise, the text will appear to run together after a merge.

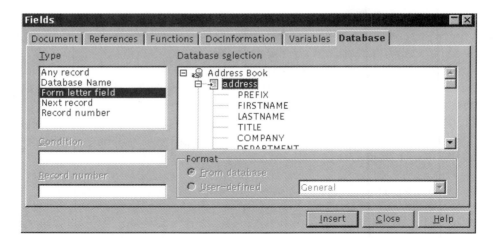

Figure 8-17. Selecting an address book field to insert into a template

---

Hands On:

MODIFYING THE CONTEMPORARY BUSINESS LETTER TEMPLATE

Continue modifying the template in the example.

1. Insert a COUNTRY field at the bottom of the recipient address.
2. Copy and paste the LASTNAME field to follow the salutation. Remember to insert a colon at the end of the line.
3. Replace the SALUTATION field with the word "Dear."
4. Save the new template by clicking File on the menu bar and navigating to Templates ➤ Save. Select the category you want the new template to appear in, name it, and click OK.
5. Close the template.

Merging Address Book Fields into Templates

This is the heart of the mail merge process. Each office application suite has its own procedure; the procedure in StarOffice is straightforward.

You merge address book fields into form letter templates in two steps. First, open the template and the address book, and check the template to make sure it works by selecting one record and clicking the Data to Fields button. Second, perform the merge by clicking the Form Letter button, and choosing which records you want to merge and what kind of output you prefer—to the printer, to a set of files, or to e-mail.

As an example, let's use the template created in the preceding "Hands On" section.

First, open the template. You'll notice that the address book automatically opens as well, in the upper part of the screen.

> **NOTE** *If you created your own mail merge template from scratch, it may not be automatically linked to the address book database. If this is the case, after opening the template, click File on the menu bar and then click Form Letter. The address book will open with its records and fields ready to be merged.*

Next, make sure the template is really going to work properly by selecting one record with the mouse and clicking the Data to Fields icon (see Figure 8-18).

Figure 8-18. Click the Data to Fields icon to test the template.

The result, in this example, should look very much like Figure 8-19. The data in the record selected is mirrored in the letter, using correct business letter format and without any disagreeable surprises. In a large or complex merge, it's wise to preview several records in this way.

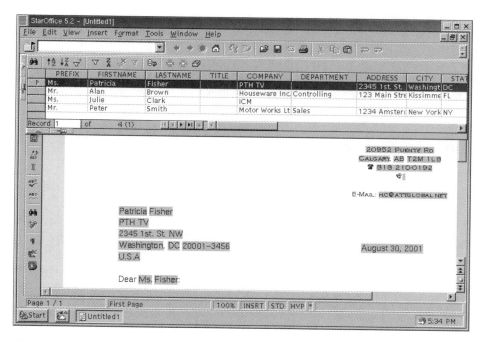

Figure 8-19. The Patricia Fisher record in a successful template test

To perform the merge, click the small Form Letter icon on the address book's toolbar (see Figure 8-20).

Figure 8-20. Click the Form Letter icon to begin a mail merge.

In the Form Letter window that opens (see Figure 8-21), you must choose the following:

- Which records to merge

- Whether to print the letters directly, e-mail them, or create files

- Whether to name the files after a database field or give them a name of your own

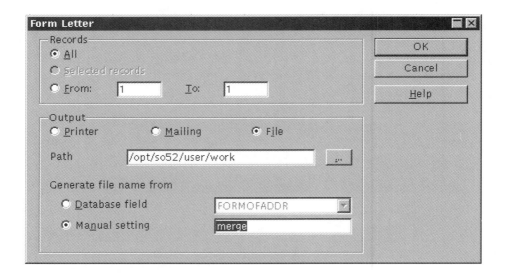

Figure 8-21. All records merged to files named "merge"

In the Form Letter window shown in Figure 8-21, the user has chosen to merge all records (meaning, every person in the address book). The user could just as easily have chosen to select individual records, using the mouse and the Shift key for contiguous records and the mouse and the Alt key for noncontiguous records. Or, the user could have chosen to select a range.

The output of the merge in this example will be saved to files in the StarOffice default save path. This path could be changed to any path on the local machine or any machine on the network with a local mount point.

Finally, the file names will all start with the word "merge." There will be a separate file for each letter produced, and since in this example all records were chosen, there will be a total of five files produced: merge1, merge2, merge3, and so on.

Once the OK button is clicked, the user is prompted for a filename again—the template itself will be saved as a separate StarOffice Writer file. The merged files are automatically created and can be checked by opening them individually.

Hands On:

MERGE ADDRESSES WITH A PRESS RELEASE

Practice a mail merge with a new template.

1. Open the Professional Press Release template from the Miscellaneous Business Documents category.

2. Using the mouse and the Ctrl key, select the first two records and the last in the address book.

3. Merge the selected records into the template, saving them to file with the name "handson."

4. Test your work.

LESSON 8-5.

CREATING SPREADSHEETS IN STAROFFICE CALC

The spreadsheet application, as much as anything, brought the PC to business. And, like word processors, most spreadsheet applications are very similar to each other.

Table 8-2 shows some of the similarities between StarOffice Calc and Microsoft Excel.

Table 8-2. Similarities between Microsoft Excel and StarOffice Calc

FUNCTION AND PROCEDURE IN MICROSOFT EXCEL	FUNCTION AND PROCEDURE IN STAROFFICE CALC		
	Menu Bar	Toolbar	Keyboard and Mouse
Opening a spreadsheet	Identical	Identical	NA
Saving a spreadsheet	Identical	Identical	NA
Starting a new spreadsheet	Similar	Different	NA
Printing a spreadsheet	Identical	Identical	NA
Inserting data	NA	NA	Identical
Inserting formulas	NA	NA	Identical
Relative and absolute addresses	NA	NA	Identical
Deleting data, cells, and so on	Similar	NA	Identical
Cutting, copying, and pasting	Identical	Identical	Identical
Formatting text	Similar	Identical	Similar
Formatting data	Similar	Similar	Similar
AutoSum feature	NA	Identical	NA
AutoFormat feature	Identical	Identical	NA
AutoFormat chart feature	Identical	Identical	NA
Multiple sheets	NA	Identical	NA
Goal seek	NA	Identical	NA
Scenarios	Different	Different	NA

Any competent operator of Microsoft Excel will feel at home in StarOffice Calc. The scenarios feature, however, is handled somewhat differently between Calc and Excel, as shown in the example that follows.

Creating Scenarios and Using Goal Seek in StarOffice Calc

Whereas goal seeking is a form of break-even analysis based on one variable, scenarios explore the results on the bottom line of one or more variables simultaneously.

In StarOffice Calc, the simplest procedure for creating scenarios is to design the spreadsheet so that the cells containing the variables are outside the main body. Figure 8-22 shows a very simplified projected income statement for a Linux company selling a boxed Linux distribution.

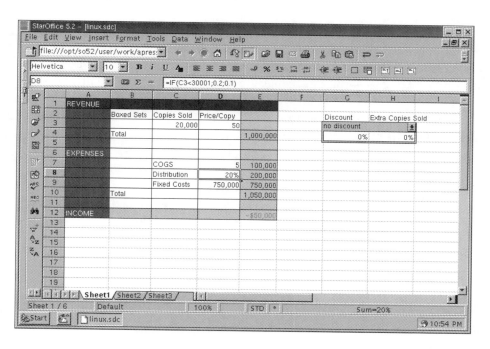

Figure 8-22. Linux projected income statement, showing a small loss, a scenario with one variable cell, and the formula in cell D8

In this spreadsheet, the number of copies sold depends on the selling price: The greater the discount, the greater the sales projection. In addition, the distributor's "take"—their percentage of the selling price—is 20 percent up to 30,000 copies sold, but only 10 percent thereafter (cell D8). The two most important variables, then, are the discount on the selling price and the projected number of copies sold.

In Figure 8-22, the formulas in cells C3 and D3 (Copies Sold and Price/Copy) are linked to two cells in the Scenario box: variable cell G4 (the discount) and a formula in cell H4 (the projected extra percentage of copies sold, which rises as the discount rises—in this case, at a rate of 2.5 times the discount).

> **NOTE** *This spreadsheet, linux.sdc, is available on the Linux Leap Web site* (`http://www.linuxleap.org`) *for those who want to inspect the formulas.*

Activating the Scenario

You should create the spreadsheet and establish the links before you activate the scenarios feature. It matters little what numbers are actually plugged into the scenario cells G4 and H4—you can change the data in scenarios in StarOffice Calc on the fly.

To activate the scenarios feature, select G4 and H4 with the mouse, and then click Tools on the menu bar and choose Scenarios.

Type in the name you would like to give the scenario—it should be descriptive, rather than just a number. The scenario cells will appear with a special border, with the name you gave it above the cells.

Now is the time to experiment. You can type in any formula or figure you like in the variable scenario cells and create a new saved scenario.

Using Goal Seek with Scenarios

Goal seek is a very simple tool that you can ally with scenarios to quickly find the exact value, or values, needed.

In the sample spreadsheet in Figure 8-22, you need to find the lowest discount necessary to boost sales to the point where zero losses are achieved—the break-even point.

To bring up the goal seek feature, first select with the mouse the formula cell that is the object of the exercise; in this case, since you're trying to bring the income (currently a loss) to zero, it would be cell E12, Income. Then click Tools on the menu bar, and choose Goal Seek. Immediately the Goal Seek window appears.

There are only three boxes to fill in, and the first already has an entry: the Formula Cell reads E12, which is the absolute address of the Income cell. In Target Value, type **0**, and then click in the Variable Cell box, and again in cell G4, the variable cell for this goal seek.

Click the OK button and the result will appear—in this case, a discount of 6 percent, as shown in Figure 8-23.

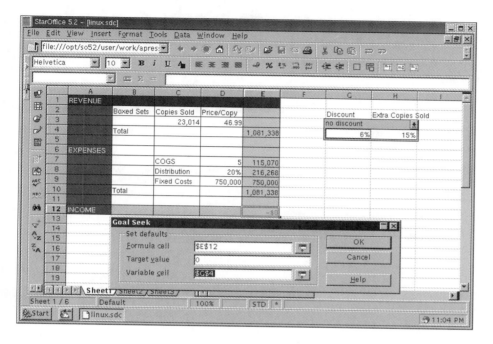

Figure 8-23. The goal achieved through goal seek: a 6 percent discount = 15 percent more copies sold = break even

You can use the scenario feature to eliminate any chance of forgetting these important numbers by selecting G4 and H4 again, choosing Tools ➤ Scenario on the menu bar, and entering a new name for the second scenario (in this case, **Break Even**). By clicking the down arrow in the upper right-hand corner, the user can cycle between scenarios.

TIP *By clicking the Explorer button in the upper left-hand corner of the editing window and choosing Explorer ➤ Samples ➤ Spreadsheets, the user can access several sample spreadsheets designed to highlight the various features of StarOffice Calc.*

LESSON 8-6.

CREATING PRESENTATIONS IN STAROFFICE IMPRESS

StarOffice Impress is the StarOffice presentations program that you can use to create overheads, handouts, and/or "live" computer-fed presentations to sell an idea or product.

Star Impress is not as slick in its own presentation as its main competitor, but it does include nearly all of its competitor's features. Table 8-3 summarizes features present in both packages.

Table 8-3. Similarities between Microsoft PowerPoint and StarOffice Impress

FUNCTION IN MICROSOFT POWERPOINT	FUNCTION IN STAROFFICE IMPRESS
Starting a New Presentation	
Outline templates	Present
Sample backgrounds	Present
Selectable output medium	Present
Editing Views	
Normal, outline, handouts, slide show	Present
Special effect transitions with speed control	Present
Ability to insert drawing, charts, and so on	Present
Preview mode	Present

Although the two applications have many features in common, the process of starting a presentation is sufficiently different to warrant a short tutorial.

Starting a New Presentation in StarOffice Impress

Upon opening StarOffice Impress, the AutoPilot is started and gives you three choices: You can open an empty presentation, a template, or an existing presentation.

Clicking Open Existing Presentation simply takes you to the file manager. This is the simplest of all options, but it's only useful when creating a new presentation if you decide to base it upon one you've already made.

Clicking the first option, Empty Presentation, is the route to go if you already have a firm idea of your presentation's organization and text, and neither need nor want it to be based on or very similar to a supplied template. It's the choice of the professional creator of presentations with confidence in his or her own creativity.

The final option, From Template, is useful if you want to explore a variety of ready-made templates, with the idea of finding one that gives you a number of ideas for your own presentation, and which will hopefully need little modification.

The following two sections walk you through the presentation creation process using the Empty Presentation and From Template methods.

Creating a Presentation Using the Empty Presentation Method

After you click the Next button, the AutoPilot prompts you for a graphic page style. There are approximately 40 premade samples to choose from, ranging f rom 1950s style to contemporary—graphic style is, of course, a matter of taste. A preview window allows you to make an informed choice (see Figure 8-24).

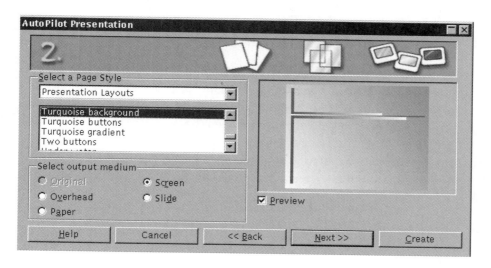

Figure 8-24. Selecting a graphic page style—step 2 of Impress' AutoPilot

In this same step, you're prompted to select the output medium:

- Overhead transparencies

- Onscreen

- Slides

- Paper handouts

Clicking Next again allows you to select what kind of transition, if any, you want to see between slides. You have approximately 40 different types of transition to choose from, and you can also select the speed. A preview window here also is included (see Figure 8-25).

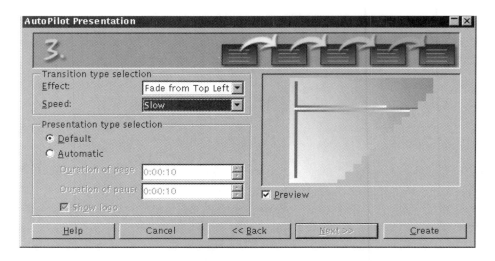

Figure 8-25. Selecting a transition type—step 3 of Impress' AutoPilot

Also in this step you can choose whether to control the speed of the presentation yourself (manually) or set it to run on a kind of automatic pilot. Choosing Automatic allows you to choose both the amount of time that each page is on the screen and the amount of time to pause between slides.

Clicking the Create button takes you to the Modify Slide screen, where you can choose a premade layout for your first, and so far, only slide. Pressing the OK button brings up the editing screen, where you can complete your presentation in any of five different views:

- Drawing View

- Outline View

- Slide View

- Notes View

- Handout View

Most users will at this point want to choose Outline View, by clicking that icon in the upper right-hand corner of the editing screen. It's a good idea to write your presentation first before you illustrate it.

Creating a Presentation Using the From Template Method

This choice offers templates—about 20 of them—from breaking bad news to presenting a new product to presenting a training seminar. The preview screen allows you to see what the default graphic background for each template looks like, although of course you can change this background later.

The next two steps are identical to the Empty Presentation method. Clicking Next brings you to graphic selection, step 2 of the AutoPilot, as shown in Figure 8-24. Step 3, transition type, as shown in Figure 8-25, follows.

The next step (step 4) prompts you to fill in the information that would typically appear on the first page on a presentation: company name, subject of presentation, and main points or ideas. In the final step (step 5) before the automatic creation of the presentation, you're prompted to choose which pages of the selected template you want to include. Figure 8-26 shows an example where the user has decided to include the title page, agenda, introduction and background, and market situation pages, but has decided to omit company differences.

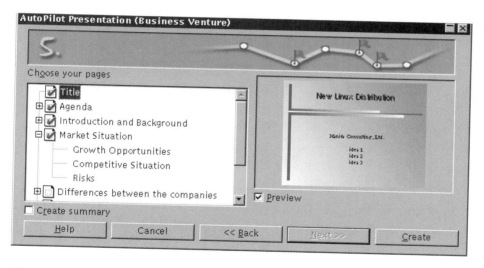

Figure 8-26. Choosing pages to include in the AutoPilot's step 5

The main editing screen that follows starts in Drawing View, showing the title slide. Below is the slide page control bar, which you can use to browse your premade slides. Choosing Outline View allows you to view the text of the complete presentation at once—if the type is too large, use the Zoom icon in the upper left-hand side of the editing screen to reduce the type size.

LESSON 8-7.

SHARING DATA BETWEEN APPLICATIONS

It's a truism that a computer application, like any tool, should be used for the purpose for which it was designed. Professional computer users, when faced with the task of sending out reports with tables attached, or of creating a presentation complete with bar graphs, would seldom decide to create the tables within StarOffice Writer or to create the bar graphs within StarOffice Impress. They would instead create the tables and graphs from StarOffice Calc spreadsheets—where no doubt the underlying data resided—and then import them into the Writer document and the Impress presentation.

Sharing data is not limited to StarOffice applications. There may be times when you want to import a graphic made or modified in The Gimp into another application. Or you may want to copy and paste e-mail from Netscape into Writer.

First, let's take a look at sharing data within StarOffice.

Importing Spreadsheets and Graphs into StarOffice Writer and Impress

You can import any part of a spreadsheet, including charts, into StarOffice Writer or Impress simply through selecting, copying, and pasting. The procedure is straightforward:

1. In StarOffice Calc, select the chart or table you want to copy and click the Copy icon on the toolbar.

2. Switch to StarOffice Writer, place the cursor in the area where you want the spreadsheet component to appear, and click the Paste icon on the toolbar.

The procedure is identical when copying and pasting a component of a spreadsheet into StarOffice Impress. In both cases, you can move and resize the pasted graphic.

There is an additional method you can use when it may be convenient to import both the spreadsheet and its related graphic into a StarOffice Writer document. Such a situation may arise when the spreadsheet itself is small enough to be conveniently presented within the same page, and when, for instance, it can be foreseen that the document may be used more than once, with updated figures.

In this case, you can import the entire spreadsheet, with graphics, as an OLE object. The procedure is as follows:

1. First, make sure that the StarOffice Calc spreadsheet is saved.

2. From within StarOffice Writer, place the cursor where you want the spreadsheet to appear.

3. Click Insert on the menu bar and navigate to Object ➤ OLE Object.

4. In the Insert OLE Object window, check the "Create from File" box and use the Search button to select the spreadsheet file. Click the OK button.

The entire spreadsheet is now inserted into the document. Double-clicking from within the imported OLE object activates the StarOffice Calc functions, rather like having a spreadsheet application embedded within a word processing application. Clicking outside the spreadsheet disables its functions. Whether they are on or off, the different elements can be resized and moved freely within the document.

Figures 8-27, 8-28, and 8-29 show the same chart, first in its parent spreadsheet in StarOffice Calc, then imported with its table as an OLE object into a StarOffice Writer document and resized (and with the table and chart switched), and finally imported into a StarOffice Impress presentation.

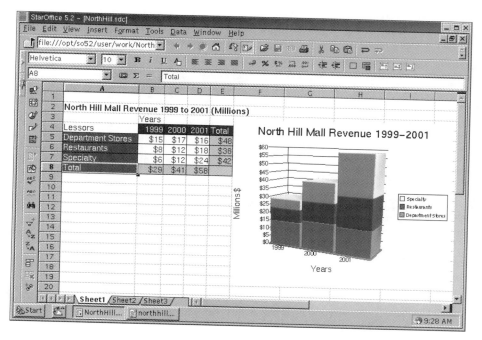

Figure 8-27. The North Hill Mall Revenue spreadsheet in StarOffice Calc

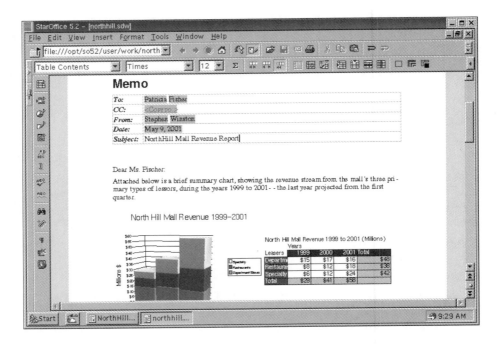

Figure 8-28. The spreadsheet imported as an OLE Object, resized, and reconfigured into a StarOffice Writer template

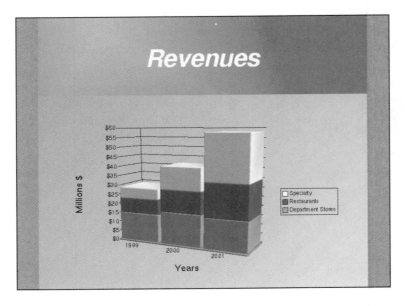

Figure 8-29. The spreadsheet's chart imported into a StarOffice Impress presentation

Hands On:

COPYING A CHART FROM STAROFFICE CALC TO WRITER AND IMPRESS

Open StarOffice Calc and build a new spreadsheet similar in design to the simple revenue statement shown in Figure 8-27.

1. Use the AutoFormat feature (select Insert ➤ Chart) to create a line or bar chart. Remember to select the appropriate rows and columns in the table first.

2. Open a template in Writer, and import the Calc spreadsheet as an OLE object. Resize as required.

3. Open a presentation template in Impress and import the Calc chart.

Sharing Data with Other Applications

The general rule is that text in text-based applications can be copied and pasted, just as if they were StarOffice applications, but graphics from graphic applications must be inserted as a separate graphic file.

Examples of text-based applications are Netscape and the VIM editor. From both applications it is possible to select text, choose copy from the menu bar, and then paste the text into StarOffice Writer.

An example of a graphic application is The Gimp. Graphics produced in this application can be copied into StarOffice applications, but only through using the Insert ➤ Graphics feature from the menu bar or main toolbar.

 TIP *When inserting a graphic, conside using the Link feature. This will reduce the size of your document and will automatically update the graphic if its appearance changes.*

LESSON 8-8.

WORKING WITH MICROSOFT OFFICE FILES

Few offices today run purely Linux applications—although the number is certain to increase. However, even in a world where Linux reigned triumphant on the desktop, it would still be necessary to import older Microsoft files.

Similar applications from different manufacturers nearly always have different file formats. The ability to export to and import from different file formats depends on filters, and the perfect filter has yet to be made. The basic rule is this: The simpler the formatting, the more successful the import.

Microsoft Office has no StarOffice filters. As a result, to be exported to Microsoft Office, StarOffice documents must either be saved in Microsoft format or saved in a third format (such as a text file) acceptable to Microsoft Office.

Fortunately, recourse to text files is seldom necessary. Table 8-4 shows the file types that StarOffice can (as of late 2001) successfully save to and open from.

Table 8-4. Microsoft Export and Import Filters in StarOffice

MICROSOFT WORD	MICROSOFT EXCEL	MICROSOFT POWERPOINT
Microsoft Word 2000	Microsoft Excel 2000	Microsoft PowerPoint 2000
Microsoft Word 97	Microsoft Excel 97	Microsoft PowerPoint 97
Microsoft Word 95	Microsoft Excel 95	
WinWord 6.0	Microsoft Excel 5.0	
WinWord 5.0	Microsoft Excel 4.0	

Of course, there are many other filters, for generic formats or for HTML, or for other applications, such as Lotus 1-2-3.

The procedure for importing and exporting in different file formats is very simple, and it's the same in all StarOffice applications.

- To import a file with a foreign format (such as a Microsoft Office file), select File ➤ Open and in the File Type box, make sure that <All> is selected.

- To export a file to a foreign format, select File ➤ Save As and choose the file type.

Figures 8-30 through 8-35 illustrate some of the (admittedly simpler) success stories of file conversion from Microsoft Office into StarOffice. In no case was the conversion perfect, but in all cases it was more than adequate. It's interesting to note that in the Word to Writer example, not only did StarOffice Writer do an excellent job of conversion, it also brought in with the document its original Word style sheet.

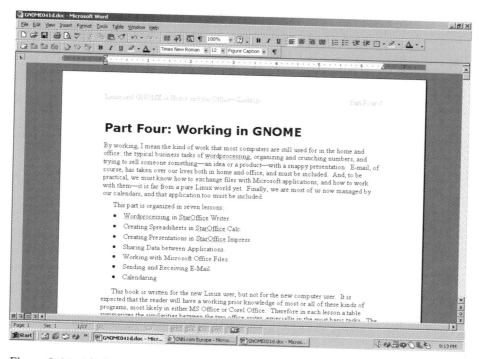

Figure 8-30. A lightly formatted document in Word, with an attached style sheet

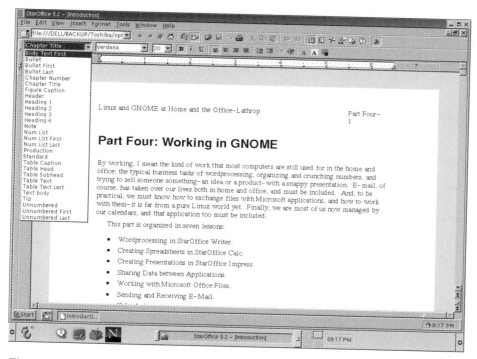

Figure 8-31. The same document imported into StarOffice Writer—along with the style sheet

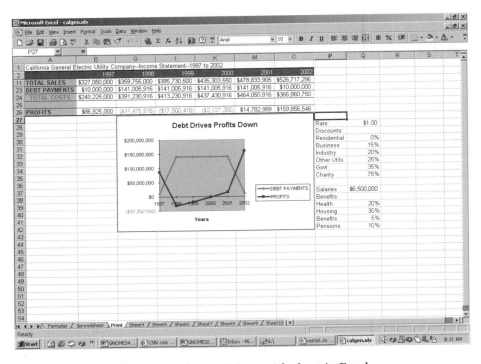

Figure 8-32. A lightly formatted spreadsheet with chart in Excel

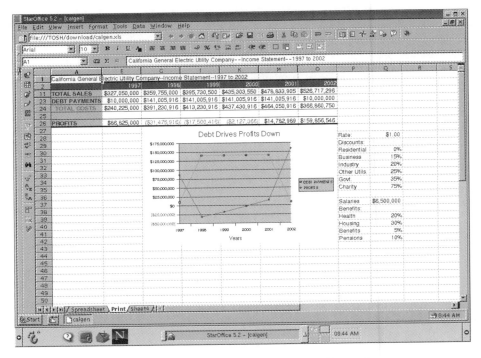

Figure 8-33. The same spreadsheet imported into StarOffice Calc

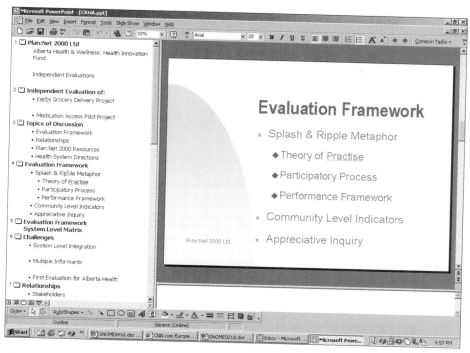

Figure 8-34. A PowerPoint presentation

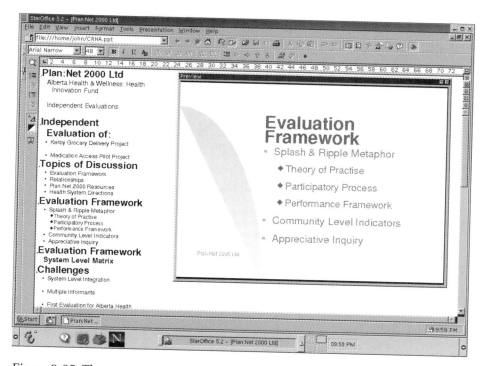

Figure 8-35. The same presentation imported into StarOffice Impress

Lesson Review

These five lessons were designed as an introduction, for the experienced user, to the major components of StarOffice. The emphasis in StarOffice Writer and Calc was on commonly used intermediate features. You learned

- The similarities between Microsoft Word and StarOffice Writer

- How to get and use Help, and how to revise documents

- How to insert graphics and drawings into a text document

- How to use and add records to StarOffice address books

- How to open and customize StarOffice Writer templates

- How to create mail merges by merging address books into templates

- The similarities between Microsoft Excel and StarOffice Calc

- How to create scenarios in StarOffice Calc, and how to use goal seek within scenarios

- The similarities between features in Microsoft PowerPoint and StarOffice Impress

- How to use the AutoPilot feature in StarOffice Impress to create a new presentation either from scratch or with a template

- How to share data between applications, through traditional cut and paste and importing

- How to import and export files to and from StarOffice and Microsoft Office successfully

LESSON 8-9.

USING NETSCAPE 4.7 AND MOZILLA E-MAIL

E-mail is the single most used Internet application and probably the most used computer application. Fortunately, several e-mail client programs are available for the Linux user to choose from. Netscape's e-mail client is virtually identical to its Windows counterpart, and its more developed (but still beta) successor, Mozilla, has the additional feature of supporting multiple e-mail accounts. Both programs are included in Red Hat 7.2, and this lesson covers both.

....

Outlook for Linux: Where Is It?

The Holy Grail of Linux e-mail applications is the all-in-one, integrated e-mail plus address book plus tasklist plus calendar program. Something remarkably like Microsoft Outlook. But where is it, in Linux?

It exists. It's called Evolution, and it's being developed under an open source license by Ximian Inc. (http://www.ximian.com). Version 1.0 was released in early December 2001. Even in this first release, Evolution gives evidence of being the program that will finally give Outlook a run for its money. Integrated with its own address book, tasklist, and calendar, it also supports multiple POP and IMAP accounts, and imports data from both Outlook and Netscape. Snappy and crisp in performance, Evolution even looks quite a lot like Outlook, and Windows users will be able to make the switch with ease.

Evolution is optimized for GNOME—which is what you'd expect in a program being developed by the same engineers who developed GNOME in the first place. Unfortunately, there's a catch: Evolution is optimized for Ximian's own version of GNOME, which is somewhat different from Red Hat's. This means that although you can download Evolution from the Ximian Web site, it entails the upgrading of approximately 20 software libraries or programs either unavailable or available in the wrong versions in Red Hat. Ximian is, however, refining their Red Carpet installer product to automate this procedure. And you can expect that an upcoming version of Red Hat Linux will include Evolution.

Most consultants would think twice before recommending that a firm change over all its e-mail clients to the 1.0 version of a highly complex open source program. Most would wait until at least 1.1. But in the interval, news of this program will spread. It may well be that, together with Sun's StarOffice 6.0, Evolution will become the killer app that finally puts Linux squarely on the desktop.

....

Using Netscape Mail

Millions have used Netscape Communicator. It's a simple and straightforward program. Using the application is even easier than setting it up—the setup was described in Lesson 8-1.

When you first open Netscape, it by default opens the browser (Navigator). In the lower right-hand corner is a "letterbox"—click it to open the e-mail client program, Netscape Messenger.

TIP *If you use Netscape primarily as an e-mail client, you may want Messenger Mailbox to open first as the default behavior. You can set this by clicking Edit on the menu bar and navigating to Preferences ➤ Appearance.*

If the application has been set up correctly, clicking the Get Msg icon on the toolbar will download your mail from your POP or IMAP server. If this is the first time you've used the program, you may be prompted for a password; it can be "remembered" by clicking Edit on the menu bar, choosing Preferences ➤ Mail Servers, selecting the incoming mail server, and clicking the Edit button. Finally, check the Remember Password box.

You can read downloaded e-mail either in the lower panel or in full-screen by double-clicking the message.

It's common for the mail folder panel on the left to be too narrow; you can widen it by dragging on the slider bar at the panel's bottom right-hand corner.

The default organization for saving incoming messages is self-explanatory. Often, however, users need to add folders to better organize their messages, dividing them into work and personal, for instance, or into further subdivisions. You can create as many subfolders of the Local Mail folder as you like simply by selecting Local Mail and clicking File ➤ New Folder. The New Folder window that opens lets you name and locate the new folder anywhere within the current folder tree.

Creating and sending messages is just as straightforward as downloading and reading them. Click New Message on the toolbar, and then, in the Compose window, click Address. Select the address, click the OK button, and type in the subject and body of the message. When you've finished, click the Send button.

You create attachments by clicking Attach on the toolbar and then selecting the desired file. Once you've made the attachment you can view it by clicking the paperclip icon on the left-hand side of the address window. Clicking the icon just below allows you to request a return receipt.

Configuring and Using Mozilla

When you start Mozilla for the first time on a computer with Netscape version 4.*x*, the newer version offers to migrate the older "profile." This includes mail settings and is a great time saver. Accept the offer.

At first glance, Mozilla does not appear significantly different from Netscape 4.78. By default it opens a browser window. The menu bar is still there, and the toolbar, although changed, is recognizable. The sidebar, which some users may find intrusive, can be hidden away simply by clicking once on the control in the middle of its right border.

Configuring Mail

Click the Mail icon in the lower left-hand corner of the screen to go to the mail window. This window looks very much as it does in Netscape 4.78. The big difference comes when you click Edit on the menu bar: There is a separate menu item for Mail/News Account Settings.

In the Account Settings window that appears, first select Outgoing (SMTP) Server, and then enter your SMTP server name in the appropriate box. In case you have more than one outgoing server (unlikely, but not impossible), you can click the Advanced button and enter the information there.

Click the New Account button and the Next button to reach the identity window, and enter your name and your e-mail address. Click the Next button again to enter your incoming—probably a POP—server information. In the next two windows, enter your user name and an account name.

When you've finished, the new account will appear in the left pane of the Account Settings window. Clicking the account name in this window brings up additional screens that you can use to edit settings (see Figure 8-36)—however, once configured, there is as yet no way to edit the POP server settings, short of eliminating the account and starting over.

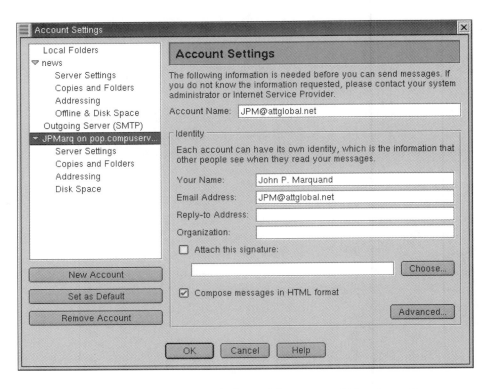

Figure 8-36. The Account Settings window, with name and identity settings

Using Mozilla

Mozilla supports multiple e-mail accounts, both POP and IMAP, and it will download mail from all accounts at once. However, the Get Msg icon on the toolbar will not be activated until you select one of the account names you created. The first time you try to download mail, you'll be prompted for your password as in Netscape, and as in Netscape you have the opportunity to have the program remember your password in the future.

Either Mozilla or Netscape 6.0, and possibly Evolution from Ximian, will probably be the Linux e-mail clients of the future. In addition, Netscape will probably remain the default Linux Web browser.

The version of Mozilla shipped with Red Hat 7.2 is a strong beta. It should be noted, however, that although Mozilla has certain definite feature advantages over previous versions of Netscape, it has two disadvantages as well: It uses far more memory, graphics, and CPU resources, and it's still buggy. Neither the enterprise nor the small business should yet depend on it exclusively for e-mail.

LESSON 8-10.

CALENDARING

The GNOME Calendar is a stand-alone program not, unfortunately, tied into an e-mail client or a contacts database. However, as a stand-alone organizer, it works well.

Start the Calendar by clicking the Start button and navigating to Programs ➤ Applications ➤ Calendar. Before you use the program, it's a good idea to set your own preferences, which you can access through Settings on the menu bar.

There are four basic calendar views, Day, Week, Month, and Year, that you can reach through the labeled tabs beneath the menu bar. The Day view is broken down into 30-minute segments. You can set new appointments and reminders in any of the views by right-clicking the mouse over the appropriate day, week, month, or year.

Starting a new appointment opens the "Create new appointment" window shown in Figure 8-37. This window lets you fine-tune the appointment time and enter a brief, descriptive summary. It also offers four different types of alarms:

- Display

- Audio

- Program

- Mail

The last two alarms are the most interesting. The Program display will start any program on the system at the alarm time. The Mail display sends an e-mail reminder to the user of choice. In Figure 8-37, Netscape is started automatically, and a mail reminder is sent to the recipient.

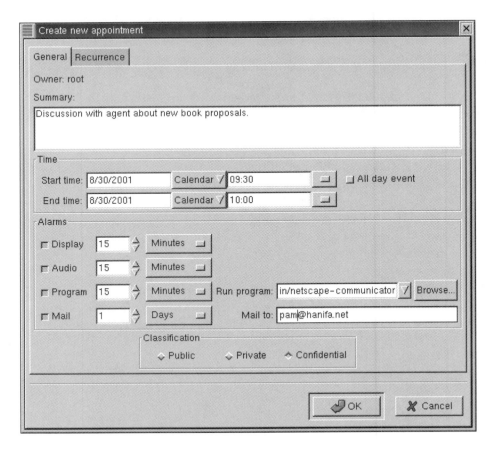

Figure 8-37. An appointment reminder with four alarms set

The alarm can also be set to recur on a daily, weekly, monthly, or even yearly basis.

Lesson Review

These two lessons covered the basics of using e-mail in Netscape and Mozilla, and the Calendar program. You learned

- The present and future of e-mail in Linux

- How to use Netscape mail in both versions currently available: 4.7 and 6.1

- How to use the GNOME Calendar

What's to Come

The next chapter covers a traditional Linux sysadmin topic, but does so largely within the desktop environment. Topics covered include the following:

- Keeping track of memory and processor usage

- Killing out –of control or recalcitrant processes

- Recovering from a desktop freeze or failure

- Manipulating start-up scripts

- Using the Red Hat Package Management (RPM) system to add and delete programs

- Using the Red Hat Network (RHN) to automate updating the system

CHAPTER NINE
System Management

By *system management* I mean managing the health and efficiency of a particular Linux computer, either a server or workstation. Entire books, of course, have been written on distinct elements of this subject. This part of the book is meant as an introduction to the topic.

Chapter Nine is organized into the following five lessons:

- Lesson 9-1. Tracking Memory and CPU Usage

- Lesson 9-2. Process Control

- Lesson 9-3. Techniques to Keep Track of System Health

- Lesson 9-4. Package Management

- Lesson 9-5. Recovering from X Window Failures and Shutting Down

A review is included at the end of the chapter.

LESSON 9-1.
TRACKING MEMORY AND CPU USAGE

Keeping track of memory and CPU usage, both the big picture and also per process, is a fundamental part of system administration. There are four basic programs that allow the user to stay on top of the memory situation: free, xosview, ps, and top (and its GNOME counterpart, GTop).

Free

The free command displays memory usage for actual RAM and for virtual memory. The program is started by typing its name in a terminal or virtual terminal. Two readouts are displayed in Figure 9-1. The first one shows the default behavior, with readouts in kilobytes, and the second is with the -m option, displaying the same information in megabytes.

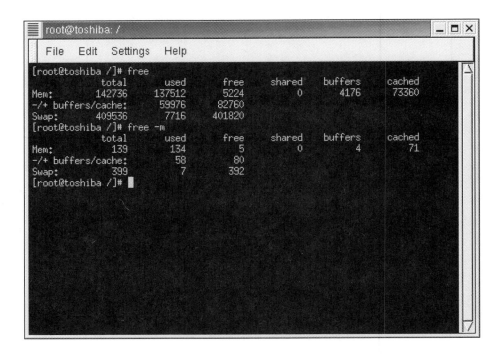

Figure 9-1. Memory readouts for RAM and virtual memory

Although the readouts in Figure 9-1 may at first sight seem obscure, they're actually straightforward. But before explaining the numbers, it might be a good idea to go over briefly the different types of memory in Linux. (Note: Memory is used in fundamentally the same way in every major operating system, including Windows.)

RAM memory falls into four basic categories: used, shared, buffers, and cache. *Used* and *shared* are similar and refer basically to memory used for running code or data—memory being used by the operating system or programs. *Buffers* refers to RAM memory set aside to temporarily hold data in RAM before it is written to disk (data is typically held briefly in RAM, before being written to disk, in order to schedule disk writes so that they have a smaller impact on the system). *Cache* is RAM that is used to hold copies of data that was recently read (or that the system expects to be read in the near future). The purpose of cache is to reduce reading from the hard disk, and so speed up operations. You can test this by opening Netscape, closing it, and then opening it again. The program will usually load much faster the second time, because much of the program data is being read from cache memory, instead of being read from the hard disk.

Of course, how much RAM is used for buffers, cache, and so on depends on many factors, such as how much RAM is present, how the system is being used, and how intensively it is being used. And, it depends on how much swap memory is available.

Swap memory, sometimes called *virtual memory,* is not RAM at all, but is a temporary substitute for RAM. Basically, when the system becomes a bit low on RAM, unused memory in RAM is "swapped out" of RAM and onto disk—in Linux, onto a specially formatted swap partition (one advantage of having a separate partition for swapping is that it does not lead to file fragmentation on the main partition—a constant problem in other operating systems). When the data on the swap partition is needed again, it is read back into RAM. Almost all systems will use some virtual memory, unless they are lightly used and very heavily supported with RAM; however, too much use of virtual memory will slow any system down.

Now back to Figure 9-1. Taking the second readout, with the -m option, line by line starting from the left:

First line: There is a total of 139MB of actual RAM on the system. Of this, 134MB is being used in some way. Only 5MB of RAM is still completely free and unused. No RAM is being used as "shared," but 4MB is set aside as buffer memory, and 71MB is being used for cache memory.

Second line: The second line acts as a kind of "reality check." The first line alone suggests that most of the memory on the system is in use. But in a low-memory situation, the cache will be reduced, and the RAM that is freed will be used for operations. In other words, cache RAM is a kind of memory store: In good times, it can be used to speed up disk read operations, but if the system needs more RAM to, say, open up a program, it use cache RAM (if there is sufficient amount) first. So this line shows 58MB actually in use for operations—this represents the 134MB from the line above, minus the amount of RAM being reserved for buffers and in uses as cache memory. The 80MB represents real RAM available, being the amount of RAM currently free, plus buffers and cache.

Third line: This line represents the swap file: 399MB of RAM is available on the swap partition, 7MB is currently in use, and 392MB is still available. Apparent errors are the result of rounding.

Free is a command-line tool, used either in virtual terminals within GNOME or KDE, or at a full terminal screen. A graphical tool that presents similar information, along with current disk usage and other data, is xosview.

Xosview

Xosview is an X Window–based program. You can start it by typing **xosview** in the Run command. It is very customizable, using a text configuration file, XOsview, within /usr/lib/X11/app-defaults. Keeping this program running full time in the corner of one of the GNOME desktops is not a bad idea, as it will give you an immediate and graphical impression of RAM and swap memory usage. Figure 9-2 shows a slightly customized xosview, presenting a memory picture only somewhat different from that of Figure 9-1.

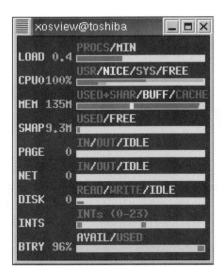

Figure 9-2. Xosview showing RAM memory and swap usage, as well as CPU, disk, and battery readouts

Note that the 100 percent CPU usage reading in Figure 9-2 is a transitory reading taken as the screen shot was captured by The Gimp.

Ps

The ps command provides a snapshot of running processes at the command line, in the order of the most recent processes to start at the bottom of the list. Although a very simple program, ps provides a fast way to make sure, for instance, that a certain process recently closed did in fact exit. Ps is often used with the x option:

```
ps x
```

to show all running processes, instead of just those within a specific terminal. The program also provides process ID numbers and a way to quickly kill recalcitrant processes. More on this later in the chapter.

Top

Top, a command-line program that you can start within a GNOME virtual terminal, like free, shows not only the same figures as free, but also both the amount, as a percentage, of CPU time and also RAM memory, that each running process is using.

An example of top is shown in Figure 9-3.

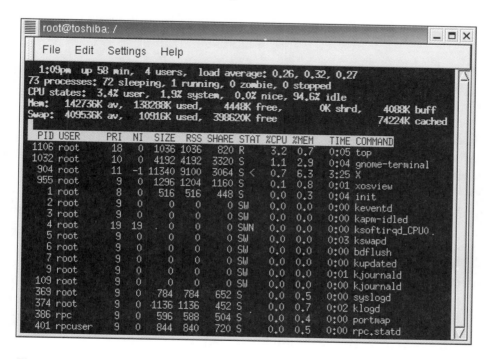

Figure 9-3. Top, showing percentages of CPU and memory being used by each process

In Figure 9-3, top itself is using the majority of CPU time, at 3.2 percent, followed by the gnome-terminal at 1.1 percent. Notice that processes are displayed organized by CPU usage. It appears that the third process on the list, the X Window System, is actually using the most memory.

A number of interactive commands are accepted by top (executed within the program while it's running) that change its readout. Some of the most useful are listed in Table 9-1.

Table 9-1.Commands That Can Be Run Interactively within Top

TOP INTERACTIVE COMMAND	RESULT
M	Sort tasks by resident memory usage
P	Sort tasks by CPU usage—the default
i	Ignore idle processes
r	Re-nice a process (more on this later)
k	Kill a process (more on this later)

Re-nicing a process refers to rescheduling the process's priority. The syntax is somewhat contradictory. After you type **r** in the top screen, you'll be prompted for a "PID to renice." "PID" refers to the process' process ID—the number that appears on the far left of the screen. After you enter the PID and press Enter, you're prompted to enter another number. Entering a positive number "causes the process to be niced to negative values, and lose priority" (the quote is from top's MAN page and is an excellent example of why Windows users are unlikely to take immediately to the help found in Linux MAN pages).

You exit top by simply entering **q**.

GTop

GTop is the graphical version of top that runs in GNOME. Start it by clicking the Start button and navigating to Programs ➤ System ➤ System Monitor. This is an excellent graphical tool that shows the same information as top (see Figure 9-4), as well as a graphical display of memory usage by process (see Figure 9-5), which can be helpful in immediately diagnosing "memory hogs."

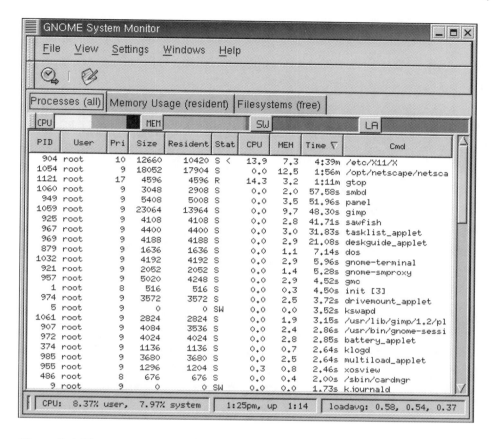

Figure 9-4. The process accounting screen of GTop, the GNOME System Monitor

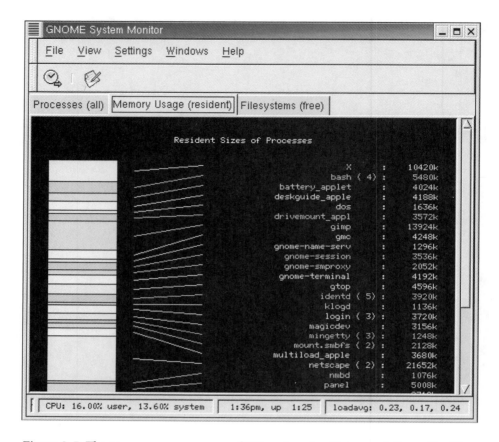

Figure 9-5. The memory usage screen of GTop, showing Netscape followed by The Gimp as the two largest users of memory

LESSON 9-2.

PROCESS CONTROL

Occasionally a process—typically, a program—will get out of control. Netscape is a well-known offender. Also, occasionally a program, even after it is closed down, will remain, at least partially, in memory—a waste of system resources. WordPerfect version 8.0 was a notorious example.

In the second situation, the downside is a perhaps minor, perhaps major waste of RAM. In the first situation, an out of control program that takes over the CPU can bring the computer to a halt. In both cases, the program has to be killed and removed from memory.

You can kill recalcitrant programs either at the command line or by using the top or GTop program.

Kill

At the command line, entering **kill** followed by the process ID number (PID) will usually kill a program. In a typical scenario, the sysadmin, after being alerted by one of the programs presented in Lesson 9-1, that a program is either out of control or wrongly still resident in memory, will use either ps or top to discover the program's PID and will then enter the kill command in a terminal, as follows:

```
kill  X
```

where X refers to the actual PID number.

The kill command, as used previously, allows the program to follow a planned shutdown routine (if it's still responding). This nice method of killing a program, by sending the SIGTERM signal, allows it to try to kill its own processes and release its memory in an orderly way. However, if the program is out of control, the "kill now" or SIGKILL command should be sent with the -s 9 option. This option will almost always exterminate any program. An example, where the offending program's PID is 1208, is as follows:

```
kill -s 9 1208
```

Killing Programs in Top and GTop

Within top, you can kill a program by entering **k**, the PID, and the desired numeric signal. The default signal, 15, sends SIGTERM. For a more drastic execution, signal 9 should be used.

GTop performs the same function, but graphically. Using the mouse to select the line relating to the process and right-clicking brings up a menu that allows you to send a variety of kill and other signals. The menu also offers a slider sub-menu to re-nice the program and extremely detailed memory maps that show both how much memory and exactly which memory addresses are being used by each program component.

LESSON 9-3.

TECHNIQUES TO KEEP TRACK OF SYSTEM HEALTH

You can use all of the programs mentioned previously to keep track of the health of your Linux system, whether it be a server or a workstation. Every administrator has his or her own preferred way of keeping track and preparing for an emergency interaction. One Linux feature that can be a great help is the fact that multiple terminals can be opened at one time, on the same machine. This applies both to virtual terminals within the X Window environment, and also, perhaps more important, to regular full-screen terminals.

Multiple Terminals

Linux is capable of having multiple full-screen terminals open at one time. This is implemented somewhat differently by different distributions, but in Red Hat, with the X Window System started on a machine, five separate full-screen terminals can be open simultaneously. It's helpful to identify the terminals by the function keys (the keys starting with the letter *F*) at the top of the keyboard.

The X Window System runs on terminal F1 but displays on terminal F7. That leaves F2 through F6 available. You can access each terminal by pressing and holding down the Ctrl and Alt keys while pressing the correct terminal key: F2 through F6 (the X Window desktop is regained by pressing Ctrl+Alt+F7). Each terminal requires a separate login and is opened as a separate process.

Why is this so useful? Because if an application in the X Window System crashes or runs out of control, it may become impossible to close it down within GNOME or KDE. But it still may be possible to quickly switch to a terminal and kill the application there, using either the kill command or the kill option within top.

Log Files

Many programs keep their own log files—that is, text files—written to and updated periodically, giving information about the health of the program in question or the system in general. A general system log file, which can be very valuable both for keeping track of what's going on and also for troubleshooting, is the /var/log/messages file.

You can use the tail command in an open terminal to keep a running display of /var/log/messages, as it is written. In a terminal, type **tail -f /var/log/messages**.

An example of this is shown in Figure 9-6. In this image, both the BIND and DHCP programs are writing to the log as a dynamic domain name server (DDNS) client first releases its lease, then renews it under the same IP address.

Figure 9-6. The tail command displaying the /var/log/messages file during a DDNS update

In a typical system management scenario, the system administrator, Stephanie, keeps top and xosview running in one of her four GNOME desktops. Xosview's graphic display keeps her up-to-date on the state of her memory, swap, and CPU usage, and top shows her immediately which programs are using most of her processor time.

Meanwhile, she keeps two terminals (F2 and F3) open, the first running tail -f /var/log/messages, so that she can keep an eye on log messages (she appreciates reading a full-screen display), and the second terminal she keeps open just as a backup, in case the X Window System hangs hopelessly and for some reason Ctrl+c doesn't close down tail as it should. In such a case, unlikely though it is, she could still use the F3 terminal to kill, one by one, the out of control and recalcitrant processes.

LESSON 9-4.

PACKAGE MANAGEMENT

Package management, meaning installing, removing, and updating programs, was for years a major problem in Linux. Eventually, it subsided to being a major irritant, and it's now only a minor irritant.

The fundamental problem was, and still is, *dependencies.* These are programs or software libraries that another program depends on to function. In the open source world, different programs and libraries are maintained by a vast array of volunteers and voluntary groups. Sometimes a volunteer has to give up the work, for one reason or another. Sometimes a group becomes leaderless or loses coordination. Or, very frequently, the maintainer of a certain program that depends on various other programs and libraries will build his or her program using the latest version of certain dependencies and earlier versions of others.

When compiling a program from its source code, error messages due to incomplete or incorrect dependencies can often be cryptic at best. Fortunately, the Red Hat Package Management (RPM) program has helped solve some, if not all, of these problems.

Ret Hat Package Management

RPM runs as both a command-line and a graphical tool under GNOME. In neither case is it problem-free, but it's such a huge improvement and boon to sysadmins that it's widely used.

The great advantages of the RPM system are that it installs binaries and default configuration files—so that the user doesn't have to compile source code—and it also provides readable messages on dependencies. Unfortunately, the command-line version is not particularly user-friendly. Even knowledgeable users will be forced to "manipulate" the program at the command line to get it to work correctly in some circumstances.

The GUI version of RPM is an improvement. To start it, click the Start button and navigate to Programs ➤ System ➤ GnoRPM. The screen that appears (which in Figure 9-7 displays the Databases submenu under Applications) allows the user to query or delete a particular package via simple point and click.

Installing a new package is straightforward. When you insert a CD containing RPM packages, you're prompted as to whether or not to automatically run GnoRPM. Choosing Yes starts the program. To install a package, click the Install icon on the toolbar. The window that eventually appears (see Figure 9-8), presents in a menu tree only those programs that are on the inserted CD and that are not currently installed on the system. Checking the desired program and clicking the Install button installs the program.

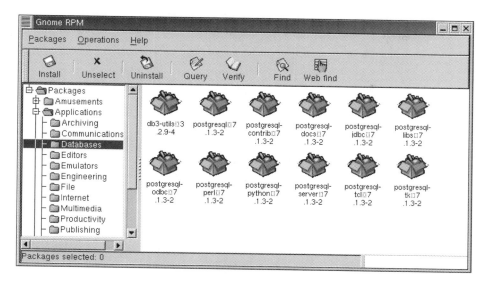

Figure 9-7. GNOME RPM opened at databases

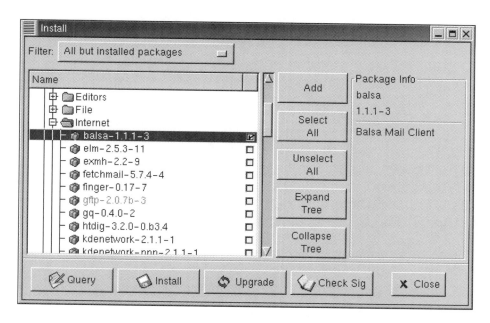

Figure 9-8. RPM program set to install the balsa mail client

The advantages to using the GUI version of RPM are as follows:

- Only programs currently not installed are displayed in the install program menu.

- Dependency problems are clearly listed.

- The query feature displays every file associated with the installed package and where the file resides on the system.

On the other hand, there is no doubt that if you simply need to "force" the installation of a certain program or package, the command-line version is preferable. Forcing installation is not uncommon, and it occurs when the RPM program gets so hopelessly confused over dependencies and versions that the GUI version literally collapses rather than install the program.

To force the installation of a program, ignoring apparent dependency conflicts, use the following command:

```
rpm -ivh --force --nodeps /mnt/cdrom/RedHat/RPMS/program.rpm
```

where program.rpm represents the name of the program you want to install, and the long directory identification represents the program location.

The Red Hat Network

The Red Hat Network (RHN) is a new service, already in its second major redesign, that is an Internet solution for managing one or more Red Hat Linux systems. The cost is as yet trivial. Basically, after signing in and registering, you may schedule automatic updates, via the Internet, to your system or systems.

From Red Hat's own Web page, the benefits of the RHN are as follows:

- Reduces the time necessary to manually track and install updates

- Minimizes security vulnerabilities by applying updates and patches as soon as they occur

- Package updates can be filtered by type, so that only the packages necessary on a particular system will be sent

Naturally, since every distribution is somewhat different, the RHN can only be guaranteed to work on the Red Hat distribution. Also, it's not clear just how accurate and effective the RHN would be on a system that had been extensively customized. It is still early days. Perhaps the best advice to give the new user or sysadmin, as of late 2001, is to give the RHN a try on a single workstation on the network, and monitor how it's doing. Should the RHN prove to work reliably, it does have the potential to be a great time-saver.

To initiate the process, open the Run command from the Start menu in GNOME, enter **rhn_register**, and click the Run button. The registration process is straightforward. After you agree to certain contractual requirements, the remote server at Red Hat creates a database of RPMS currently installed on your system—a profile of your computer.

To manually start the upgrade process, click the Start button and navigate to Programs ➤ System ➤ Update Agent. The program lists all available updates to the current system, including a description of each program and the actual advisory that describes the nature of the update: a security advisory, a bug fix, or simply a package enhancement. You may select the packages you desire, and then choose to have the RHN automatically download and install them. First, a dependency-checking program runs (see Figure 9-9), and then each program is downloaded.

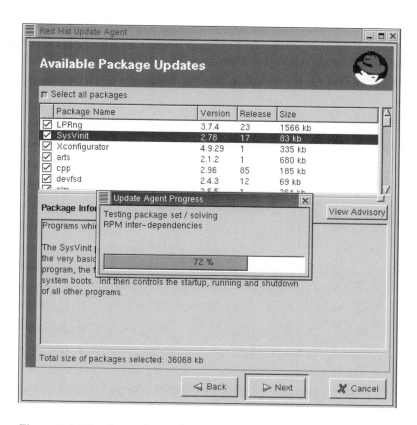

Figure 9-9. The dependency check prior to automatically downloading and installing through the RHN

After downloading the programs, the RHN prompts you to actually install them.

The RHN Web site displays a list of systems that you've registered, as well as the packages available to be updated. You can view, update, and configure registered systems in a variety of ways from the RHN site.

LESSON 9-5.

RECOVERING FROM X WINDOW FAILURES AND SHUTTING DOWN

Although it's a rare occurrence, the X Window System can freeze up. You can usually correct this problem by switching to a terminal and killing off the X process. However, this takes time, and in very rare circumstances it may not be possible to switch to a terminal at all.

In such a case, there is a simple keystroke combination that will kill the X Window System. It is Ctrl+Alt+Backspace—in other words, the Ctrl, Alt, and Backspace keys all held down at the same time. That should kill the display on F7 and return the screen to the F1 terminal (this is, of course, if the computer was started in terminal mode, which this book suggests).

In the very rare situation where the entire system is hopelessly locked up, the Ctrl+Alt+Delete key combination will generally suffice to reboot the computer.

Shutting the System Down

There are no fewer than four commands you can use at the command line to shut down Linux. They are as follows:

- halt

- reboot

- poweroff

- shutdown

The first three of these commands are relative newcomers, and in fact the first two, in most cases, trigger the last command, with the necessary options to either halt or reboot the system.

All are safe commands to use, but the last, shutdown, is both slightly more direct and more capable of customization.

When the shutdown command is given, via halt, reboot, or shutdown, all running programs are first notified that the system is about to be turned off, which gives them time to save open files and exit gracefully. (Note: This applies to command-line processes and may not always apply perfectly to programs running in the X Window System.) Then the operating system is gradually brought to a halt.

The shutdown command is generally used in one of the following two ways:

```
shutdown now -r
shutdown now -h
```

The first line commences an immediate shutdown and reboots the computer, while the second line halts the system after an immediate shutdown.

Some of the more useful options available to the shutdown command are listed in Table 9-2.

Table 9-2. Options for the shutdown Command

SHUTDOWN OPTION	RESULT
-r	Reboot the machine.
-h	Bring the machine to a halt.
-F	Force a check of the file system when the system is started next.
time	The actual time to shutdown. Examples include the following: now; 7:25, meaning 7:25 in the morning; and +10, meaning in ten minutes.
message	A warning message to all users.

Lesson Review

These five short lessons were devoted to some of the basics of system management, either on a workstation or on the server for a small LAN. You learned

- How to track memory and CPU usage, both in terminals and within the X Window System, using the free, xosview, ps, top, and GTop programs

- How to kill out of control or recalcitrant programs using the kill, top, and GTop programs

- How to use programs such as top and ps in terminals to keep track of system health, as well as to keep an eye on log files, especially with the tail command

- How to use the Red Hat Package Management (RPM) program to install, uninstall, and upgrade programs, and how the Red Hat Network (RHN) is evolving into a time-saving system management feature

- Techniques you can use to recover from a freeze-up of the X Window System, and a variety of ways to shut the system down

What's to Come

The next section of the book leaves GNOME and the X Window System behind completely and focuses on an introduction to command-line operations. It's rather like learning to drive a manual shift car, even when a vehicle with an automatic transmission is freely available. It's such a pain to learn at first that many will be unable to understand or empathize with your motivation. However, there is a good chance that, as you eventually build your skills, you'll come to enjoy it, and there's no doubt at all that it will give you increased control over your machines' mechanical systems and performance.

CHAPTER TEN
Command-Line Operations

This chapter is presented for two reasons. First, even with today's desktops—GNOME and KDE—there are still some system administration tasks that are best undertaken at the command line. Second, for a competent typist, command-line operations are still usually faster than mouse-driven point and click.

Command-line operations are traditionally the purview of the system administrator. However, all users who work on a Linux desktop will find at least some of the techniques in this chapter—particularly navigating the system, and manipulating and editing files—useful and profitable to learn.

Chapter Ten consists of four lessons:

- Lesson 10-1. Linux Directories and Navigation

- Lesson 10-2. Manipulating and Editing Files

- Lesson 10-3. Mounting Partitions and Network Shares

- Lesson 10-4. Command-Line Networking

There are two reviews—the first after Lesson 10-2 and the second after Lesson 10-4.

LESSON 10-1.
LINUX DIRECTORIES AND NAVIGATION

It usually saves time, before driving into a new city or town, to take a look at a road map first. In the same way, it's wise to have an overall view of the Linux directory structure before driving in and manipulating files.

The Linux Directory Structure

Computer files are arranged in a computer the same way that ordinary files are arranged in an office: in a set of folders. In a computer, of course, the folders are electronic, but in Microsoft Windows they're still called "folders." In the DOS and UNIX/Linux worlds, they're called "directories." Both terms mean the same thing.

A directory may contain files or other directories (subdirectories). Very often a directory contains both. The very top of the directory tree is called the *root directory.*

The directory arrangement in all Linux distributions is very similar. It follows the Filesystem Hierarchy Standard (FHS, which you can find at `http://www.pathname.com/fhs/`), which is a guide for all UNIX operating systems and Linux distributions.

Each user of a Linux system has his or her own home directory meant for the data files—letters, spreadsheets, presentations, and so on—that the user uses and creates. Most users will only be interested in their own home directories and directories meant for shared data. The system administrator will also be interested in the /etc directory, because of its configuration files, and perhaps in the /mnt and /opt directories, for mounting drives and installing application programs. If the administrator is interested in upgrading the kernel, he or she will also be interested in the /boot, /usr/src, and /lib directories. Most program upgrades, however, are now done automatically and do not require manual digging around in the directory system.

To take a look at your top-level directories, open up a terminal and navigate to the root directory by typing **cd /** and pressing the Enter key. Then, type **ls** and press the Enter key again. The directories in Figure 10-1 should appear.

Figure 10-1. Standard root directories revealed by the ls command

Each directory is meant to contain specific types of files and subdirectories. A description of each follows, organized by directory type.

User Directories

These are the private directories belonging to each individual user.

/home: This directory contains user home directories. For security reasons on a multiuser system, most directories are restricted (i.e., they are off bounds to most users). A typical user only has access to a limited number of directories, often just his or her "home" directory and a few shared directories containing shared data files. On Pam's personal system, for instance, Pam's home directory would be /home/pam. This directory could easily be mirrored on a file server.

/root: This is the home directory for the root user—the system administrator.

System Administration Directories

These directories are off bounds to most users, but they're where the administrator will spend much of his or her time.

/etc: This directory contains configuration files. This is an important directory for administrators. Configuration files for LILO and the boot loader, as well as for the X Window System, Samba, and networking, are all either in /etc or one of its subdirectories. This directory will be frequently accessed by the system administrator, at least during initial configuration.

/mnt: This directory contains the mount points for temporarily mounted file systems and drives—for example, CD-ROMs and floppy disks.

/opt: This directory is where the add-on applications go—StarOffice and WordPerfect, for example.

/boot: The kernel—the actual operating system—and other files necessary for booting (i.e., starting) Linux are in this directory. (Note: Configuration files for the kernel, such as lilo.conf, are in the /etc directory.) Users who update their kernels will access this directory, the /usr directory, and perhaps the /lib directory.

/usr: This directory contains read-only files meant to be shared among several users. If you look into this directory, you'll find many of the top-level directory names mirrored here.

/lib: This directory contains shared libraries (software) and kernel modules needed to boot the system and run basic system commands.

Rarely Accessed Directories

The following top-level directories will rarely need to be accessed, even by the system administrator.

/bin: This directory contains essential binaries (the actual program files) for command-line operations. These include, for instance, such programs as cp, kill, ls, mkdir, rmdir, and mount.

/sbin: This directory contains system binaries for command-line operations normally used only by the root user.

/dev: This is the directory for device files. These are files the operating system uses to interface with the computer. Most users will never need to get into this directory.

/proc: This directory contains files that allow a programmer or Linux guru to closely monitor the computer, at a very detailed level, and even to change certain kernel variables. Most users will never use it.

/tmp: This directory contains temporary files.

/var: This directory contains variable data files. A major use for it is automatically generating process accounting log files—files that tell the system administrator how a particular program is operating.

Creating and Removing Directories

This is a job usually done by the root user. The commands used are mkdir, rmdir, and rm.

The mkdir command's syntax is mkdir *directoryname*. For instance, if the user wanted to make a directory called "invoices" within the /home/steve directory, he or she would type **mkdir /home/steve/invoices**. Of course, if the user was already within the /home/steve subdirectory, he or she would simply enter **mkdir invoices** and press Enter.

The rmdir command's syntax is identical, but it will only remove empty directories. The rm command can be used to both remove directories, and subdirectories, with the -r option. For instance, if the user wanted to remove /opt/so52/user/work/consulting, along with all the subdirectories and the files under the "consulting" subdirectory, he or she would type **rm -r /opt/so52/user/work/consulting/*** and then **rmdir /opt/so52/user/work/consulting**.

The first command would also result in the user being prompted before removing every file. To avoid this, the user would add the -f option.

Navigation

Navigating through the directory structure from the command line is a basic skill useful for all users and necessary for administrators. Always faster than the mouse for competent typists, command-line navigation is necessary when for some reason the X Window environment does not start or becomes disabled.

NOTE *The* superuser *is UNIX-speak for the system administrator. Many commands can normally only be performed by the administrator. This is one of Linux's natural security features that prevents both unwanted user access to directories and files and also keeps certain commands in reserve for only those who need them. However, not even the system administrator is going to want to always log in as the administrator—it's simply too dangerous. All it takes with superuser privileges is one slipup to destroy an entire system. Fortunately, it's possible to log on as a regular user and then "switch identity" (i.e., become the administrator) as long as you know the administrator's password.*

The su command allows any user to temporarily become another user, as long as he or she knows the other user's password. To use this command to become the system administrator, simply type **su** *and press the Enter key. You will be prompted for the correct password. To switch back to your regular identity, simply type* **exit***.*

Command-Line Operations: Case and Space

All commands in Linux, like UNIX, are case sensitive. This means, as an example, that the common command to change directory, cd, must be lowercase:

```
cd = Correct
CD = Incorrect
Cd = Incorrect
```

Linux commands are not only case sensitive, they are also space sensitive. This means, for example, that the command to move to the root directory, the very top of the directory system, cd /, must have a space between the "cd" and the "/":

```
cd / = Correct
cd/ = Incorrect
```

In general, the demand for complete accuracy is a major cause of problems both at the command line and in shell scripts (executable text files). A good example is a common shell script used to kill a dial-up Internet connection, PPP-off:

```
DEVICE=ppp0
If [ -r /var/run/$DEVICE.pid ]; then
kill -INT `cat /var/run$DEVICE.pid`
fi
```

This four-line shell script contains the seeds for several types of errors: capitalization, spacing, and even the substitution of the grave (`) for the more common apostrophe (').

The `ls`, `pwd`, `cd`, and `clear` Commands

Navigation starts with discovering where in the directory structure you are. For this, use the List Directory (ls) and Print Working Directory (pwd) commands. The Change Directory (cd) command does just that, and it's easily the most used command at the terminal. Finally, the Clear (clear) command clears the screen of typed commands and scrolled output.

ls

Figure 10-1 is an example of screen output produced by using the ls command. Used alone, ls displays directories and files. Like many Linux commands, however, ls comes with many options. Three common options are -l, for long list format; -h, for human readable; and -a, for all files, including hidden files. As an example of how this works, navigate again to your top-level directory, type **ls -l -h** and press the Enter key. A directory listing similar to that in Figure 10-2 should appear.

Since you've used the -l option, a great deal of information on each directory is displayed. This includes, from the left, the directory's permissions, the number of subdirectories at the next level down, the directory's owner, and its size. Since you've used the -h option, the size is shown in kilobytes.

This command can also be used to display information on a single file. If you change to the /etc directory and type **ls -l -h pine.conf** you'll be shown the size in kilobytes of pine.conf, the configuration file for the Pine e-mail program.

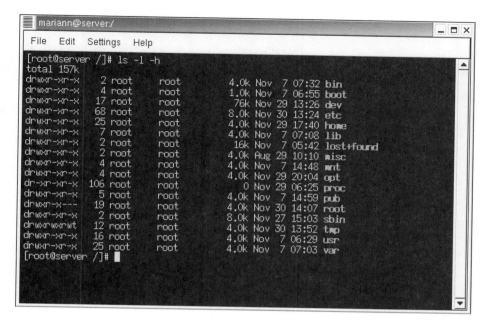

Figure 10-2. Root-level directories displayed using the long list (-l) and human readable (-h) options

pwd

Use the pwd command to print the name of the current working directory on the terminal screen. When at the root directory, for instance, typing **pwd** and pressing the Enter key produces a simple /. This is the sign for the root directory. There are times, however, when you can be several subdirectories down into the file system structure and need to have a reminder of exactly where you are. At such a moment the pwd command can come in very handy.

> **NOTE** *The command prompt only shows the current directory, but it does at least give you an indication of where you are in the directory structure. If the current directory is preceded by a slash, you're at the top of one of the root level directories. For example:*
>
> [john@hanifa.net /etc]$
>
> *indicates that you're at the /etc directory, which is one of the root level directories. If, however, you go down to /etc/X11, the command prompt shows*
>
> [john@hanifa.net X11]$
>
> *without the slash. This is at least an indication of depth. However, when you're deep into the file system, it's very easy to lose your exact location, and this is where pwd is most profitably used.*

cd

Use the cd command to change the working directory and to navigate through the file system. Used by itself, it simply takes the user to their home directory under /home. However, when combined with directory names, the / sign and double periods, the cd command can take a user anywhere (permissions allowed) within the directory structure.

Table 10-1 presents some of the most common ways to navigate using cd. In the table, "X" stands for a directory name.

Table 10-1. Syntax of the Change Directory (cd) Command

COMMAND SYNTAX	NAVIGATION DIRECTION AND SPEED
Moving Down	
cd X	Move down one directory, to the X directory.
cd Xa/Xb	Move down two directories, to the Xb directory.
cd Xa/Xb/Xc	Move down three directories, to the Xc directory—this is an extendable pattern.
Moving Up	
cd ..	Move up one level through the directory tree.
cd ../	Move up two levels through the directory tree.
cd ../../..	Move up three levels through the directory tree—this is an extendable pattern.
cd ../../Xa	Move up two levels, and down one, to the Xa subdirectory.
cd /	Move up from whatever level to the top-level root directory.
cd	Move up from whatever level to the user's home directory: /root.

A few examples can be helpful to see how this works. To take moving down first, if, at the root directory, you type **cd etc** and press the Enter key, you'll see immediately that you've moved down one level to the /etc directory. If you then decide to go one step lower, into the X11 subdirectory, you can repeat the process by typing **cd X11**.

You could have performed this two-step process in one step by originally typing **cd etc/X11**. Similarly, you could go down three levels with one step by entering **cd etc/X11/AnotherLevel**.

NOTE *Directories are sometimes all lowercase, sometimes all uppercase, and sometimes mixed case. When you type a directory name, you must be perfectly accurate—case counts.*

Moving up is just as straightforward. At the previous directory location, typing **cd ..** and pressing Enter will bring you back up one level, to /etc/X11. To go up two levels at a time, simply enter **cd ../..**; as the table indicates, this is an extendable pattern.

When you want to move right back up to the root directory in one step, type **cd /**. This will immediately take you back to the root directory, from wherever you are in the directory structure. Similarly, typing just **cd** will take you to your home directory.

 TIP *The asterisk wildcard can be used with the cd command. This can be extremely useful, because directory names can sometimes be long and complex. The directory automatically created for the BIND installation program is bind-9.2.0rc10. To move into it from an otherwise empty directory, simply type:* **cd b***.

clear

This simple command does exactly what its name suggests: It clears the terminal screen of typed input and scrolled output—of anything, in fact, that's on the display. To use it, simply type the command and press Enter. The command prompt will reappear at the very top of an otherwise blank screen.

 TIP *For those who would rather press two keys than type five letters, pressing the Ctrl key and L at the same time also clears the screen.*

LESSON 10-2.

MANIPULATING AND EDITING FILES

File manipulation is so easy to master that even remotely competent typists, once they've learned command-line copy and paste, may find themselves performing file operations at a terminal window more often than in a graphical file manager.

The cp, mv, rm, and mtools Commands

The basic command-line file operations produce the same results as their point-and-click counterparts in the GMC file manager: copying and pasting, renaming, and deleting (removing) files. In addition, there is a whole set of commands that allow you to deal with older DOS and Microsoft Windows files without mounting media (more on mounting shortly).

cp

Use the cp command to copy files and directories from one location to another. You can also rename the copied file, if you want. The syntax is quite simple. For instance, to copy a file named "hosts" from the current working directory to the /home/mariann directory, you would type **cp hosts /home/mariann** and press the Enter key. Similarly, if you were at /home/john and wanted to copy the hosts file from /etc to /mnt/floppy, you would type **cp /etc/hosts /mnt/floppy**.

A common use of the cp command is to take advantage of the renaming facility to make a backup file. You could make a backup copy of the hosts file, with a .bak extension, and place it in the /backup directory by typing **cp /etc/hosts /backup/hosts.bak**.

You can use wildcards (see the following Note) and also several options. Two of the most useful of these are -f, for force the copy, and -r, for copy "recursively." The default behavior of cp is to ask you if you really want to copy a file if it means copying over an existing file with the same name. The -f option disables this query behavior. *Recursive* simply means to copy a selected directory and everything—both files and subdirectories—under that directory.

As an example of how to use these two options, suppose you wanted to make a backup of your home directory's contents (your home directory being /home/mariann) onto another machine—a Linux server, mounted via NFS on /SERVER.

In this example, you want to copy all the files and subdirectories (and the subdirectories' files) within /home/mariann to /SERVER/mb/. What's more, you do this on a regular basis, so many files and directories have previously been backed up. Some have been altered since the last backup, and there are also some new files.

In order not to be queried every time an existing file is to be copied over, you would use the -f option to force the copy without a prompt. And in order to recursively copy every file and subdirectory beneath /home/mariann, you would use the -r option. Starting from /home/mariann as the working directory, you would type **cp -f -r * /SERVER/mb** and press the Enter key.

NOTE *There is in fact only one wildcard, the asterisk (*). But this one wildcard can represent any number of files and directories. As an example of how * is used, suppose you had to copy 20 files, all with different names but all with the same .rpm extension, to the /C directory. (For a discussion of the .rpm extension and what it means, see the "Package Management" section in Chapter Nine.)*

In such a case, if there were no other files at all in the current working directory, you could simply type **cp * /C** *and press the Enter key. Every file would be copied to /C. On the other hand, if there were other files in the directory that you didn't want to copy— and none of them had the .rpm extension—then you would type* **cp *rpm /C** *and press Enter. Only the files with the .rpm extension would be copied. Notice in this case that the period before "rpm" is not necessary.*

What if you had 25 files with the rpm extension, and you only wanted to copy the 20 with "i386" before the extension? In that case, you would type **cp *i386.rpm /C**, *thus saving yourself several minutes of command-line tedium.*

mv

Use the mv command to move (as opposed to copying) and also to rename files and directories. The syntax for the mv command is identical to the cp command: It is the command followed by the file's name and location (if it isn't in the current working directory), and then the destination directory, or new name.

As an example, to move the budget.xls file from /home/pam to /E, you would type **mv budget.xls /E** from the /home/pam directory and press Enter. If you wanted simply to rename the file to budget.xls.old and keep it in the original directory, you would enter **mv budget.xls budget.xls.old** from /home/pam. Finally, if you wanted to both move and rename the file, you would type **mv budget.xls /E/budget.xls.old**.

The mv command, like cp, also has a number of options, but -r is not among them. It's not needed. If you wanted to move the /home/john directory, for instance, and all of its subdirectories and files to /SERVER/dc5, you would simply type **mv john /SERVER/dc5** from the /home directory and press the Enter key.

CAUTION *Because of the automatic recursive behavior, and also because the mv command accepts wildcards, it's important to think carefully before using it. Used improperly, it can be as dangerous as the remove (rm) command.*

rm

Use the rm command to remove—delete—files and directories. The syntax is identical to the cp command. As an example, to remove the /home/bob/budget.xls file, you would, from the /home/bob directory, type **rm budget.xls** and press the Enter key.

Like the cp command, rm uses both the -f and the -r options, thereby making it the most dangerous terminal command available. From the root directory, typing **rm -f -r *** and pressing Enter will erase, without hope of recovery from the selected partition, every file and directory on that partition and, for that matter, on any other mounted partitions on that hard drive.

> **NOTE** *There is no "unerase" feature at a Linux terminal. When, at the command line, a file or directory is erased by the rm command, it's erased for good.*

mtools

Mtools allows you to copy, move, delete, rename, and read DOS files to and from a DOS formatted floppy disk—without having to first mount the disk drive.

One of the longest standing irritants in the Linux world has been the need to "mount" floppy drives before copying data to and from them. Nowadays in either GNOME or KDE, you can mount (access) a floppy just by clicking an icon. But for command-line work, it's still necessary to enter a special command—floppy drives are not automatically accessible.

Mtools eliminates this irritant for DOS-formatted floppies. By "DOS-formatted floppies" I mean floppy disks that are formatted by any version of DOS or Microsoft Windows. (Floppies that are specially formatted with the Linux file system must be accessed using the mount command. See Chapter Three of this book for more information.)

The mtools commands are identical to the old DOS commands, except for having "m" in front of each. Table 10-2 makes this clear.

Table 10-2. DOS and Mtools Commands

DOS COMMAND	MTOOLS COMMAND	ACTION
cd	mcd	Changes directory
copy	mcopy	Copies file or files
del	mdel	Deletes file or files
deltree	mdeltree	Deletes directories and subdirectories
dir	mdir	Lists contents of directory
format	mformat	Formats a floppy disk
ren	mren	Renames a file

As an example of how these commands work, if you wanted to copy a file named "profit2001" from the /reports directory on the floppy to the /home/mariann/ directory on the Linux machine, you would type (as root) **mcopy a:/reports/profit2001 /home/mariann/**.

Similarly, if you wanted to copy a file to the floppy, perhaps the /home/john/staff file, you would enter **mcopy /home/john/staff a:** and press the Enter key. Finally, if you just wanted to list the contents of the floppy, you would type simply **mdir a:**.

Editing Files with Vi

Vi is the command-line text editor that has been used for many years by programmers and system administrators. Being completely keyboard oriented, it has the advantage of being simple and fast, and of course it has the disadvantages of all keyboard-oriented text editors: It takes a little while to learn the commands.

Fortunately, a very short list of commands is all that's necessary to create and edit text files with speed and accuracy. It is, however, necessary to know that vi has two distinct "modes": input mode, in which the user can actually insert (and delete) text, and command mode, in which the user can perform certain editing functions and save the file.

To start the vi editor, just type **vi** and press Enter. To start it and automatically open a file for editing, type **vi** *filename*.

Table 10-3 presents some of the most useful vi commands under each mode.

Table 10-3. Common Commands in the Vi Text Editor

COMMAND	ACTION
Input Mode	
i	Enters input mode and inserts text
Normal typing	Enters text
Backspace key	Deletes text to the left of the cursor
Delete key	Deletes text to the right of the cursor
Enter key	Starts new line
Command Mode	
Escape key	Enters command mode
x	Deletes the character above the cursor
u	Undoes the previous action
dd	Deletes an entire line
:r filename and Enter	Reads another file in the system and appends it beneath the cursor
ZZ and Enter editor	Writes the file, if it has been modified, and exits the vi
:w	Writes the file, but doesn't exit
:q	Exits without saving the file

You can start the GNOME version of the vi editor simply by clicking the Start button, opening Run, and typing **gvim**.

Lesson Review

The previous two lessons were devoted to the Linux directory structure and navigation, and manipulating and editing files. You learned

- The main user directories and the contents of the system administration directories

- How to create and remove directories

- The various navigation commands and how to use them

- The most common commands for manipulating files and directories, including the mtools commands for Windows formatted floppies

- How to edit files with the vi text editor

LESSON 10-3.

MOUNTING PARTITIONS AND NETWORK SHARES

Windows workstations that are converted to Linux workstations are likely to remain dual-boot machines for some time while the user gets used to the new OS. In this situation, mounting the Windows partition from within Linux is likely to be useful, since the chances are good that a number of files will need to be transferred to the new system.

Using Samba to mount a Linux server's shared directories from within Windows was covered in Chapter Six. However, there are times when Linux users—either on a Linux workstation or server—may want to mount a Windows directory. This is also done through Samba.

Mounting Windows Partitions within Linux on a Dual-Boot Machine

This is easier than the lengthy section title would make it seem. All that is required is a mount point on the Linux file system and the appropriate entry in the /etc/fstab file.

The mount point is simply a directory name. A useful place for it could be within the user's home directory. Since the drive is likely to be C under Microsoft Windows, a typical mountpoint might be /mnt/C. (You can create this with the mkdir command.) Navigating to this directory, after mounting it, would take the user to their Microsoft Windows drives on the Windows C drive. The user could then open, move, copy, edit, or delete files and directories there.

The required entry within the /etc/fstab file is a single line that includes the device number of the Windows partition, the mount point within Linux, the type of file system to be mounted, and whether or not it should be mounted at system boot. Here's a typical example:

```
/dev/hda1     /mnt/C     vfat     noauto     0 0
```

In this example, the Windows partition is device /dev/hda1—the first primary partition. This is typical on a system that started out as a Windows workstation or server and was converted to a dual-boot Linux/Windows machine. The mount point is /mnt/C, and the partition type is vfat, meaning the Windows file system. The noauto means that the partition will not be automatically mounted at system boot, but will require manual mounting by the user. Finally, the two zeros indicate that the drive does not have to be backed up by the dump command, and that it does not have to be checked by the fsck program.

Actually mounting such a partition only requires the user to type **mount /mnt/C** and press Enter. Note that this does not require a system reboot: The /etc/fstab file can be edited with the vi editor, and then the partition can be mounted, without ever having to reboot the Linux computer.

Unmounting the partition is just as simple. Type **umount /mnt/C**.

Mounting a Windows Share on the LAN from within Linux

Mounting a Windows share from within Linux is very similar to mounting a local partition. The first steps are as follows:

1. Make sure that the user and password used on the Windows machine is mirrored by an identical user and password on the Linux machine.

2. Check that the partition to be shared on the Windows machine is configured to be shared.

3. Ensure that the /etc/smb.conf file is correctly configured.

4. Make sure a mount point on the Linux machine exists.

5. Check that Samba is running on the Linux machine.

Steps 1, 2, and 3 are covered in Chapter Six of this book. Step 4 is simply a matter of creating the appropriate directory entry, using the mkdir command, as in Lesson 10-1. Step 5 is accomplished either by enabling Samba at start-up, by checking it in the Setup program, or by starting it manually after boot-up with the /etc/init.d/smb start command.

The smbmount command is used to mount a Windows partition within Linux. The Windows network share and the mount point, as well as the user name and password, should be included in the command. If, for instance, the user wants to mount the C partition of a networked Windows machine called hp5, on the mount point /mnt/windows/C he or she would type **smbmount //hp5/c /mnt/windows/C -o username=john,password=xyz123**.

This would mount the c partition of the computer with the hostname of hp5 on the mount point /mnt/windows/C. The -o stands for "options," which in this case are both the user name john and the password. Note that Samba operates somewhat differently with Windows versions 95, 98, and 2000; however, the preceding example should generally work on all three.

To unmount the Samba share, the user would simply type **smbumount /mnt/windows/C** and press Enter.

Of course, typing all that in is a terribly tedious job and is very liable to error. Automating the process is fortunately straightforward. Simply add the appropriate line in the /etc/fstab file. In the case of the preceding example, the line would read as follows:

```
//hp5/c     /mnt/windows/C     smbfs     username=john,password=xys123     0 0
```

Now the user can automatically mount and unmount Samba shares from Linux, exactly as he or she would nfs shares: with the netfs file. To automatically mount them, type **/etc/init.d/netfs start**. To unmount them, type **/etc/init.d/netfs stop**. If netfs is started at system boot (this can be configured through setup), then the Samba shares will be automatically mounted with zero user intervention each time the computer starts.

LESSON 10-4.

COMMAND-LINE NETWORKING

Two of the oldest command-line programs to upload and download files and to manipulate files on remote computers are FTP and Telnet. In the past few years, a huge amount of effort and money has been expended to shield computer users from these two programs. Nowadays, users download files from the Web by pointing and clicking, and nearly every Web hosting company has either an off-the-shelf or in-house developed program to allow clients to manipulate Web pages without the necessity of accessing a terminal.

However, like all command-line operations, these, too, are often faster than their GUI counterparts—if the user knows what he or she is doing.

FTP

The File Transfer Protocol (FTP) is, as its name suggests, used for transferring files to and from networked workstations and servers. Linux starts with FTP automatically enabled. Its basic usage is quite simple. Suppose, for instance, that Mariann, the sysadmin for Hanifa Consulting, Ltd., wanted to download the latest BIND release from the Internet Software Consortium's FTP site. She would enter ftp

ftp.isc.org and press Enter. Prompted for her name, she would type in "anonymous"—the convention for logging into a public FTP site. She would enter her user name. (For a public FTP site, the standard name to use to log in for downloading is "anonymous.") She would then enter her password, and when she's finished she's presented with the sparse and somewhat intimidating FTP command line, as shown in Figure 10-3.

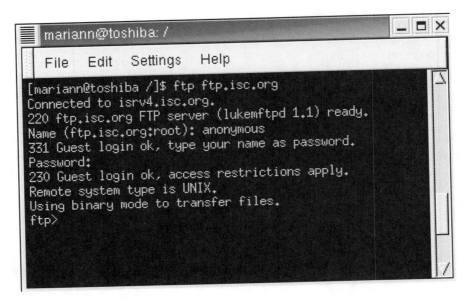

Figure 10-3. Logging in via FTP

The most useful FTP commands are in two categories: navigation and transfer. Table 10-4 presents the most common commands.

Table 10-4. Common FTP Commands

CATEGORY	COMMAND
Navigation	
lcd	By itself, prints the directory on the local machine. Also changes the local directory.
pwd	Prints the directory on the remote machine.
cd	Changes the directory on the remote machine.
ls	Lists the files and directories on the remote machine.

Table 10-4. Common FTP Commands (continued)

CATEGORY	COMMAND
Transfer	
get	Transfers files from the remote machine to the local machine.
put	Transfers files from the local machine to the remote machine.
mget	Transfers more than one file at a time, using wildcards.
mput	Transfers more than one file at a time, using wildcards.

As an example of how FTP works, suppose Mariann has started in her home directory, /home/mariann. But she wants to download the files she desires into her /home/mariann/download directory. To move there, she would type **lcd download** and press the Enter key. To be sure she's in the correct directory, she could enter **lcd** by itself. The FTP server would respond by printing her complete local directory: /home/mariann/download.

At this point, she wants to navigate to the subdirectory on the FTP server that houses the program she wants to download. In this case, it's the /isc/bind9/9.2.0rc2/ subdirectory. She would enter **cd /isc/bind9/9.2.0rc2**.

If she managed to type that in correctly, the FTP server at the ISC site would respond with the following message: CWD command successful.

Just to make sure, the user could type in **pwd** to get a print out of the current remote directory. At this point, it could be a good idea to make sure that the desired file is in the directory accessed. Just typing the ls command will reveal the contents. To actually download the file, the user would enter **get *filename*. (In this case, **get bind-9.2.0rc2.tar.gz**.) To logoff, the user types **bye**.

There are several possible refinements to this sort of scenario. The mget and mput commands both allow the use of the * wildcard, which can be used to simplify uploading and downloading a file with a long and complex filename and can also be used to upload and download multiple files. By default, the FTP server will ask the user whether or not he or she wants to download the next file in a list of files requested; this can be extremely tedious when the user wants to download a large number of files within a directory, and can be turned off by logging on with the -i option, as follows:

```
ftp -i ftp.isc.org
```

The FTP program can be useful not only on remote servers, but also to quickly transfer files to and from a server and clients on a local network. Although obviously not a first choice for anyone used to drag and drop, some time spent at the command line will convince many system administrators of FTP's usefulness.

Telnet

Telnet is used for manipulating directories and files on a remote host. It isn't used for uploading or downloading files—that's the job of FTP. It is used, however, for moving, copying, creating, deleting, and renaming files and directories on the remote computer.

Because of its administrative nature, there are no "public" Telnet sites, as there are FTP sites. Instead, Telnet is used to manipulate directories and files on machines on which the user has password access. One of the most common uses of Telnet is still to manipulate HTML files on remote Web servers, although this use has greatly diminished during the past few years with the adoption of specialized GUIs developed for just this purpose.

To start a Telnet session, simply type **telnet**, followed by the hostname of the computer. The user is prompted for a login name and password. Once in, most of the normal command-line commands apply. To close the session, type **exit**.

Lesson Review

These two lessons were devoted to the mounting of various shares and to ommand-line networking. You learned

- The technique behind mounting a Windows partition from within Linux on a dual-boot Linux/Windows computer

- How to mount, manually and automatically, a networked Windows share from within a Linux workstation

- How to transfer files using FTP, and how to manipulate files on a remote computer using Telnet

APPENDIX A

Making a Boot Disk

The normal method of installing Linux is to boot the computer from a Linux installation CD. However, some older PCs will only boot from either the hard drive or a floppy disk. Fortunately this is not a problem. You can easily create a Linux boot disk from a floppy, so that the computer will boot up from the Linux boot disk, and then, once started, continue the installation process from the CD.

 NOTE *The directories shown hold true for Red Hat 7.2.*

1. Install a blank, formatted floppy disk into a Windows machine, and also insert the first Linux installation CD.

2. Open a command prompt, and type, where d is the CD-ROM's drive letter (press the Enter key after each line):

   ```
   d:
   cd dosutils
   rawrite -f d:\images\boot.img
   ```

3. At this point, the system will prompt you to enter a target diskette drive. Just type **a** and press Enter.

4. Follow instructions to insert the floppy, if you haven't already done so, and press Enter again.

Insert both the CD and the floppy into the computer you want to install Linux onto and reboot. The installation process will start from the floppy disk and proceed from the CD.

APPENDIX B

Linux Configuration Files

This appendix is a list of configuration files that are mentioned in this book organized by the purpose (type of networking or type of service) they support. This list is not exhaustive. An exhaustive list would be much longer and would cover many files that most sysadmins would rarely, if ever, have to touch. This list does, however, contain the files most likely to need some configuration in a heterogeneous networking environment, including those files likely to be automatically configured through a GUI administration tool, such as Network Configurator.

The differentiation between Linux server and Linux workstation files is taken from the scenario in Chapters Five and Six. In fact, a Linux workstation on a LAN can have both server and client functions, as required, and many of the server files may be duplicated on the client.

Files downloadable from the Linux Leap Web site (http://www.linuxleap.org) are bolded.

This appendix is for those users interested in exploring, and perhaps even editing, configuration files at the command line.

 NOTE *etc/init.d is linked to the /etc/rc.d/init.d directory, where so many of the (start-up) scripts in Table B-1 reside. This means that copying or moving a file to /etc/init.d is the same as copying or moving it to /etc/rc.d/init.d—a useful time-saver.*

Table B-1. Configuration Files

PROGRAM OR PROTOCOL	CHAPTER	GUI PROGRAM	LINUX SERVER	LINUX WORKSTATION
Network hardware	Four		/etc/modules.conf	
Internet: PPP or ADSL	Four	internet-config	/etc/ppp/options	
		internet-config	/etc/ppp/pap-secrets	
		internet-config	/etc/ppp/ppoe.conf	
			/sbin/ifup	
DHCP	Five	netcfg	/etc/resolv.conf	/etc/resolv.conf
		netcfg	/etc/hosts	/etc/hosts
		netcfg	/etc/sysconfig/ network-scripts/ ifcfg-eth0	/etc/sysconfig/ network-scripts/ ifcfg-eth0
			/etc/rc.d/init.d/dhcpd	
			/etc/dhcpd.conf	
			/var/lib/dhcp/dhcpd.leases	
		ntsysv	/etc/rc.d/init.d/dhcpd	
DNS	Five	ntsysv	/etc/rc.d/init.d/named	
		bindconf	/etc/named.conf	
		bindconf	/var/named/[Forward Master Zone File]	
		bindconf	/var/named/ [Reverse Master Zone File]	
		netcfg		/etc/resolv.conf
NAT	Six		**/etc/rc.d/rc.local**	
		netcfg	/etc/resolv.conf	
		netcfg	/etc/sysconfig/network	
		netcfg	/etc/hosts	/etc/hosts
NFS	Six		**/etc/exports**	/etc/fstab

Table B-1. Configuration Files (continued)

PROGRAM OR PROTOCOL	CHAPTER	GUI PROGRAM	LINUX SERVER	LINUX WORKSTATION
		ntsysv	/etc/rc.d/init.d/nfs	
		ntsysv	/etc/rc.d/init.d/nfslock	
		ntsysv	/etc/rc.d/init.d/portmap	
Samba	Six	ntsysv	/etc/rc.d/init.d/smb	
			/etc/samba/smb.conf	
		ntsysv	/etc/rc.d/init.d/netfs	
Sendmail	Six		**/etc/mail/sendmail.mc**	
		ntsysv	/etc/rc.d/init.d/xinetd	
		ntsysv	/etc/rc.d/init.d/sendmail	
Apache	Six	ntsysv	/etc/rc.d/init.d/httpd	
PostgreSQL	Six		**/etc/rc.d/init.d/postgresql**	
			/var/lib/pgsql/data/ pg_hba.conf	
Firewall	Seven		**/etc/rc.d/rc.local**	

(Note: This is the same as the NAT file in Chapter Six.)

PROGRAM OR PROTOCOL	CHAPTER	GUI PROGRAM	LINUX SERVER	LINUX WORKSTATION
StarOffice Calc	Eight		**linux.sdc**	

(Note: This is the sample spreadsheet for Chapter Nine.)

Dynamic Domain Name Service (DDNS)

DDNS is the result of the marriage of DHCP and DNS—both of which are explained in Chapter Five of this book. It ensures that the IP addresses dynamically assigned by the DHCP server are copied to the DNS server, assuring reliable hostname lookups across the network, without the administrative and technical hassle involved with manually assigned static addresses. This completely frees the system administrator from the day-to-day necessity of administering IP addresses for computers on the network, either computers permanently on the network, or computers, such as laptops belonging to consultants or sales staff, that travel part of the time and connect to the office network at regular or irregular intervals. It also greatly simplifies network expansion.

Unfortunately, it's also very time-consuming to set up—so time-consuming that the sysadmins of many small offices may not want to be bothered. Certainly, putting in the time and effort to implement DDNS may not be high on the list for many small businesses. But, once it's done, the organization will have not only a highly robust system capable of easy expansion, but also a system that, on a day-to-day basis, is largely maintenance-free.

NOTE *Although DDNS does increase the work for initial configuration, both on the server and on the Linux clients, it also simplifies one aspect of setting up DHCP. It is no longer necessary to enter all the client computers' information in the /etc/dhcpd.conf file. See the following section, "Configuring the Linux Server Files," and compare the script to Chapter Five's Figure 5-12.*

Setting up a DHCP server, and DNS, as was done in Chapter Five, is one part of the job. The other is to insert the necessary extra lines into the /etc/dhcpd.conf and /etc/named.conf files to enable DHCP and DNS to work together, so that the IP addresses in the DNS zone files are updated to match the IP addresses newly assigned by the DHCP server. Among other things, this means generating a security "key" used by both programs.

This appendix presents the procedure used for the latest version of BIND and DHCP available from the ISC. You can find these versions on the ISC Web site (http://www.isc.org). The versions used for this appendix (rc stands for "release candidate") are

- BIND 9.2.0rc3

- DHCP 3.0rc12

RPM packages are available for DHCP from the ISC Web site. BIND will have to be compiled. Instructions for that are not give here, since it's assumed that anyone willing to take on DDNS will already know how to compile software packages. Very thorough instructions for this particular package are presented on http://www.isc.org.

Linux Server Configuration

The Linux server configuration described in this section will dynamically update both Linux and Windows clients on the LAN.

Producing the Security Key

To make certain that the DNS server is not updated by the wrong DHCP server, both use a security key. The same security key is also used by any Linux workstation on the network that takes advantage of DDNS. To generate a key, use the dnssec-keygen program.

On the server, perform the following steps. At the command line, type **dnssec-keygen -a HMAC-MD5 -b 128 -n USER mykey**. This will produce two files, which will look something like this:

```
Kmykey.+157+17138.key
Kmykey.+157+17138.private
```

The numbers after +157+ will change each time the command is run. The actual key is within these files. Use the cat or less command to view them. Figure C-1 shows an example of using the cat command to view the contents of both files, which have been created in the root directory. Notice that the wildcard (*) has been used to avoid the tedium of typing out the full filenames.

The actual key in this case, which of course will be different each time the command is run, is seen in both files. It is

```
Qcehmcwc7VMN/6n46KkC4g==
```

You should write this down. This key will be used in both the /etc/dhcpd.conf and the /etc/named.conf files on the server, and also in the /etc/dhclient.conf file on the Linux workstations.

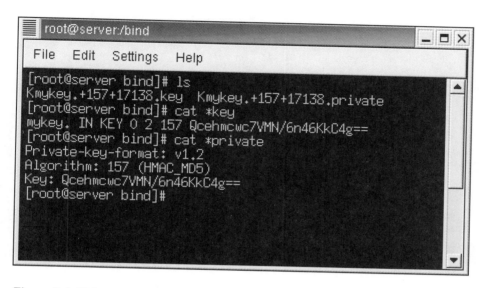

Figure C-1. Using cat to read the contents of the security key files

Configuring the Linux Server Files

The configuration files for both DHCP and DNS have to be altered for DDNS. An example of the DHCP configuration file, /etc/dhcpd.conf, is provided in Listing C-1.

Listing C-1. A Sample /etc/dhcpd.conf File

```
# dhcpd.conf
authoritative;

default-lease-time 2592000;
max-lease-time 2592000;

# default gateway
option routers 192.168.0.1;
option subnet-mask 255.255.255.0;
option broadcast-address 192.168.0.255;
```

```
# dynamic updates
ddns-update-style ad-hoc;
ddns-updates on;
ddns-domainname "dev.org";
ddns-rev-domainname "in-addr.arpa";

option domain-name "dev.org";
option domain-name-servers 192.168.0.1;

subnet 192.168.0.0 netmask 255.255.255.0 {
range 192.168.0.1 192.168.0.40;
}

# security
# key generated by dnssec-keygen command from bind

key mykey {
algorithm hmac-md5;
secret /ZBJ/r1TKDIcmnKFVU9GpQ==;
};

zone dev.org. {
    primary 192.168.0.1;
    key mykey;
}
zone 0.168.192.in-addr.arpa. {
    primary 192.168.0.1;
    key mykey;
}

# Making sure that the server keeps its fixed address
host server.dev.org {
hardware ethernet XX:XX:XX:XX:XX:XX;
fixed-address 192.168.0.1;
}
```

It will be useful to compare this to the /etc/dhcpd.conf file presented in Chapter Five. The same scenario is used for both, except in the preceding file, all machines on the LAN are given dynamically assigned IP addresses from the 192.168.0.1 to 192.168.0.40 pool, except for the server, which is given the static address of 192.168.0.1.

The /etc/named.conf file in this scenario would need three additions: the identical key statement as the /etc/dhcpd.conf file, and allow-update statements appended to two of the zone statements. The additions are shown in Listing C-2, with the actual additional lines in bold.

Listing C-2. Additions to the /etc/named.conf File for the Same Scenario

```
key mykey {
algorithm hmac-md5;
secret /ZBJ/r1TKDIcmnKFVU9GpQ==;
};

zone "dev.org" {
    type master;
    file "dev.org.zone";
    allow-update {key mykey;};
};

zone "0.168.192.in-addr/arpa" {
    type master;
    file "0.168.192..in-addr.arpa.zone";
    allow-update {key mykey;};
};
```

A good way to update this file is to create it using the bind.conf tool, then open it in an editing program such as gedit, and add the key and all-update sections.

Linux Workstation Configuration

Linux workstations can participate in DDNS, but they need more configuration than Windows workstations. You need to create two files: /etc/dhclient.conf and /var/lib/dhcp/dhclient.leases. You can create the latter file (initially empty) with the touch command:

```
touch /var/lib/dhcp/dhclient.leases
```

(Note that you may have to create the /var/lib/dhcp subdirectory first.)

You must write the configuration file with an editing program. Listing C-3 shows an example.

Listing C-3. The /etc/dhclient.conf File for Use on a Linux Workstation

```
interface "eth0" {
}
key mykey {
algorithm hmac-md5;
secret /ZBJ/r1TKDIcmnKFVU9GpQ==;
};

zone dev.org {
    primary 192.168.0.1;
    key mykey;
}

zone 0.168.192.in-addr/arpa {
    primary 192.168.0.1;
    key mykey;
}

send fqdn.fqdn "dc3.dev.org.";
send fqdn.encoded on;
send fqdn.server-update on;
```

Note that in Listing C-3, dc3.dev.org is the FQDN of the Linux workstation.

In addition, in Red Hat Linux, the /sbin/ifup file needs to be edited. This is because Red Hat uses, by default, a program called "pump" to start networking, rather than the dhclient program. There are two lines you need to edit. In Listing C-4, the original lines are presented in a group of four, and beneath it, the same group of four, with the edited lines in bold.

Listing C-4. The /sbin/ifup File for Use on a Linux Workstation

```
if [ -x /sbin/pump ] && /sbin/pump ${PUMPARGS} -i ${DEVICE} ; then
    echo $" done."
elif [ -x /sbin/dhcpcd ] && /sbin/dhcpcd ${DHCPCDARGS} ${DEVICE} ; then
    echo $" done."

if [ -x /sbin/dhclient ]  ${DEVICE} ; then
    echo $" done."
elif [ -x /sbin/pump ] && /sbin/pump ${PUMPARGS} ${DEVICE} ; then
    echo $" done."
```

Windows Workstation Configuration

This is the simplest part. In Windows 2000 Local Area Connections, configure the Internet Protocol (TCP/IP) Properties box with Obtain an IP Address Automatically checked.

Starting DDNS

The server should be turned on first, followed by the workstations. Windows workstations should pose no problem, but Linux workstations may need their initial networking turned off, as follows:

```
ifdown eth0
```

and then

```
dhclient
```

It may sometimes be necessary to "flush" the client's DNS and DHCP records on the server. You can do so by typing:

```
dhclient -r
```

and then

```
dhclient
```

This first releases the IP address, and then establishes it again.

Taking a look at the /var/log/message file on the server will tell you what is happening via DHCP and DNS. The log file messages are not bad and will frequently lead you to the source of any problem, which will often be a typo in one of the configuration files. On the Linux workstation, both the /var/log/messages file and the readout from dhclient will often give good troubleshooting advice.

For more information on DDNS, I suggest reading either a recent book on the subject or the MAN pages for the servers. The mailing list on the ISC Web page is also a good source of information, for it seems that many users are having difficulty in configuring these programs to work together.

Once it's working, however, your hours of typing, and perhaps frustration, will pay off in a dramatically decreased administrative workload.

Index

Symbols

* (asterisk) wildcard
    examples of usage, 267
    using with the cd command, 265

A

-a option, for ls command, 262
Account Configuration screen, setting up
    passwords in, 27–28
Account Settings window, in Mozilla,
    233–234
Add New Record button, in StarOffice, 207
Address Book
    adding a record to in StarOffice, 207
    using in StarOffice, 206–207
address book fields, merging into
    templates, 210–213
address books
    importing from Windows Netscape,
    192
    importing from Windows Outlook, 191
addresses. *See* IP addresses
Advanced Options (PostgreSQL) window,
    configuring, 166
Apache Configuration Tool
    default directories and, 157–158
    opening screen, 158
Apache Web server, 156–158, starting and
    stopping, 157
applets, customizing the panel and, 51–54
Applets submenu, Linux desktop, 46
Application menu, adding StarOffice to,
    197–198

applications, sharing data between,
    222–225
attachments, adding to Netscape mail, 232
Authentication Configuration screen, 28
automatic partitioning, Red Hat Linux
    version 7.2, 21–24
AutoPilot presentation window, selecting a
    graphic page style in, 219–220

B

backup copies, creating for the hosts file,
    266
balsa mail client, RPM program set to
    install, 251
/bin directory, 260
BIND, configuring to start at system boot,
    114
BIND Configuration Tool, setting up a
    nameserver with, 179
/boot directory, system administration
    directory, 259
boot disk, creating, 277
Boot Loader Installation screen, accessing,
    24–25
BootMagic (PowerQuest's), 31
Bridged DSL service, 68–69
    common problem with static IPs, 73
Bridged dynamic IP connection, setting up
    for DSL service, 69–71
Bridged static IP connection, setting up for
    DSL service, 71–73

U

V

W

Notes

Notes

Notes

Apress Titles

ISBN	PRICE	AUTHOR	TITLE
1-893115-73-9	$34.95	Abbott	Voice Enabling Web Applications: VoiceXML and Beyond
1-893115-01-1	$39.95	Appleman	Appleman's Win32 API Puzzle Book and Tutorial for Visual Basic Programmers
1-893115-23-2	$29.95	Appleman	How Computer Programming Works
1-893115-97-6	$39.95	Appleman	Moving to VB. NET: Strategies, Concepts, and Code
1-893115-09-7	$29.95	Baum	Dave Baum's Definitive Guide to LEGO MINDSTORMS
1-893115-84-4	$29.95	Baum, Gasperi, Hempel, and Villa	Extreme MINDSTORMS: An Advanced Guide to LEGO MINDSTORMS
1-893115-82-8	$59.95	Ben-Gan/Moreau	Advanced Transact-SQL for SQL Server 2000
1-893115-48-8	$29.95	Bischof	The .NET Languages: A Quick Translation Guide
1-893115-67-4	$49.95	Borge	Managing Enterprise Systems with the Windows Script Host
1-893115-28-3	$44.95	Challa/Laksberg	Essential Guide to Managed Extensions for C++
1-893115-44-5	$29.95	Cook	Robot Building for Beginners
1-893115-99-2	$39.95	Cornell/Morrison	Programming VB .NET: A Guide for Experienced Programmers
1-893115-72-0	$39.95	Curtin	Developing Trust: Online Privacy and Security
1-59059-008-2	$29.95	Duncan	The Career Programmer: Guerilla Tactics for an Imperfect World
1-893115-71-2	$39.95	Ferguson	Mobile .NET
1-893115-90-9	$44.95	Finsel	The Handbook for Reluctant Database Administrators
1-893115-85-2	$34.95	Gilmore	A Programmer's Introduction to PHP 4.0
1-893115-36-4	$34.95	Goodwill	Apache Jakarta-Tomcat
1-893115-17-8	$59.95	Gross	A Programmer's Introduction to Windows DNA
1-893115-62-3	$39.95	Gunnerson	A Programmer's Introduction to C#, Second Edition
1-893115-30-5	$49.95	Harkins/Reid	SQL: Access to SQL Server
1-893115-10-0	$34.95	Holub	Taming Java Threads
1-893115-04-6	$34.95	Hyman/Vaddadi	Mike and Phani's Essential C++ Techniques
1-893115-96-8	$59.95	Jorelid	J2EE FrontEnd Technologies: A Programmer's Guide to Servlets, JavaServer Pages, and Enterprise JavaBeans
1-893115-49-6	$39.95	Kilburn	Palm Programming in Basic
1-893115-50-X	$34.95	Knudsen	Wireless Java: Developing with Java 2, Micro Edition
1-893115-79-8	$49.95	Kofler	Definitive Guide to Excel VBA

ISBN	PRICE	AUTHOR	TITLE
1-893115-57-7	$39.95	Kofler	MySQL
1-893115-87-9	$39.95	Kurata	Doing Web Development: Client-Side Techniques
1-893115-75-5	$44.95	Kurniawan	Internet Programming with VB
1-893115-46-1	$36.95	Lathrop	Linux in Small Business: A Practical User's Guide
1-893115-19-4	$49.95	Macdonald	Serious ADO: Universal Data Access with Visual Basic
1-893115-06-2	$39.95	Marquis/Smith	A Visual Basic 6.0 Programmer's Toolkit
1-893115-22-4	$27.95	McCarter	David McCarter's VB Tips and Techniques
1-893115-76-3	$49.95	Morrison	C++ For VB Programmers
1-893115-80-1	$39.95	Newmarch	A Programmer's Guide to Jini Technology
1-893115-58-5	$49.95	Oellermann	Architecting Web Services
1-893115-81-X	$39.95	Pike	SQL Server: Common Problems, Tested Solutions
1-893115-20-8	$34.95	Rischpater	Wireless Web Development
1-893115-93-3	$34.95	Rischpater	Wireless Web Development with PHP and WAP
1-893115-89-5	$59.95	Shemitz	Kylix: The Professional Developer's Guide and Reference
1-893115-40-2	$39.95	Sill	An Introduction to qmail
1-893115-24-0	$49.95	Sinclair	From Access to SQL Server
1-893115-94-1	$29.95	Spolsky	User Interface Design for Programmers
1-893115-53-4	$39.95	Sweeney	Visual Basic for Testers
1-59059-002-3	$44.95	Symmonds	Internationalization and Localization Using Microsoft .NET
1-893115-29-1	$44.95	Thomsen	Database Programming with Visual Basic .NET
1-893115-65-8	$39.95	Tiffany	Pocket PC Database Development with eMbedded Visual Basic
1-893115-59-3	$59.95	Troelsen	C# and the .NET Platform
1-893115-26-7	$59.95	Troelsen	Visual Basic .NET and the .NET Platform
1-893115-54-2	$49.95	Trueblood/Lovett	Data Mining and Statistical Analysis Using SQL
1-893115-16-X	$49.95	Vaughn	ADO Examples and Best Practices
1-893115-68-2	$49.95	Vaughn	ADO.NET and ADO Examples and Best Practices for Visual Basic Programmers, Second Edition
1-59059-012-0	$34.95	Vaughn/Blackburn	ADO.NET Examples and Best Practices for C# Programmers
1-893115-83-6	$44.95	Wells	Code Centric: T-SQL Programming with Stored Procedures and Triggers
1-893115-95-X	$49.95	Welschenbach	Cryptography in C and C++
1-893115-05-4	$39.95	Williamson	Writing Cross-Browser Dynamic HTML
1-893115-78-X	$49.95	Zukowski	Definitive Guide to Swing for Java 2, Second Edition
1-893115-92-5	$49.95	Zukowski	Java Collections

Available at bookstores nationwide or from Springer Verlag New York, Inc. at 1-800-777-4643; fax 1-212-533-3503. Contact us for more information at sales@apress.com.

Apress Titles Publishing SOON!

ISBN	AUTHOR	TITLE
1-893115-91-7	Birmingham/Perry	Software Development on a Leash
1-893115-39-9	Chand	A Programmer's Guide to ADO.NET in C#
1-893115-42-9	Foo/Lee	XML Programming Using the Microsoft XML Parser
1-893115-55-0	Frenz	Visual Basic for Scientists
1-59059-009-0	Harris/Macdonald	Moving to ASP.NET
1-59059-016-3	Hubbard	Windows Forms in C#
1-893115-38-0	Lafler	Power AOL: A Survival Guide
1-893115-43-7	Stephenson	Standard VB: An Enterprise Developer's Reference for VB 6 and VB .NET
1-59059-007-4	Thomsen	Building Web Services with VB .NET
1-59059-010-4	Thomsen	Database Programming with C#
1-59059-011-2	Troelsen	COM and .NET Interoperability
1-893115-98-4	Zukowski	Learn Java with JBuilder 6

Available at bookstores nationwide or from Springer Verlag New York, Inc. at 1-800-777-4643; fax 1-212-533-3503. Contact us for more information at sales@apress.com.

books for professionals by professionals™

About Apress

Apress, located in Berkeley, CA, is an innovative publishing company devoted to meeting the needs of existing and potential programming professionals. Simply put, the "A" in Apress stands for the "Author's Press™." Apress' unique author-centric approach to publishing grew from conversations between Dan Appleman and Gary Cornell, authors of best-selling, highly regarded computer books. In 1998, they set out to create a publishing company that emphasized quality above all else, a company with books that would be considered the best in their market. Dan and Gary's vision has resulted in over 30 widely acclaimed titles by some of the industry's leading software professionals.

Do You Have What It Takes to Write for Apress?

Apress is rapidly expanding its publishing program. If you can write and refuse to compromise on the quality of your work, if you believe in doing more than rehashing existing documentation, and if you're looking for opportunities and rewards that go far beyond those offered by traditional publishing houses, we want to hear from you!

Consider these innovations that we offer all of our authors:

- **Top royalties with *no* hidden switch statements**
  Authors typically only receive half of their normal royalty rate on foreign sales. In contrast, Apress' royalty rate remains the same for both foreign and domestic sales.

- **A mechanism for authors to obtain equity in Apress**
  Unlike the software industry, where stock options are essential to motivate and retain software professionals, the publishing industry has adhered to an outdated compensation model based on royalties alone. In the spirit of most software companies, Apress reserves a significant portion of its equity for authors.

- **Serious treatment of the technical review process**
  Each Apress book has a technical reviewing team whose remuneration depends in part on the success of the book since they too receive royalties.

Moreover, through a partnership with Springer-Verlag, one of the world's major publishing houses, Apress has significant venture capital behind it. Thus, we have the resources to produce the highest quality books *and* market them aggressively.

If you fit the model of the Apress author who can write a book that gives the "professional what he or she needs to know™," then please contact one of our Editorial Directors, Gary Cornell (gary_cornell@apress.com), Dan Appleman (dan_appleman@apress.com), Karen Watterson (karen_watterson@apress.com) or Jason Gilmore (jason_gilmore@apress.com) for more information.